SHALLOW GRAVES

SHALLOW GRAVES

True stories of my life as a Forensic Scientist
on Britain's Biggest Cases

Ray Fysh

Published by John Blake Publishing,
an imprint of Bonnier Books UK
4th Floor, Victoria House
Bloomsbury Square
London, WC1B 4DA

Owned by Bonnier Books
Sveavägen 56, Stockholm, Sweden

www.facebook.com/johnblakebooks
twitter.com/jblakebooks

Paperback: 978-1-78946-602-7
Ebook: 978-1-78946-603-4
Audio: 978-1-78946-633-1

Design by www.envydesign.co.uk

Printed and bound in Great Britain by Clays Ltd, Elcograf S.p.A

1 3 5 7 9 10 8 6 4 2

John Blake Publishing is an imprint of Bonnier Books UK
www.bonnierbooks.co.uk

To my late mother and father, Beryl Fysh
and Reuben Fysh

CONTENTS

FOREWORD
BY ANDRÉ BAKER

'The greatest honour of any detective is to investigate the death of another human being.'

In an era when the police are being challenged in their methodologies and processes, forensic evidence so often proves key.

Some forensic evidence is very difficult to question: if DNA testing says there's a one-in-500-million chance of a single sample belonging to a suspect, this – along with other details – amounts to a fact. Whereas other pieces of evidence, such as blood splatter, require careful interpretation and analysis before they can be used or even prove helpful to a case.

That makes an experienced forensics specialist essential to police investigations.

I've known Ray Fysh since he was a toxicologist, then as a specialist advisor working with enquiry teams in all areas of forensic evidence gathering. I count Ray as a dear friend, and we often catch up with other colleagues over a beer, reminiscing over old cases, putting them right and challenging one another as to 'what would you do…'

Over forty years, Ray's dedication and service to forensics has been invaluable. He has contributed to the development and enhancement of forensic science and is a true stalwart of his profession. I've counted on his expertise many times throughout my career, but several occasions and cases spring to mind.

The first was at the turn of the millennium. London was recording around two hundred murders per year – one-quarter of the national annual numbers. The Metropolitan Police Service (MPS) was also under increased scrutiny, following the handling of the investigation into the murder of Stephen Lawrence in south London. The spotlight was on policing in general and on the MPS in particular: we had to do things better, in a more open way and to much higher standards. We needed to attain better detection rates, to work more closely with families and communities and, of course, to reduce the number of victims of murder.

The MPS took on the challenge with a Murder Prevention Programme, which I oversaw as the Service's first Head of Homicide Investigations at Scotland Yard. The idea was to identify and tackle key incidents and acts of violence which, if left unaddressed, could escalate to murder.

A senior analyst, along with a team of six newly recruited, high-potential graduates and a couple of police officers, broke down murders into sixteen 'strands' – including domestic violence, knife crime and ritual – and worked on finding ways to stop that violence.

A key part of the team's intelligence came from forensics work. While the painting of a full forensics picture may not always have been possible given the evidence my team was working with, the integration of forensics intelligence helped to form scenarios on what may have happened, or was used to identify other opportunities for investigation. Ray was the specialist advisor to the MPS on murder. He was very much a part of my team.

Along with other initiatives, the programme saw London's murder rate fall from 200 to 125 people per year. That meant seventy-five fewer victims and seventy-five fewer sets of bereaved families and friends. The programme was later extended to the rest of the UK, to Europe and beyond, with Ray a key part of its development.

Another case was the ritual murder of a little boy whose body was found floating in the River Thames in 2001. Ray's contribution to the investigation springs to mind because he proved himself to be a true team player – perhaps reflecting his days as a keen sportsman. He worked closely with the police in what proved to be a particularly difficult case.

The case affected us all. We had what we thought was an unidentifiable young child, mutilated and thrown into the Thames. No family or community members were asking questions and we had minimal evidence to go on, beyond what could be gleaned from his small torso and a pair of shorts. Within a few months, senior police officers were reporting that this case was not yielding any suspects, that the victim could not be identified and that other cases were coming in that were putting us under pressure and needed to be investigated. One senior officer directed that the case should be closed. I wasn't having that… we had to try our best.

I set Ray and the Senior Investigating Officer (SIO), Will O'Reilly, the challenge of obtaining as much forensic evidence as possible. To support them in this task, more than sixty forensic experts from the UK and beyond got together at a weekend conference at Bramshill Police Staff College. It was a conference like no other: the gloves were off, brains were engaged and everyone was encouraged to shout out any ideas – however far-fetched, different or bizarre they were. Such an unusual murder required an unusual approach.

From the weekend conference and the team's incredible work throughout, ground-breaking developments were made in using the isotopic analysis of bones. This has gone on to be used in many other cases.

Another case that owes a lot to Ray's pioneering forensic work is Operation Minstead, the investigation into a predatory gerontophile who burgled and sexually assaulted more than one hundred elderly people in south London, Surrey and Kent over almost two decades. To help solve the case, we used Ray and his forensic team's pioneering and progressive work on familial DNA.

There is no doubt that Ray was considered by the SIOs as a saviour who, quite frankly, helped them to solve some difficult cases that without his input would have not been brought before the courts.

I trust that you enjoy the read, and also recognise Ray for what he deserves. Well done Ray and thank you from the people of London and beyond.

Andy B
Queen's Police Medal, former Commander
Metropolitan Police Service

'Wherever he steps, whatever he touches, whatever he leaves, even unconsciously, will serve as a silent witness against him. Not only his fingerprints or his footprints, but his hair, the fibres from his clothes, the glass he breaks, the toolmark he leaves, the paint he scratches, the blood or semen he deposits or collects.

'All of these and more, bear mute witness against him. This is evidence that does not forget. It is not confused by the excitement of the moment. It is not absent because human witnesses are. It is factual evidence.

'Physical evidence cannot be wrong. It cannot perjure itself, it cannot be wholly absent. Only human failure to find it, study and understand it, can diminish its value.'

Locard's exchange principle, as explained
by criminologist Paul L. Kirk

PROLOGUE

This is the story of a working-class kid from south-east London who happened to land the best job in the world.

For almost two decades, I helped investigate some of the UK's most high-profile crimes – from the murders of Sarah Payne and Billie-Jo Jenkins to London's 7/7 and 21/7 transport bombings and the poisoning of Alexander Litvinenko.

Better still, in most cases I helped to catch the culprits.

I'm not a detective. I'm a forensic scientist who, in the mid-1990s, happened to find myself in the right place, at the right time. Until then, cops did the investigating and boffins like me did the corroborating. We were faceless geeks in sterile labs whose sole function was to confirm or eliminate evidence.

Then, all that changed. The Forensic Science Service (FSS), formed in 1991, placed forensic science at the heart of major investigations and hired people like me to make it happen.

In 1996, I became the Service's specialist advisor (SA) for major crime. My patch: south London and the south-east of England. My job: to assist major, high-profile investigations from day one in identifying and exploiting forensic opportunities to help solve these crimes.

As a result, forensics 'came in from the cold' to become an integral part of these investigations. As specialist advisor, I became privy to every critical decision and evolving theory, the suspects and the pressures, the red herrings and breakthroughs, living every high and low with the inquiry team.

But the specialist advisor role worked! Forensics became a proactive force during these investigations, developing and driving key lines of police inquiry. For the first time in forensic science, we ventured outside criminal expertise to explore scientific breakthroughs in academia, archaeology and industry, which we then applied to live investigations. We pushed the science we did know – like DNA, chemistry and fibre identification – into bold new areas.

None of this could've happened without the brilliant scientists who worked with me. Their ingenuity, diligence and perseverance – often under immense pressure – deserves to be known and recognised. And, as their tormentor-in-chief, it is only right that I get them the credit they are overdue.

It wasn't all plain sailing. We made mistakes that I want to own up to. On a personal level, I encountered snobbery and resistance to change in the most surprising quarters.

But, thanks to those colleagues who came on board, we ensured that forensic science helped crack some of the most iconic, disturbing and perplexing cases this country has ever known. These are my recollections of those cases and the role forensics played in solving them.

CHAPTER ONE

OPERATION 'GET OUT OF MANAGEMENT' – 1994 TO 1996

My professional 'midlife crisis' came in my early forties, so right on cue.

A quarter of a century earlier – in 1971 – I'd joined the Met Police forensic science lab straight from school as a long-haired, eighteen-year-old oik from the London suburbs who just needed a job. I had no idea what I wanted to do and certainly never envisaged myself in a white coat performing experiments.

Every morning, I'd get the train from my family home in Belvedere, south-east London to Charing Cross. Then, because I couldn't afford the tube or bus fare, I'd walk to the Metropolitan Police lab in Holborn. Along the way, I'd pass through the clanging and banter of Covent Garden – then a heaving fruit and veg market, where the smells of fresh produce intermingled with the stale whiff of pubs open since 3 a.m. to service the traders.

As I approached Holborn, I'd stop for a real Italian coffee in one of the numerous family-owned cafes in the area, which felt like a real community. I'd then start my day at the lab as a lowly assistant, performing the most mundane of tasks and wondering if I'd made the right career choice.

Then, one morning, a team of detectives from Hertfordshire came barrelling into the lab for an urgent case conference. The resulting forensic tests truly opened my eyes to the radical and sometimes critical work that went on there.

The lab's toxicology department examined the organs of a suspected murder victim and – in a world first – the yet-to-be-scattered ashes of another. The toxins they discovered led to the exposure of a twenty-four-year-old factory tea boy as a serial poisoner and murderer. A year later, in 1972, notorious 'Teacup Poisoner' Graham Young was convicted of murdering two elderly colleagues with the toxin thallium and poisoning dozens more. During his trial, it emerged that a decade earlier, he'd been sent to Broadmoor psychiatric hospital for poisoning members of his own family, including a stepmother who later died.

That was me hooked. I joined the toxicology department, desperate to become one of the reporting officers who got involved in police casework and the resulting criminal trials. However, as I soon realised, unless I got a degree I'd spend the rest of my career studying samples of cannabis. With the lab's help, I studied part time at Woolwich and North London polytechnics, securing a degree in chemistry. Mum and Dad attended my graduation – a family first – and we shared a toast to my old chemistry teacher Mr Maxwell.

Many years earlier, on passing my O levels, I'd wanted to achieve another 'family first' by getting A levels. But Dad needed reassurances and went into the school to get them: was Ray bright enough to pass his A levels? Thanks to teachers like Mr Maxwell vouching for me, I wouldn't be following Dad into a factory. Instead, I found myself assisting the police in investigations ranging from suspicious deaths and attempted murders to date rapes and blackmail

* * *

I'd always been fascinated by CID officers: the way they talk and think, the whole concept of setting up a hypothesis and testing it. Case briefings with cops brought my days alive. I discovered that by understanding a case – the context, the characters, the leads – I could offer up not only forensic solutions but also suggestions as to how it might be solved. My managers thought I was doing such a good job that, in 1994, they bumped me up to Head of Toxicology.

And that's where the problems started.

I'd somehow become a manager of people. And I don't particularly like people. Especially moaners. Despite making this very clear, I still had a revolving queue of scientists grumbling that they were 'stressed out from too much casework'. Every day, I'd observe these same 'stressed out' staff stroll in at 9 a.m., break for coffee between 10.30 and 11, take lunch between 1 and 2 and stop for another break from 3.30 to 4, before bailing out at 5 on the dot. I must say, I struggled to sympathise, especially having watched my dad slog his guts out at the Vickers factory in Crayford, Kent, for almost forty years.

I wanted out of management. But, in 1995, a fresh development threatened to consign me there until retirement. The Home Office announced that the Met Lab would be merging with other labs around the country to form the Forensic Science Service.

'You're a shoo-in for National Head of Toxicology,' my line manager cheerfully informed me. More staff, more moaning; the prospect represented everything I desperately wanted to escape. But what else could I do?

Then I saw my chance.

The idea for the role of specialist advisor stemmed from one of the police force's darkest episodes – the bodged Yorkshire Ripper inquiry of the late 1970s. During this five-year investigation, detectives had serial killer Peter Sutcliffe in their clutches on no fewer than nine separate occasions, only to let him slip through the net to attack more women. The inquiry team had simply become so overwhelmed by sheer volume – of suspects, of leads and the resulting paperwork – that they couldn't see the killer, even when he was stood right in front of them. In the end, they caught Peter Sutcliffe purely by chance.

An inquiry into how the Ripper investigation had gone so spectacularly wrong led to an exhaustive report with a series of recommendations. One of the Byford Report's key proposals was that a senior scientist – only later dubbed a specialist advisor – should be attached to every major police investigation. The role of the SA would be to coordinate all of the forensic science work, from the crime scene to the lab, from day one of the inquiry right through to the conclusion of any court proceedings.

And not before time.

Until then, crime scenes had been something of a free-for-all. As a toxicologist, I remember attending the scene of a shooting to find myself jockeying for space with a firearms expert, a biologist, a chemist, a DNA specialist and a small army of scenes-of-crimes officers (SOCOs). To be fair, we were all diligently doing our bit, but nobody was stepping back to take an overall strategic view.

As a scientist on the ground, I knew nothing about Byford's recommendation until 1996, when I learned that the Home Office had been piloting a specialist advisor trial in north-west England. Participating police forces had given it a ringing endorsement and the rumours swirled: would they roll the SA scheme out across the country?

Finally an internal ad appeared, seeking senior scientists to fill eight SA roles across the UK, including three in the Met Police area. Each SA had two basic roles: number 1, to give advice to local police forces on the use of forensic science in their inquiries and number 2, to lead a team of forensic scientists both inside and outside the Forensic Science Service to deliver that science.

I showed the ad to my wife Jackie, who was all for me applying. After all, she'd seen first-hand how management had eroded me.

As I told my interviewers, this was all I'd ever wanted – to get out there on the ground and apply our forensic knowledge and skills to live investigations. Why shouldn't cops be able to deploy forensics not just to prove a case later, but to help them solve it in the first place?

I couldn't stress enough how much working directly with the police excited me, and I left my interviewers in no doubt that I wanted this role and I wanted it badly.

To my intense relief, they entrusted me with the job. The fire in my belly was back.

CHAPTER TWO

OPERATION CATHEDRAL – SATURDAY, FEBRUARY 15, 1997

During my first decade as specialist advisor, almost every summer came to be dominated by a child murder. No social history of the era would be complete without reference to Sarah Payne and Damilola Taylor in 2000; Danielle Jones in 2001; the Soham murders and Milly Dowler in 2002. The list goes on: Rhys Daniels, Baby P, Victoria Climbié – it felt like every year had its own tragic, true-life summer blockbuster. Accompanying each of these cases was an iconic image of the victim that, through constant media exposure, would become indelibly carved in our minds.

This case was no different. If you were around in 1997, then you can most likely still close your eyes and summon up that image of Billie-Jo Jenkins in her school uniform, her pretty, smiling face oblivious to the fate that awaited her.

I first heard about her killing while watching the Sunday mid-morning TV news in my sitting room in south-east London.

'A schoolgirl has been found battered to death in the back garden of her home in Hastings, East Sussex. Billie-Jo Jenkins, thirteen, suffered horrific head injuries in the seemingly random attack yesterday afternoon…'

Certain crimes stop you in your tracks. How could this happen in broad daylight? In an ordinary, suburban back garden? To a thirteen-year-old girl? And why?

I felt the sudden surge of adrenaline to which, over the next decade and a half, I'd have to become accustomed.

I can do something about this. I can help!

I stared at the trendy new cordless phone on the sideboard, willing it to ring.

'Come on, Brian…' I said, urging that phone to ring, 'give me a call.'

I'd been specialist advisor at the Forensic Science Service for nine months now and was beginning to feel the pressure. I needed a big case like this; as cynical as it may sound, I knew it would take a high-profile murder to put me and my new role on the map.

I still hadn't proven myself or the point of this swanky new job.

God knows, I'd been trying. I'd really put myself out there, meeting senior investigating officers and scientific support managers in London, Sussex and Kent to sell what the FSS and its new SA – me – could bring to a major investigation. The trouble was, I couldn't just turn up and barge into an incident room. I had to be invited by someone of rank to join an inquiry. So far, to my intense frustration, most of those senior rankers seemed openly sceptical about the concept. Some suspected it was a dastardly FSS plot to take over crime scene management. Others questioned how I – as a toxicologist – could possibly make a call on the best strategy moving forward in other disciplines like biology, chemistry and ballistics. Senior cops looked irritated at the prospect of a 'civvy' coming into his or her incident room and disrupting the flow. And so I'd spent the best part of a year nowhere near a live investigation, but instead stuck in the office liaising between police forces and the FSS on a range of unsolved, long-running cases.

A glorified messenger boy.

I'd even started following the news closely, waiting for big cases to break. If I knew the cop in charge, I'd call them to directly offer my help. 'Ambulance-chasing', in other words.

'I think we've got all we need, Ray,' would come the inevitable response, or, 'We'll call you if we need you.'

So why should this case be different? When I'd been out 'pressing the flesh' and selling my role, I'd got the feeling that one senior scientific manager immediately recognised the role's merit. Detective Inspector Brian Cook and I had got along. Refreshingly, he seemed more concerned with catching criminals than staying within his annual budget – a trait that was becoming regrettably rare. And he'd gone out of his way to introduce me to senior detectives on his patch. That patch included East Sussex, and in that patch is the historic town of Hastings – where Billie-Jo Jenkins had been tragically murdered yesterday afternoon.

'Come on, Brian…' I again urged the phone. 'Give me a call.'

I decided that if I hadn't heard from Brian by 2 p.m., I would call him. If that made me look desperate, then so be it. I was!

As I picked at a light lunch, I felt the familiar yet nerve-shredding buzz of the pager on my belt. I glanced at the screen and saw the message – simply a phone number with the area code 01424. I'd already checked. That's Hastings! I called right away.

'Hi Brian, it's Ray Fysh.'

'Hi Ray. Listen, I haven't got long but can you be in the Billie-Jo Jenkins incident room for the 8 a.m. briefing tomorrow?'

'I think I can manage that, Brian,' I said, feigning nonchalance.

MONDAY, FEBRUARY 17, 1997 – 5 A.M.

I crept out of our house in Belvedere so as not to wake Jackie. All the way to Hastings, the car radio spoke of little else but the murder of Billie-Jo.

> Thirteen-year-old Billie-Jo had been painting a pair of French doors at the rear of the house when she was attacked. The killer struck with an eighteen-inch metal tent peg that had been removed from a garden shed that morning during a clear-out. Her foster-father Siôn and two sisters returned home from an errand to find Billie-Jo with fatal head injuries. The forensic medical examiner, who was called to certify death, said the suspect would've been covered in blood.

I felt certain that detectives would be taking a good look at Billie-Jo's foster family: in any search for suspects, close relatives need to be excluded as soon as possible. Another detail had snagged on my mind: if Billie-Jo's killer had been covered in blood, then how come nobody had spotted them? It was mid-afternoon on a Saturday. Someone roaming the streets covered in blood would garner some attention. Then, an intriguing fresh lead.

> Billie-Jo's foster dad – Siôn Jenkins – revealed yesterday that his family had been concerned in recent months by a snooper hanging about in and around their home. Now police are hunting for a suspect who knocked on the front door of a neighbouring house on Lower Park Road at about 3 p.m. Saturday afternoon looking for accommodation. The suspect then walked on in the direction of the Jenkins home. Siôn Jenkins reported getting back to the house some time around 3.30 p.m. to discover Billie-Jo had been attacked.

Police are very keen to trace the man seen walking along Lower Park Road between 3 and 3.30 Saturday afternoon.

He is described as dishevelled, with a distinctive scar or birthmark on his forehead and nose. He's in his forties, about five feet ten and with wispy short hair.

Police believe the killer hid behind a hedge in the garden of a derelict house next door watching Billie-Jo, who was painting the patio doors. He lay in wait until the family went out and then struck.

I ordered myself to keep an open mind. But I couldn't help thinking that if this was a totally random attack, then the lack of a motive and witnesses would make forensics absolutely crucial in connecting the suspect to the scene and to that improvised metal weapon. Only one thing puzzled me: why had the police not tracked down this character yet? How far could a dishevelled man covered in blood have got?

The squeal of seagulls and smell of the sea told me I'd reached Hastings; a series of black-and-white street signs directed me to the police station. To my surprise, it sat next to the magistrates' court and the town's main fire station on a narrow roadway already jammed with parked cars, both sides. I didn't have a pass to get through to the car park to the rear of the police station and so began the tedious process of cruising up and down that narrow road, waiting for a space to appear – a circuit of hell, broken only by the need for a neck-contusing three-point turn at the bottom end. I was struck, suddenly, by a flood of doubt. Is this my life now? Barging in where I'm not necessarily wanted or welcome? Should SA really stand for Spare Appendage? Because that's how I'd been feeling these past nine months. Like an outsider trying to break into a closed and suspicious secret world.

I finally parked the Cavalier but felt anything but. As I walked towards reception, a blast of cool sea air snapped me out of my fug.

'Come on, Ray,' I told myself. 'Just find ways to be useful.'

Brian Cook led me straight into the incident room, the nerve centre of the investigation. As he went to fetch coffees, I took a good look around. On a desk in the centre lay a stack of daily newspapers.

'Billie-Jo Murder: Hunt for Scarface,' reported the *Daily Mail*. 'Find the Scarface Killer of Billie-Jo,' demanded the *Daily Mirror*.

Detectives talked urgently in knots. Some squinted at computers and pointed out details to colleagues. Others bashed keyboards or phones. Bins already heaved with used coffee cups and paper plates. All leave had been cancelled. These police officers were already living the case and would continue to do so until – to use the phrase so beloved of senior investigating officers – they'd broken the back of it. I wondered if I could ever impose such a responsive culture at the Forensic Science Service. Knowing some of the scientists and their civil service cultures, I doubted it. But I'd give it a bloody good go one day.

Brian brought drinks, snacks and Nick Craggs, the principal SOCO. They told me things were moving so fast that my briefing this morning would be with just them, which was fine by me. I knew the senior detectives probably had too much on their plates already. And, as I'd been at pains to stress over the previous nine months, I was just there to help.

Brian and Nick talked me through the Jenkins family dynamic. Siôn and his wife Lois had four biological daughters: Annie, twelve; Charlotte, ten; Esther, nine; and Maya, seven. Siôn and Lois (who, entirely by coincidence, shared the same surname with Billie) took Billie-Jo Jenkins out of care and into their home in 1992 and became her legal guardians four years later in December 1996, just three months before her murder. Siôn was deputy headmaster at the prestigious local William Parker School, Lois a social worker.

They then ran me through the forensic efforts. SOCOs had been searching the Jenkins home and gardens since Saturday evening, as well as the adjoining derelict house where the assailant may have hidden.

They'd invited my colleague at the Forensic Science Service, Martyn Ismail, to examine the scene in order to interpret the blood spatter. Police divers were still searching ponds in Alexandra Park, directly across the road from the Jenkins home. The postmortem – performed by pathologist Dr Ian Hill – had taken place the previous day. Dr Hill found that Billie-Jo had suffered at least six blows to the head, delivered by the metal tent peg, which had fractured the top half of her skull 'a bit like an egg shatters'. He calculated that two of her head injuries had been caused by more than one blow.

Brian and Nick suggested I follow them to the murder scene, take a look for myself. Although loath to lose my precious parking spot, I tailed Brian to Lower Park Road and into the inevitable media circus. Donning forensic armour by my open car boot, I wondered why hearing reporters constantly repeating the horrors that had gone on here had the curious effect of making it all seem less real. Somehow, the presence of the mass media had turned what should feel like a tragedy into a grotesque sort of carnival. I couldn't wait to reach the sombre peace on the other side of that police tape.

Number 48 sits sixteen steps up from Lower Park Road on top of an almost vertical front garden. The house is imposing – red-brick, three-storey, semi-detached, boasting six front windows. I climbed those steps and followed a narrowing path that leads up the left-hand, detached side of the house.

After twelve feet or so, I reached the home's main door on the side of the building. Ten feet farther along, the laneway was filled by the wooden frame of a six-foot-high, thick wooden gate, currently open. I got to the end of the house, turned right around the back, past a back door and a shed to a small, open terrace with alternate black and red floor tiles. On the way, Nick pointed out the cover of a coal bunker.

'The eldest girl, Annie, had been clearing out the shed and left a metal tent peg here, on top of this coal bunker,' he said.

'So, whoever killed Billie-Jo must have picked up the tent peg from here before attacking her.'

As half a dozen SOCOs milled about me, I took a few moments to take in the murder scene. My first thought was that the attack had been frenzied. Although Billie-Jo had been removed, blood from her wounds had sprayed the tiles and French doors she'd been painting. A number of fresh white paint splashes on the floor tiles also stood out.

As ever at a murder scene, I became too engrossed in the forensic detail to let emotion sneak in. I'd long since reconciled myself with one pragmatic reality – the only thing I could ever do for a crime victim was help catch the bastard who did it. I checked out egress points from the dilapidated house next door and the rear of the garden, before giving Martyn Ismail a call to find out what he'd learned from the blood spatter.

Returning to the incident room, we were greeted with news that officers had just arrested the 'Scarface' suspect at his home in St Leonards, a couple of miles west of Hastings – but only after he put up a hell of a fight. Thanks to the morning's publicity, several local nurses had rung in with his name and details. It turned out he'd been suffering serious mental health issues for years. And just last Friday – a day before Billie-Jo's murder – social workers had sent a rapid response team to the man's home to have him sectioned, only to discover he wasn't there.

On arresting Scarface earlier that day, officers had found blue plastic bags in his pockets and stuffed down his underwear. Later, in custody, he was observed poking blue plastic up his nose 'to keep out germs' – which alarmed anyone privy to the Billie-Jo murder scene. What hadn't been made public yet was the fact that – somewhat bizarrely – similar material had been found inserted in Billie-Jo's nostrils. A neighbour, Denise Lancaster, who'd tended to Billie-Jo before paramedics arrived, described how part of a black bin liner lying beneath the girl's body had been stuffed up her nose. When Denise removed the plastic, blood had poured from her nostrils. Did Scarface's similar use of plastic connect him to Billie-Jo's murder?

As the incident room buzzed about us, Brian wanted to glean my thoughts on the likelihood of Scarface being Billie-Jo's killer. I had already begun to mull over the case and had noticed a few odd things.

First, I couldn't imagine a man with serious mental health issues hiding out in next-door's back garden, biding his time until everyone except Billie-Jo had left the Jenkins home. Besides, if her killer had been in next-door's garden waiting to pounce, he needed to scale either a wall or a fence to get into the Jenkins property, then grab the metal tent peg – all without Billie-Jo noticing or reacting. Also – at least to me – the sheer level of violence involved suggested it was more a 'heat of the moment' attack.

Other details perplexed me about the 'stranger' killer hypothesis. Without a motive or witnesses, a murder weapon would be one of the few things that would connect a killer to their crime. So, why had Billie-Jo's attacker left the murder weapon at the scene? I'd checked his most likely means of escape from the back garden. The foliage at the back – behind the back garden fence – was way too dense for anyone to have fled through there. The only viable exit option was the pathway to the front of the house. If he'd left this way, then surely he would've taken the metal tent peg with him for two compelling reasons. First, in case he encountered anyone. Second, so he could later dispose of such an incriminating piece of evidence.

But there was something else that troubled me – a detail that may have wrong-footed detectives from the get-go.

'Earlier today, I heard the forensic medical examiner tell the media that the suspect would've been covered in blood,' I said. 'When I called Martyn Ismail, the blood-spatter expert, he told me that the attacker was garden-side of Billie-Jo throughout the attack, as all the blood spatter had radiated towards the French doors and house.

'According to Martyn, the killer wouldn't have been covered in blood. He may have had little or none of Billie-Jo's blood on him.'

Brian and Nick looked at each other, then back at me.

'The detectives are keen, if possible, to eliminate or implicate the foster-dad, Siôn Jenkins,' said Nick, handing me a bundle of paper.

I opened it up to find a timeline of Saturday, the day Billie-Jo was murdered. They explained that this timeline was based on two things. First, interviews conducted on Sunday afternoon with Billie-Jo's sisters Annie and Charlotte, who, along with Siôn, had found her body. The timeline was also based on informal chats with Siôn, Lois and Denise Lancaster.

The timeline started in the morning. Siôn Jenkins had promised Billie-Jo she could go into town with a friend to buy some new trainers. However, Lois had scuppered the plan, telling Billie-Jo that she needed to earn the money by doing some jobs around the house. This apparently enraged Billie-Jo, who stormed out of the room muttering. Lois then scolded Siôn for giving Billie-Jo more than his 'natural' daughters.

The timeline then jumped to 2.30 p.m. Lois and the two younger children – Esther and Maya – were in Hastings town centre, Charlotte at a clarinet lesson. Siôn was at home with Billie-Jo and Annie. Both girls had agreed to complete specific tasks to earn pocket money. The plan was for Billie-Jo to paint the French doors and for Annie to clean the family's Opel saloon car. Annie had already cleared out the shed, putting items including the eighteen-inch metal tent peg on top of the coal bunker.

Siôn showed Billie-Jo how to paint the French doors and Annie how to wash the car. But, every time Siôn checked on Billie-Jo, he encountered a fresh crisis with his reluctant painter. First, she started painting the inside of the doors instead of the outside. Then she got paint on the glass panes, on the terrace tiles and, later, on Siôn's shirt.

It's safe to say Billie-Jo was making her point, and that Siôn regretted ever letting her near a paintbrush.

Just after 3 p.m., Siôn and Annie went to pick up Charlotte from her clarinet lesson. Before leaving, Siôn ensured that the side gate – the only access to the rear garden – was wedged shut with a bag of fertiliser, leaving Billie-Jo on the back terrace painting and listening to the radio. Siôn and Annie picked up Charlotte and a friend of hers from the lesson, dropping the friend off at her home first. Siôn, Annie and Charlotte then returned home. Charlotte put her clarinet away in her bedroom and came downstairs. And here's where things started to get odd.

Siôn told Annie and Charlotte that they needed to leave the house again to buy white spirit from a local DIY store, complaining that Billie-Jo had spilled paint on the patio tiles. Annie described how she and Charlotte waited outside the front of the house for their dad to emerge.

Siôn insisted he take his white MG sports car, which had its soft-top down, to the Do It All DIY store some two miles away, ignoring the fact that a shop up the road sold white spirit. He then drove the long way around the park towards the store, only to change his mind at a junction and turn back towards home.

He told the girls that it was too late for any more painting today. Annie complained that she had been promised 'a go'. Registering her disappointment, Siôn agreed that they'd go to the DIY store after all, once again looping the park the long way round.

On pulling up in the Do It All car park, Siôn discovered he'd forgotten his wallet and, after much hunting, failed to find any change in the car. So, the trio headed back home without white spirit. Siôn allowed the girls to run into the house ahead of him, which was when they discovered Billie-Jo lying on the terrace with extensive head trauma. Brian spelled it out for me.

'Some of the detectives think it's highly suspicious that Siôn brought the girls on an extended and pointless trip to a DIY store without his wallet. Especially as one of the first things we found in the house was a bottle of white spirit next to all the painting materials. They're beginning to wonder if he was creating an elaborate alibi. Could it be that Billie-Jo already lay dead on the terrace when they set off on that fruitless trip to the DIY store?'

I tried not to look confused.

'What if,' Nick said, picking up the thread, 'after Siôn, Annie and Charlotte had returned from the clarinet lesson – Siôn had gone out the back to check on Billie-Jo, found that she'd messed up again and lost it? He grabbed whatever was to hand – the metal tent peg – and whacked her over the head? Remember, the girls were waiting for him outside the front of the house, perhaps for a couple of minutes. Was the trip to the DIY store the only ruse he could think of to distance himself from the terrible crime he'd just committed?'

It certainly made a lot more sense to me than an opportunistic stranger attack.

But how could we ever go about proving this hypothesis?

It was now that I discovered the smart work of a quick-thinking detective constable on the night of Billie-Jo's murder. Amid all the shock and chaos, he somehow persuaded Siôn Jenkins to hand over his clothes and shoes to be bagged and tested. The DC had explained to Siôn that this was purely procedural so that they could eliminate him from enquiries. I was impressed. Approaching a grieving relative with such a delicate request requires real tact and balls.

Brian and Nick told me these clothes and shoes were ready to be tested at the lab – which was at my official place of work, the FSS HQ in Lambeth, south London. As was the suspected murder weapon, along with other key items from the murder scene, many of which had captured blood spatter.

'But we need a favour.'

'Name it,' I said.

'The thing is, Ray, we can't have these exhibits sitting in some scientist's in-box for two weeks. Especially the clothes. We need them dealt with right away. We need you to make this happen. Can you do that?'

'Leave it to me,' I said confidently, but I knew this was my first big test as SA.

* * *

This special request touched on something that, since joining the FSS, I knew had to be addressed. To tailor the FSS for modern policing, we needed to impose wholesale cultural change. Our pay, benefits, holidays and promotions were all based on the civil service model that served all government departments. Staff worked 9 to 5, five days a week. With that came a civil service mindset. People didn't want, need or expect to work overtime. If the job had to wait till Monday, it waited till Monday. This model worked fine for most civil service departments, but when it came to catching criminals, it simply didn't cut it.

The process of in-tray ping-pong before an exhibit was even tested could take anything from three to ten days, and always left us behind with investigations and constantly snowed under. In my early days as SA, every time I went to a meeting I'd come back to find my computer screen covered in Post-it notes, each one asking me to call a detective in urgent need of a result. No wonder the police used us for corroboration purposes and little else.

But now, if we were going to run in tandem with live, ever-evolving murder cases, we needed to find an express system for getting the most vital, game-changing exhibits tested right away. We could no longer be lagging behind. In the long term, my dream was to set up a dedicated major crime team that would drop everything as soon as a big case came in. But for now I had to fall back on that tried-and-tested formula: beg, borrow and steal.

I called my boss at the FSS HQ in Lambeth and explained the situation: I needed a senior scientist attached to this case full time and right away. I told him who I had in mind – a meticulous, experienced and confident biologist called Adrian Wain. I knew Adrian wasn't part of the old-guard, 9-to-5 club and that he would relish taking personal responsibility for such a high-profile case. I suspected there'd be ructions later when some of the senior scientists found out that I'd not followed procedure. But a thirteen-year-old girl was lying on a slab. Who cared about the egos of a few crusty old boffins?

My boss took a diplomatic stance: 'If Adrian's OK with that, then I'm OK with that.'

I called Adrian immediately. He agreed to drop everything and the exhibits were blue-lighted directly to his lab in Lambeth.

Next morning, we met early in his lab and talked through a plan of action. With his mousy hair, glasses and meticulous tone, Adrian came across as the archetypal studious forensic scientist. But as I got to know him, his offbeat humour shone through. He once told me that a fly defecates every time it lands and takes off! I quickly realised he had a quietly confident edge, which made him formidable as an expert and a colleague. For the first of many times that week, Adrian asked me to leave him alone so he could get on with it.

FRIDAY, FEBRUARY 21 – 6 DAYS AFTER BILLIE-JO'S MURDER

'If there's blood on these exhibits, we'll know by three this afternoon.'

With that pledge from Adrian Wain ringing in my ears, I headed back down to Hastings on another promise – there had been significant developments in the Billie-Jo case.

After my by-now customary slow-motion grand tour of the packed car park, I found myself back in the airless and messy incident room, sitting opposite a clearly worried Brian and Nick. They explained how Scarface had been eliminated from enquiries three days earlier – on Tuesday – and promptly sectioned for his own good. That same day, officers finally persuaded Siôn and Lois to give a press conference appealing for witnesses and information to help identify Billie-Jo's killer. In murder investigations, putting parents up in front of TV cameras had become standard practice. Not only did it generate publicity, it acted as a litmus test for flushing out potential parental guilt. Anyone who'd seen the couple's joint public appeal on Tuesday, February 18 – three days after Billie-Jo's murder – couldn't have missed the hostility between Siôn and Lois. Throughout twenty excruciating minutes, they didn't touch or share a single glance, the significance of which the police were still trying to figure out…

Nick and Brian shuffled in their seats, indicating that all this had been a mere prelude to a more significant development.

'They had Siôn in making his statement Wednesday and Thursday,' said Nick. 'The thing is, some of his behaviour in the immediate aftermath of discovering Billie-Jo's body is, well, let's see what you think.'

They explained how, after finding Billie-Jo's body, Siôn placed Annie and Charlotte in a playroom towards the front of the house to shield them from the grisly scene out back. Siôn then spent a couple of minutes faffing about before dialling 999 from a landline in the hallway. They played me the 999 call, made to the emergency services at 3.38 p.m.

Siôn gave his address, adding: 'And it is an emergency.'

'What happened?'

'I don't, I don't really know. My daughter's fallen, or she's got head injuries, there's blood everywhere, she's lying on the floor.'

'Is she conscious?'

'No, she's not conscious, I've just run. I'm going to go back for her now.'

'You say she's unconscious, is she breathing all right?'

'I don't know. I don't know, I haven't looked.'

'Right, OK, and did this happen while you were out of the house, then?'

'Yes, it, I've just, I've just this minute got back.'

'Oh, right, so you don't know how long…'

'I don't know how, well, in the next, in the last, I don't know – half an hour, three-quarters of an hour.'

The operator then instructed Siôn to place Billie-Jo on her side and check if she was breathing – and to call straight back if she wasn't.

Siôn used the same landline phone to call a neighbour, Denise Lancaster, who came quickly to the house. Between them, Siôn and Denise took turns either comforting the crying girls in the playroom or tending to Billie-Jo's body on the outside terrace. Siôn then did something that would raise the eyebrow of any detective.

After paramedics and police had arrived at the Jenkins home and begun tending to Billie-Jo, Siôn walked out of the house, leaving his two traumatised daughters, along with his dying foster-daughter, to go and sit in his MG sports car parked up on the street outside. To me, as a forensic scientist, this didn't just raise an eyebrow; it came as a full-on revelation. This was the same car he'd just used to take Annie and Charlotte on their abortive trip to the DIY store. Why would he have done this?

Sticking with the theory that Siôn had battered Billie-Jo to death before driving Annie and Charlotte to the DIY store in the MG, had Siôn suddenly realised that he may have left traces of blood from the crime scene in the car? If forensics were to find traces of blood in the MG, how would he explain that away? The only way to ensure this wouldn't become a problem was to sit in the car again now, after he'd 'discovered' Billie-Jo's body. Then, any blood found in the car could be put down to this.

When challenged by detectives as to why he'd left the scene and got into his car, Siôn claimed that, as it looked like rain, he wanted to close the car roof. Officers were not only struck by the breathtaking emotional detachment of this explanation, they also realised it contained a glaring omission. He didn't need to sit inside the MG to close the roof. He could've done so from the pavement. Incidentally, traces of blood were found on the steering wheel of the MG but, because of the minuscule amount, it was not possible to identify whose blood it was.

These actions seemed odd – unless carried out in the context of a cover-up. But we needed something more concrete than irrational behaviour that – Siôn could argue – came about as a result of shock. What else might point to Siôn's guilt in this case? His DNA or prints on the murder weapon would mean nothing. After all, the metal tent peg had come from the home where he lived.

We realised it all came down to what Siôn Jenkins wore that day. The only way we could ever connect him to – or exonerate him from – Billie-Jo's murder would be through those clothes and shoes that a sweet-talking DC had persuaded him to part with on Saturday evening.

I paced the car park, phone in hand, thinking 3 p.m. would never come. At least Adrian was punctual.

'I've found several tiny spots of blood on the lower right leg of Siôn's trousers and on the lower left sleeve of his fleece jacket,' he said flatly, in his own deadpan style.

'Now, I'm talking very, very fine that you could never see with the naked eye, Ray. You could almost think of them like the spray from an aerosol can. These spots are typical of those I would expect to find following an impact onto a surface that is already wet with blood. The size of the spots indicates that the force of the impact was considerable and that the wearer of the clothes was close to the impact.'

'What does this mean, Adrian?'

'The blood spatter on Siôn Jenkins's clothes is what I'd expect to find on Billie-Jo's attacker.'

'Blimey, you kept that quiet!'

'Well, I didn't want you getting overexcited, Ray, and jumping the gun.'

'Who, me?'

It was one of those moments where every sinew of my body seemed to punch the air in unison. We had delivered! What's more, by making this breakthrough so early, the murder squad could use the information to narrow down and refocus their investigation.

I gathered myself and went through it with Adrian again. I knew I'd have to answer a lot of questions from Brian and Nick.

Using a microscope, he'd detected a total of 158 tiny blood spots on Siôn's clothing. There were seventy-six spots on the trousers; seventy on the lower right leg, four higher up and two small spots on the left leg. On Siôn's blue fleece jacket there were seventy-two spots: forty-eight in the chest area, twenty-one on the left sleeve and three on the right sleeve. There were ten more on his left shoe.

Adrian explained that, as Billie-Jo had been bludgeoned at close range, the force of the blows was considerable. Swinging the metal peg would cause larger blood drops to shoot forward, and would also create a fine spray of smaller droplets, which would go upwards and backwards towards the assailant. The smaller spots would not travel far, indicating that the wearer was very close. The first blow would not have produced a spray, because at that moment there would've been no exposed blood. Subsequent blows, if aimed at the same area where blood was pooling, would've created this spray or mist of tiny droplets.

The postmortem found two of Billie-Jo's head injuries had been caused by more than one blow – and this would've created the 'fine spray' effect Adrian had just described.

'But could there be another explanation for this blood spatter?' I asked. 'Could Siôn Jenkins have got these splashes when he tended to her? He did say that, as he handled her, he saw a bubble of blood come from her nose and burst.'

'These droplets aren't consistent with blood staining from that kind of contact,' Adrian explained. 'Even if he'd jumped in a pool of her fresh blood, it wouldn't have created a mist this fine. That's my firm opinion. I'd be only too happy to accept an alternative explanation, but that seems far and away the most likely to me.'

I told Adrian to get it in writing and over on fax to Detective Superintendent Jeremy Paine, the officer in charge – and to expect an instant call back. I then told Brian and Nick the news. They were ecstatic. So much hard work had already gone into this case. Cracking it now looked like it was down to specks of blood smaller than the prick of a needle.

Police arrested Siôn Jenkins the following Monday morning, February 24 – nine days after Billie-Jo's murder. A day later, detectives shared the details of the new forensic evidence with his wife Lois.

'If he's charged, I will start to tell you some stuff,' she told detectives.

It turned out that Lois had suspected Siôn of being Billie-Jo's killer since the press conference a week earlier. She just couldn't bring herself to confront such an unthinkable horror. However, a police report filed after Siôn's arrest reveals she'd changed tack.

Lois then went on to tell us he has a violent temper and has hit her in the past. She has also expressed concern re. his heavy-handed smacking of his natural children. (At no point is she aware that he has ever hit Billie-Jo, he was very aware of where the boundary was with her being a foster-child.)

She says he has hit her throughout their marriage and that she has come to accept this as the norm, believing this is usual in a relationship. She has considered leaving him and has discussed it with Annie [their eldest biological daughter] who is aware that her mum is frightened of Siôn. However, she does not know if Annie has actually seen Siôn hit her. She said he does not need much of a trigger to lose his temper but can just snap for no apparent reason and after losing his temper cannot recall the event. It is as if it did not happen... She commented that she always thought it would be her, and found it difficult to believe not that Siôn had done this but that he had done it to Billie.

Lois went on to accuse Siôn of trying to dispose of the evidence that now appeared to incriminate him. She told police how the family had gone to Denise Lancaster's home nearby on the night of the murder – where Siôn had made strenuous efforts to shed the fleece jacket on which we'd now found Billie-Jo's blood. Her claim was backed up by Denise.

On the might of the murder, Lois recalls that Siôn had taken his blue fleece off. As they left Denise's house (where the family went on the evening of Billie-Jo's murder), Lois saw that Siôn was not going to put it on. She told him to put it on because it was cold, but he said he didn't want to and Denise went after him with it and gave it to him. Denise was with Lois while we were talking about this and recalls it too. In hindsight, Lois thought this was odd...

Lois had one last accusation to make against her husband. She claimed that, in the days after the murder, he was constantly conducting private chats with Annie and Charlotte – with whom he'd found Billie-Jo's body. She believed he was 'coaching' them on what to tell the police so as not to incriminate him.

Meanwhile, the forensic case against Siôn was strengthening. Adrian Wain confirmed that the blood spots found on Siôn's clothing were a match to Billie-Jo's. Adrian had also found mist/ spray samples of Billie-Jo's blood on her leggings. According to Adrian, this blood spray on both sets of clothes could only have been created by the same impact on pooled blood. He examined the clothing of other people who'd tended to stricken Billie-Jo – neighbour Denise Lancaster and two paramedics – and found no similar blood patterns on them. Adrian felt this proved something important – that this blood spatter could only have come from high-impact blows on a bloody surface, and not from simple contact. A check revealed nothing in Siôn's statements or accounts that could give any other explanation for these aerosol-like blood sprays. In our view, this was because there could only be one explanation: Siôn Jenkins had murdered Billie-Jo.

* * *

On March 14, 1997 – less than a month after her killing – Siôn Jenkins was charged with murdering Billie-Jo. The prosecution appeared to largely hinge on Adrian's discovery and interpretation of the blood spatter on the clothing of Siôn and Billie-Jo. It seemed obvious to me that the first thing Siôn's defence team would do was set out to contest Adrian's findings. They'd hire a private forensics firm and a scientist to critically re-examine Adrian's work and seek out any weaknesses or flaws. After all, under the UK system, it is up to the prosecution to prove the case. Thanks to our exacting standard of criminal guilt as 'beyond reasonable doubt', all the defence has to do is plant that seed of doubt in the minds of the jury.

I decided we should beat Siôn's defence team to it.

My plan was to get the most prominent defence experts we could find. Forensic Alliance had been founded by a brilliant former FSS scientist, Angela Gallop, and was fast gaining a reputation as the best private company in the business. If anyone could find fault with what we did, Forensic Alliance would.

I wanted Sussex Police to hire them, but first I needed to run it past Adrian. He'd done such a sterling job, locating and interpreting this critical blood spatter. By getting someone from outside to check his work, would he feel that I was doubting or undermining him? Inside the FSS HQ at Lambeth, we already had plenty of scientists objecting to me and my new role. I was under strict instructions to try to build bridges with scientists. After all, I couldn't perform my role properly without them. Was I torching the first decent bridge I'd built?

I broached it delicately.

'Adrian, I wonder if we should get some defence people to take a look at it, you know, so that we can anticipate what might be coming?'

He looked at me blankly.

'We're not disbelieving anything you found, Adrian. The science speaks for itself, but maybe we could get another scientist to back you up.'

'Makes sense,' he said finally. 'We should go for Forensic Alliance.'

It was typical of Adrian's humility not to kick up a fuss. This had been one of the reasons I'd hand-picked him for the job in the first place.

In May 1997, Adrian and Forensic Alliance's top biologist Russell Stockdale agreed that they needed to find a way to exhibit the behaviour of pooled blood during a frenzied assault on a human skull. But this posed a challenge. Smashing an actual human skull was clearly out of the question. Physiologically, a monkey skull would work – but this was not something they could get their hands on. So, they acquired a pig – the skull of which is physiologically close to that of a human. They then coated the pig's head with wet blood and proceeded to batter it with an identical tent peg. Alas, the pig's ears kept flapping up and down, ruining their experiment. So, they lopped them off.

The pig in question, you'll be relieved to learn, was already dead!

Having proceeded with what some might have viewed as a rather unorthodox experiment, Russell Stockdale came to exactly the same conclusions as Adrian. I felt so confident in the science that I didn't bother attending Siôn Jenkins's murder trial.

JULY 2, 1998 – 17 MONTHS AFTER BILLIE-JO'S MURDER

I was in the lab when a late-afternoon call came in from Brian Cook; Siôn Jenkins had been found guilty of murder.

'Well done, Ray,' he said, 'and be sure to pass the good news on to Adrian.'

I switched on the news to learn that the jury of eight men and four women had taken just over ten hours to reach a unanimous verdict. This is how the news was reported:

Sentencing Jenkins to life, Mr Justice Gage told the defendant: 'Siôn Jenkins, the jury have convicted you of murder in what, in my judgment, was compelling evidence.

'On the fifteenth of February last year, you battered your foster-daughter with an iron bar. It was a furious assault, the motive for which only you now know.'

As the foreman announced the verdict, there were shouts of 'Yes' from the packed public gallery where Billie-Jo's natural father and mother Bill and Debbie Jenkins sat.

The nineteen-day trial heard testimony from fifteen witnesses including Jenkins himself. He said that he did not know who killed Billie-Jo, and admitted that he was confused at the time of the attack. He claimed that blood on his clothes came from a bubble bursting in Billie-Jo's nose as he tended to her. A paediatrician called the defence impossible. Another paediatrician said the distribution of blood was consistent with the wearer of the clothes delivering several blows to the head.

I went for a quiet pint to reflect. It felt good knowing we had the ability to react quickly to a fast-moving, live investigation. Adrian's work had been exemplary. Yet I couldn't help thinking that this was just the start. I knew we had it in us to deliver so much more. I craved something more complex. A protracted investigation that we could take over and drive forensically until we got a result.

Little did I know that the Billie-Jo Jenkins case was far from over, or that it would come back to haunt us some six years later.

CHAPTER THREE

OPERATION STURDY – JUNE 1998

Stuck in snarled-up south London traffic, I suddenly remembered my last encounter with Detective Chief Inspector (DCI) Steve Kupis and guffawed.

I had been sitting in the foyer of Camberwell Magistrates' Court waiting to appear as an expert witness when Steve walked in, plonked a young man down next to me and said: 'I've got things to do, Ray. Can you keep an eye on this kid? Give him anything he wants except drugs!'

There I remained all morning, a toxicologist due to give evidence in an assault case, effectively babysitting a witness I'd never met before.

I'd known Steve since my days at the Met Lab. He was a hard-nosed south London copper who you wouldn't want to tangle with, yet we'd 'clicked' right away. In fact, I tended to connect better with detectives than with some of my fellow scientists at the Forensic Science Service.

Maybe it was because, like me, most detectives had learned their craft 'on the job'. I joined the Met Lab as a long-haired, flowery-shirted school leaver who liked football, cricket and beer. Ultimately, I think this is why I got the job. One of the people who interviewed me – a no-nonsense Aussie head of chemistry, Dr Shirley Wilson – seemed to like the fact I was more interested in the football league table than the periodic table. Perhaps Shirley felt the place needed a cultural reboot – 'less geeks and more geezers'!

I never felt like a stereotypical lab 'anorak' and prided myself on being able to translate complex scientific processes into plain English for the cops I dealt with. This had always set us off on a solid footing.

I had taken the job of specialist advisor convinced that the strong working relationships I'd formed with senior detectives throughout the Met Police would have me run off my feet. But, in the eighteen months I'd been in the job – apart from the Billie-Jo Jenkins case – the phone had hardly rung. On the rare occasion a Met detective did call me, it was invariably a request to expedite either a DNA test or result. After almost two years as specialist advisor, I felt more like a DNA delivery boy.

In my darkest hours, I found myself asking the same question: did senior detectives involved in live investigations actually need me? I knew my bosses at the FSS were watching like hawks. Slashing costs often seemed to be their only function. How they'd love to get my salary off their books…

Thankfully, I was picking up some 'real' work from Kent and Sussex Police. I had always 'delivered' for them, and comforted myself in the certainty that word of my general usefulness would spread. Or something so grisly and shocking would happen in London that they'd be left with no option but to get me on board.

And so it came to pass, in the summer of 1998.

After the cold-blooded fatal shooting of a young mum in her south London home, police feared they had some sort of twisted execution gang on the loose. I got a call asking me to meet my old pal, DCI Steve Kupis, at the scene of the gang's first known murder in Tulse Hill, just south of Brixton.

I arrived at Cressingham Gardens to find a baffling maze of low-rise yellow-brick blocks. By the time I'd tracked down Crosby Walk, Steve was already waiting for me. He got straight down to business.

At about 10.30 on the night of Friday, June 25, Kirk Johnson, twenty-nine, heard a double knock on his front door at Number 4. His wife Avril and two daughters, Ashanti, six and eighteen-month-old Zhana, were in an upstairs bedroom watching TV. He could see a figure that he didn't recognise through the glass of the front door.

'Next-door neighbour,' the man said.

Kirk opened the door, and suddenly found himself confronted by three men in baseball caps, one of them carrying a gun.

'Don't make a noise or I'll kill you,' said the gunman, barging inside with the others. 'Where's your money?'

Kirk was forced upstairs at gunpoint to the bedroom where Avril and the kids lay on a double bed. The gunman ordered the youngest of the gang to turn up the volume on the TV. He then pointed his gun directly into Kirk's face. Fearing something awful was about to happen, Kirk made a grab for the weapon. As he and the gunman wrestled, Kirk felt a sudden, sharp pain in his neck. Another gang member had jabbed him with a knife.

The gunman forced Kirk onto the bed with his family. The youngest of the intruders then followed the gunman's order and placed baby Zhana under the bed. As the gunman stood over Kirk, Avril and Ashanti, the younger man snatched all of their jewellery and watches, including a ring Kirk wore with a metal head in the shape of Africa. The raiders then set about ransacking the room, pocketing jewellery and cash. It was at this point Kirk noticed that all three men were not wearing gloves. Having asked Kirk where more money could be found, one of the gunman ran downstairs, reappearing minutes later with £100 in cash, which he waved furiously under Kirk's nose, clearly annoyed that there wasn't more money to be accessed.

The gunman ordered the youngest raider to tie Kirk's hands with a nearby phone charger and his feet with a set of curling tongs. Kirk now noticed Avril was standing by the bed and there was no sign of Ashanti. He realised his wife had bravely shuffled the six-year-old girl under the bed to be with her baby sister. The gunman ordered Avril to get back on the bed while another tied her hands and feet with electrical flex.

To Kirk's horror, the men weren't leaving. Instead, the gunman handed the knifeman his firearm and gave him a nod. The knifeman pocketed his blade and walked around the bed towards Avril. He raised the pistol to her forehead. Before Kirk could say a word, a deafening shot rang out. Kirk closed his eyes. A second shot blasted. Kirk kept his eyes shut and didn't open them again until he heard the front door slam shut behind them.

He turned to find Avril's face covered in blood. Later that night, she died from her injuries.

* * *

As Steve led me around the bedroom murder scene, I could see that just a few dry bloodstains on the carpet now remained of this cold-blooded and utterly mindless killing. And, as Steve pointed out, a hole in the wall.

'The second shot was aimed at Kirk but missed him,' he said, 'it went through the mattress and a magazine rack before lodging here. He did a good job playing dead.

'But the killing of Avril, it was an execution. That's the only way I can describe it. All for a few hundred quid, some cheap jewellery and mobile phones. They're unhinged, Ray. We've got to catch these people.'

'Did Kirk or Avril know them?' I asked.

'Kirk thinks he recognised two of the three suspects. He says he saw them around Brixton with a Jamaican who he vaguely knows and who goes by the street names Junior and Lyrics. The three of them were with some disabled guy in one of those mobility cars, he thinks it was a Renault Clio.

'The thing is, Ray, the Met has an intelligence cell working on this type of crime and they've got informants inside the Black community but no one has come up with any names.'

It was clear from the lack of items in the bedroom that the SOCOs had been and gone.

'You say this gang ransacked the room and wore no gloves, Steve,' I said. 'Why have all these boxes in the closet been left behind? Shouldn't they be testing everything for prints?'

'That's why we've brought you in, Ray. We need you to review the forensics in this and all the linked cases and suggest a way forward. Because at the moment, we're struggling.'

Steve explained that, unknown to the public, they were linking the murder of Avril to a robbery and vicious rape at a flat in nearby Stockwell ten days earlier. And the parallels were chilling.

This time, an eighteen-year-old girl had answered the front door of the third-floor flat while her boyfriend, twenty-four, sat on the sitting-room couch.

A man wearing a black baseball cap grabbed her wrists, forcing her arms behind her back, and marched her towards the sitting room. Two other men entered: one wore a red-and-black baseball cap, the other had a gun in his hand.

The gunman ordered the man on the sofa to lie on the floor. He picked up the man's mobile phone, put it in his pocket and said: 'You have something for me.'

As they tied his feet and hands with electrical flex, the man fought back and was cracked across the head with the gun.

The intruders then searched the flat, throwing things around, apparently looking for either large amounts of cash or drugs. They found a small amount of money and threatened the man, demanding more money.

When he told them that there was more stashed in his wardrobe, two of the suspects dragged his bound body into the bedroom and started ransacking the wardrobe.

Meanwhile, the third intruder dragged the girl into the kitchen and frisked her, taking a £20 note out of her jeans pocket. He then pulled out his penis and, despite her pleas, raped her. He dragged her back to the living room and tied her up with electrical cord. To her horror, another of the men untied her and pulled her back to the kitchen. After hitting her across the face, he forced her to perform oral sex on him. Meanwhile her boyfriend, still in the bedroom, was being kicked and punched by the other two men, frustrated at finding little cash and no drugs. As he lost consciousness, he saw one of them produce a knife.

After the attackers left, the young woman managed to free her hands and found that her boyfriend had been stabbed, once in the back and once in the chest, piercing his lung. The couple staggered to an upstairs flat, where a friend dialled 999.

'The suspects in both cases were Jamaican and the descriptions match,' said Steve.

'The MO is the same. They were armed with a handgun and a knife, tied the suspects with electrical flex and stole mobile phones. And, in both robberies, the gang seemed to be working on intel that the victims had a lot of either cash or drugs on the premises.'

'Anything else linking the victims?' I asked.

'Not yet,' said Steve.

'What about DNA?'

'Vaginal swabs of the girl did give us a DNA profile of the rapist,' said Steve, 'but it doesn't match anything on the system.

That's hardly surprising though is it, Ray, with what's been going on in recent years.'

* * *

Steve was referring to the explosion in so-called 'Yardie' violence. It all began in the late 1980s: blood-chilling reports from New York, where agencies logged more than six hundred Yardie murders in the previous three years and monthly earnings of $9 million from the sale of crack cocaine.

'Yardies' started to make their presence felt in London. Of course, our police don't carry guns, and customs rarely seemed to spot the fake passports of convicted Jamaican criminals, so Britain was considered a soft touch. They pumped crack cocaine into housing estates and used guns and knives with terrifying spontaneity. Soon, places such as Brixton and Harlesden in London and Handsworth in Birmingham were like the Wild West, with each new cowboy behaving like Ivan Martin from the film *The Harder They Come*.

The litany of extreme and random violence was chilling: a man intervening in a row at an illegal drinking den shot four times and left for dead on the roadside. A woman arguing with a crack dealer marched at gunpoint up three flights of stairs, beaten over the head and tossed off the balcony. A seventeen-year-old blasted in the face with a shotgun for selling hooky gear.

All the time, more 'Yardies' flew into London. And their crimes grew more horrific. Using a red-hot iron on a rebellious woman courier; strangling a senior official from the US embassy to stop her exposing a phony visa racket. Few of these crimes were reported. Police only heard about them on the streets and could never find weapons or eyewitnesses.

Police efforts to infiltrate and control this closed underworld had largely failed. It was just a few years since the Brixton riots and, amid accusations of racism and heavy-handedness, the Met kept chopping and changing strategies, one year targeting 'Yardies' with all they had, the next denying that they were a threat at all.

In the meantime, gun violence soared, often carried out by Jamaicans who'd just arrived in the UK on fake passports and were known only by their street names. Just like 'Lyrics' and/or 'Junior', the man Kirk Johnson had seen in Brixton with the two men who would later shoot his wife dead. How were we supposed to trace any of these suspects when all we had was a street alias? 'Like gripping jelly in your hands,' said Roy Ramm, the first senior police officer in Britain to try to tackle the Yardie phenomenon.

Steve Kupis summed it up well: 'Unless we get the Black community onside, we've got no chance of solving this crime.'

JUNE 30, 1998 – 5 DAYS AFTER AVRIL JOHNSON'S MURDER

The fact that something had gone terribly wrong for thirty-year-old Michelle Carby only came to light on the morning of June 30. That's when neighbours on Alma Street in Stratford, east London, were approached by her three children – aged twelve, ten and four – and asked to help 'wake up our mum'.

Exactly what happened to Michelle is not known because there were no witnesses. However, based on evidence at the scene, police pieced together a likely sequence of events. Late the previous night, dressed in her nightwear, she'd opened her front door to the killers while her three kids slept upstairs. She was hit in the mouth, kicked in the legs, bound to a chair with electrical flex and gagged. She was then shot twice in the back of the head at close range. Incredibly and thankfully, her children had slept through the entire ordeal. Rings were missing from her fingers and jewellery from her ransacked home.

Ballistics were able to quickly link the murder of Michelle

Carby to that of Avril Johnson less than a week earlier. Two 9mm Parabellum cartridge cases found in Michelle's living room had been fired by the same reactivated Winchester handgun that had killed Avril. What detectives needed to figure out now was why the gang had specifically targeted these victims. What was the all-important connection between Michelle, Avril and the couple in Stockwell?

And where were this gang going to strike next?

The police needed information and the only place to get it was from the Black communities of London. But the latter viewed the police with suspicion, and justifiably so. There had been a spate of Black people dying in police custody. And the Met Police had still failed to arrest anyone for the racist murder of Black teenager Stephen Lawrence five years earlier.

However, the cold-blooded shooting of two young mothers had horrified local people, and DCI Kupis saw his chance. This was the time to mend bridges. He told Black community leaders that, if they came on board, he would track down the killers of these women. According to these leaders, no senior Met Police officer had ever made them a straightforward promise like that. They went for it.

Prominent figures in the communities of south London threw their weight behind the police operation. They toured their own neighbourhoods, shoulder to shoulder with officers wearing the Met badge, urging anyone with information to call Crimestoppers or the incident room. Race rights activist Lee Jasper – one of the Met Police's fiercest critics – made a game-changing appeal at a Scotland Yard news conference.

'It is time for the Black community to stand up and be counted,' he said. 'This gang has committed wildcat robberies using lethal force. This level of callousness is not acceptable to the Black community. We are witnessing a terror campaign.'

Local citizens responded by calling in a number of street names they believed to be connected to these murders, the most prominent being 'Pepe' and 'Irone'. It might not sound like much but, when it came to crime in south London, detectives often lacked even somewhere to start.

Meanwhile, back at my office at FSS HQ, I reviewed forensics in the three cases – Stockwell, Tulse Hill and Stratford – to see if we could identify any fresh leads.

First, looking at the attempted murder and rape in Stockwell, I was surprised to see that one of the suspects had left a baseball cap at the scene. The lab had carried out tests on the cap but failed to get a DNA profile. I told them to try again.

I also seized upon one curious detail. The female rape victim in Stockwell had noticed one of the gloveless intruders walking around the property picking up and inspecting photos. I struggled to think of a single logical reason why he would've done this, but that didn't matter. I made sure that the photos and frames at all three scenes were dusted for prints.

Third, from the flat in Tulse Hill where Avril Johnson had been shot dead, fingerprints from one suspect had been found on drawers, the magazine rack and a bedside cabinet. However, these prints matched nothing on our databases, confirming that the gang members had likely just arrived in the UK. So, as it stood, these prints would only be useful *after* we'd apprehended the suspects. Even then, they would merely confirm the presence of one of them inside the Johnsons' flat. We needed more.

I then became aware of a fine example of forensic sleuthing at the Avril Johnson murder scene. The SOCOs had checked all hard surfaces for fresh footwear marks. They then cross-referenced the designs with the library of shoe soles maintained at the Forensic Science Service. What they found were curved bars that matched the sole of a Reebok Ripple trainer shoe – neither Kirk nor Avril Johnson had owned a pair. They also found angled geometric blocks with arrowhead-shaped studs and the letters 'i', 'd' and 'a', which most likely belonged to Adidas Falcon running shoes.

I then noticed something intriguing from the police photos of Michelle Carby's flat in Stratford. There was a mark on the bathroom door where it had been kicked in. I checked and this foot mark had been gel-lifted. Examination revealed it to have curved bars from a Reebok Ripple shoe, just like the mark lifted from the lino flooring at Avril Johnson's flat.

This discovery chimed with a very important trend we'd picked up about Yardie gangsters over the years. They may destroy or dispose of their weapons, phones and clothes, but they never get rid of their very expensive trainers.

Dozens of other items retrieved from all three crime scenes – such as cigarette butts, the flex used to tie up victims, drink cans, tiny bloodstains – were still in the process of being tested for DNA. Meanwhile, the three cases were formally linked and an officer placed in overall charge. I made a comprehensive list of all exhibits for DCS Dave Cox, adding an explanatory note beside the most promising items that I was personally chasing up at the lab. If nothing else, having me on board would at least speed up response times from the Forensic Science Service.

JULY 17, 1998 – 8.30 P.M. – 17 DAYS AFTER MICHELLE CARBY'S MURDER HIGHFIELD AVENUE, KINGSBURY, NORTH-WEST LONDON

Primrose John Baptiste, thirty-four, had just run a bath for her two-year-old daughter Tiana when the front doorbell rang.

She opened it to be greeted by two men she'd never met before, one about thirty, the other maybe ten years younger.

'Is Fergie there?' asked the older man cheerfully, referring to her husband, Patrick Ferguson, a plasterer, who was due home any minute.

Primrose couldn't help but notice how fidgety the younger man seemed.

'He's not here,' she told them.

The men turned to walk away. And Primrose blurted out something she'd regret saying for the rest of her life.

'He'll be back soon because he's going to pick us up.'

The older man turned back.

'Shall I tell him who called?' asked Primrose.

'Tony.' He smiled.

At about 9 p.m., Patrick, thirty-four, returned from work just as Primrose and Tiana got into the bath. Tiana called out from the bathroom, telling him that he had just missed the visitors but he could possibly still catch them if he hurried outside.

With that she heard the door slam as Patrick left the house for a few minutes, then returned. He sounded agitated muttering to himself as he moved around the flat.

The doorbell rang. On hearing Patrick go to answer it, Primrose pushed the bathroom door shut.

'It must have been about 9.30 p.m. by now and I was still washing Tiana, who was being her chatty self,' Primrose later told police.

'There was a shuffling sound outside. I heard Patrick saying, "I told you, I don't want anything from you. I don't have anything here," and then he said, "What do you want?" The sound of feet was now a scuffling sound. I got out of the bath and grabbed a towel. It was the combination of the scuffling and Patrick's desperate tone that made me feel sick and I realised something was horribly wrong.

'I saw Patrick and another, who I had never seen before, at

arm's-length holding each other by their throats. Turning to my left, I shouted, "What the hell's going on here?" At this point, Man Two [the younger man from earlier] appeared from my bedroom. Patrick is saying, "I told you, I don't have anything here."

'Everything went into slow motion. Patrick and Man Three broke apart, separated. Man Three is near to my bedroom door, no more than an arm's length from me. I saw Man Three turn to his right to look over his shoulder to where the other two are – his left hand, with which he'd held Patrick, dropped down and from nowhere his right hand came up… his arm is outstretched, pointing at Patrick and in his hand, for the first time, I saw a gun. It was black, squared off in shape and about eight inches long – I've never seen a gun before. I shouted, "Oh my God, please, no!" Patrick then said "Who sent you?" I'd never heard such desperation in his voice. Those were his last words when the gun fired. It was deafening. I saw Patrick falling straight back. My ears were ringing. I heard him hit the ground. I looked to my left to see Man Three leaving – the others had gone. I screamed, "Oh my God no, Patrick." He was not moving. I remember saying, "Why have you done this to us? God no, Patrick no, don't leave us"…'

The bullet that killed Patrick Ferguson went in above his left cheek and exited the lower right-hand portion of his neck. It came from the same gun that had killed Michelle and Avril – which led to all three investigations being linked. This psychotic execution gang had killed for a third time in less than three weeks.

DCS Dave Cox – the officer in charge of the linked cases – asked me to attend the scene with DCI Sue Akers, the senior investigating officer in the Ferguson case, together with the exhibits officer for the inquiry.

'Ray, make sure everything is being done to trace these killers,' were Cox's parting words.

I arrived at the house, a classic 1930s semi-detached suburban residence that had been divided into two flats. After I'd reached the scene on the ground floor, the exhibits officer explained what forensic work had been carried out. He told us that the fingerprint officer was under the impression that the offenders hadn't got far inside the house, and so had focused his efforts around the front door. I couldn't understand this thinking.

'But according to the dead man's wife, Primrose, she saw one of the men come out of their bedroom,' I explained. 'He could've gone into any number of rooms while Patrick was dealing with the gunman. This gang's MO is rifling through homes looking for stuff to sell. We need to check everything for prints, including every photo and frame in the house.'

The exhibits officer threw me a quizzical look.

'One of this gang's weird foibles is picking up and examining photos,' I explained, 'it's happened at one of the other scenes. What about the internal doors?'

'The fingerprint officer said that, as all the internal doors were wedged open, it's unlikely the suspects would've touched them. But he powdered them all anyway, just in case.'

'We should get the Serious Crimes Unit in,' I said. 'They can use chemicals and light sources to recover marks that powder misses. They can bring a lot of extra weapons to a scene like this.'

And I should know, having volunteered for the Serious Crime Unit (SCU) in 1990. Back then, I saw it as my chance to get out there and become involved in crimes on the frontline, something that I'd craved. SCU's role was to bring – literally in a van – the very latest science to crime scenes to help develop fingerprints, marks in blood and any other possible forensic leads. It taught me so much and instilled in me one primary belief: everything that can be done at a crime scene should be done. To me, that's the least a senior investigating officer deserves. If there's

even a one-in-a-billion chance to get a fingerprint, do it. Because
that print might be the one and only chance we have to identify
the culprit. And what if we miss something that is later
found? I'd struggle to imagine anything more humiliating for a
forensic professional.

With Dave Cox's battle cry still ringing in my ear – make
sure *everything* is being done – and knowing that this gang was
out there, no doubt plotting their next atrocity, I was in no mood
for shortcuts.

The wallpaper in the hallway had caught my attention. It was of
the flock variety, old fashioned, but probably still favoured by your
nan. Four men had stood in this cramped hallway. I felt there was
a good chance one of them might have touched the wall.

'Have they checked the wallpaper for prints?' I asked the
exhibits officer.

'Like I said, detectives told me they didn't get in very far, so no
they didn't.'

'Like I said, I think the SCU could use chemicals and lights to
get something out of that. Can you send a sample to the lab for us
to check out?'

I then noticed lots of bloody footwear marks on the wooden
hallway floor.

'Who made all of those?' I asked, suppressing my irritation.

'Paramedics, police. It's a tight space and he was lying in the
middle, so everyone had to walk around him.'

We'd picked up and identified shoe marks at two of the other
scenes. I sensed that this evidence could end up being a crucial
plank of a prosecution case in the future. But any chances of us
finding the same here had been scuppered by what I considered
poor scene-of-crime management. It's fair to say I came away from
Highfield Avenue a little irritated.

Next day, I was sat at my desk in the FSS HQ when one of the bosses, Dr Les Russell, came in.

'I've had a written complaint, Ray,' he said, placing a sheet of paper in front of me. 'About you.'

The first thing I saw was the signature. This letter had been written and signed by the senior identification officer – who'd left the scene by the time I'd arrived the day before. I then saw that he'd copied in the scenes-of-crime branch at Scotland Yard.

I sighed. 'We should at least keep this stuff in-house.'

The complaint went like this:

Mr Fysh, by involving himself in the way he has, has created a great deal of mistrust between certain police officers on 2 Area and this unit. He has also created tension between ourselves and the Serious Crime Unit. Mr Fysh should not imply that work has not been properly carried out without speaking to those involved and he should not offer unrealistic results prior to speaking to the providers.

I would like to suggest to you that had Mr Fysh been more diplomatic, he would have informed the scientific support manager on this Area that he intended visiting the scene and arrangements could have been made for a meeting with the key personnel present.

I sincerely hope that all parties can learn from this experience. However, before progress can be made, Mr Fysh must understand that a little courtesy can go a long way.

I put the sheet of paper down and ordered myself not to swear. I was furious. First, I knew this man. Yet, he chose to publicly air his beef not just to my bosses at the FSS but to Scotland Yard. He could've just picked up the phone! Second, he was suggesting I had undermined his expertise. That was never my intention.

I just wanted to ensure we did the best job possible. Third, there was a gang of homicidal lunatics running around London shooting innocent people in their homes. Surely, in such desperate circumstances, his ego could've taken a back seat, just this once.

'I'll have to respond to it, Ray, you know, keep the peace,' said Les.

'Can I have a copy of this, please? And would it be OK if you did nothing for a couple of days?'

'Of course,' he said.

I picked up the phone.

'I need to see you, Dave, it's not about the case but it is important.'

'Come on up to Hendon, Ray,' said DCS Dave Cox, 'if my door's closed, I'm busy but if it's open, just walk right in.'

I knew I had to nip this in the bud. Yes, I probably should've called the senior identification officer in advance of attending the scene. But DCS Cox hadn't said to me: 'Let's get a date in the diary.' He'd sent me there directly. As a specialist advisor, I needed to be able to attend a scene when requested and call it as I saw it. Otherwise, how could I do my job?

I needed Dave Cox to back me on this. I needed the police to support me and the role of SA. If they didn't back me here – if they didn't insist that I could attend any scene they saw fit and to operate independently – then my role was untenable. Instead of supporting the police, I'd be just another forensics boffin at an already overcrowded crime scene offering an opinion. I didn't want to sound melodramatic, but my authority had to be beyond question.

At Hendon, I found Dave's door open, walked in and handed him a copy of the letter. He read it, handed it back and said: 'I'll deal with this.'

He turned to his computer and started bashing the keyboard.

'This isn't your crime scene. It's my crime scene,' he said, in rhythm with his furious two-finger typing. 'I'm the officer in overall command of the case and if I ask Ray to go to a crime scene and make sure everything is being done, then I expect you and your team to accommodate him in any way you can and action all of his suggestions. If you have any problem with this, call me at your earliest convenience.'

I got back to the lab and sought out Dr Les Russell.

'It's all sorted,' I said to him, 'you won't be hearing any more from our friend.'

A few days later, the senior identification officer who'd made the complaint rather smugly reported that all of my suggestions at the Ferguson murder scene had drawn a blank. But once again he had missed the point. We may not have made any breakthroughs, but one thing we could be sure of: we'd done all we could, result or no result.

Now forensics had drawn a blank, the detectives turned to other means of investigation. It wasn't long before they made a major breakthrough. Steve Kupis called me at work with the update. When they traced the call histories of mobile phones stolen in the first two robberies committed by this gang, records showed that they had been used to call several numbers in Jamaica – and that two particular numbers had been called by both phones. This was it: we had a connection!

The inquiry team contacted detectives in Jamaica, who discovered that one of the numbers called by both phones belonged to a woman who happened to be the sister of twenty-eight-year-old Hyrone Hart – a convicted armed robber who had escaped custody in Jamaica. Police intelligence in Kingston believed that Hyrone was in the UK – and using the street name Irone. This had been one of the names anonymously called in to police after our public appeal.

In a separate development, detectives raiding a property in Clapham, south London, found a photo of a man wearing a ring in the shape of Africa, identical to one stolen in the raid on Kirk and Avril Johnson's flat. A check with Jamaican police revealed the man to be Kurt Roberts, nineteen, a criminal with the street name Pepe – which had also been called in to the London inquiry.

Meanwhile, the Met's network of informers inside the community helped police make another breakthrough. Kirk Johnson had vaguely recognised two of the men who raided his house and subsequently shot dead his wife Avril. He described seeing them being driven around Brixton in a white Renault Clio that had been modified for a disabled driver.

Intelligence revealed this disabled driver to be a twenty-two-year-old paraplegic named Adrian Francis, aka Prento, who had used a wheelchair since 1995 when he was shot in Notting Hill, west London. The bullet, aimed at someone else, had struck Francis in the spine. Since then, his modified disability vehicle had proven perfect cover for the illicit activities of a deadly Yardie gang. After all, what cop is going to stop a person driving a disability vehicle?

Perhaps the prospect of serving a prison sentence had persuaded Francis to talk. He admitted driving Hyrone Hart and Kurt Roberts to the home of Kirk and Avril Johnson. Francis insisted he had no idea what they'd planned at the Johnson address, otherwise he would never have taken them there. Four days later, Irone and Pepe had threatened to kill him if he didn't drive them to Carby's home in east London. Detectives took Francis on a tour of south London so that he could point out other locations where he'd picked up or dropped off the suspects. During this tour, he'd shown them a flat on Weir Road in Balham.

The net was closing in on the killers. But although we had the names of the suspects, we did not know their whereabouts and had no solid evidence to tie them to these vicious crimes. This is where I hoped forensics would come in and prove my worth to the investigation.

A few days later, I was driving through Blackheath in south-east London when I received a call from Steve Kupis. Their tech people had traced the calls made from the phones stolen in the first two attacks to an address at Weir Road, Balham – and it was the same flat pointed out by Adrian 'Prento' Francis.

'We think this is where Hyrone Hart and Kurt Roberts had been staying. Can you get the Serious Crimes Unit over there to lift all the footwear marks? If we can match the shoe marks from this flat to the ones found at the Johnson flat or at Michelle Carby's, we'll know they've been staying at this flat.'

Checking an empty address for footwear marks was a first for us. So far, we only had fingerprints for one suspect, lifted at the flat of Kirk and Avril Johnson in Tulse Hill. But given the way that the cases had developed, it was easy to see why the footwear marks at the Johnson and Carby murder scenes had become so crucial.

The most common method for replicating latent or invisible shoe marks is electrostatic lifting. It's often applied first because, if it fails, it doesn't impact any other lifting techniques. It uses a foil that has a black side and an aluminium-coated side; the black side is placed against the impression and a high-voltage charge applied to the film, resulting in the transfer of the dry dust or residue impression. This then needs to be examined in a darkened room with a high-intensity light source placed at an oblique angle.

Another method commonly used is a gelatine lifter, which is a sheet of rubber with a low-adhesive gelatine layer on one side that can lift prints from almost any surface. Where a foot or tyre has left an imprint in a soft surface like soil, we can make a cast of it, which can then be compared with police records. The lab's exhaustive database of soles had a proud record in helping to establish the brands of shoes left at crime scenes. The 'wear and tear' on that sole is a distinct signature that – if we find the actual shoe – can provide irrefutable proof.

My team reported to me that electrostatic lifting at the Weir Road flat in Balham had provided a dramatic breakthrough. The same pairs of Reebok Ripple and Adidas Falcon shoes identified at the Tulse Hill flat of Kirk and Avril Johnson had recently been in this Weir Road flat.

Exploiting his tendency to constantly call friends and family in Jamaica, detectives were able to trace Hyrone Hart to an address at Junction Road in Handsworth, Birmingham. Next morning, police sent in an armed unit to arrest him. Forensics found at the address two tiny specks of blood on a pair of Nike trainers that had been worn by Hart. Tests showed the blood matched that of Patrick Ferguson. They took Hart's fingerprints and, in a breakthrough that particularly satisfied me, found it matched a print left on a photo frame at the Stockwell flat where the eighteen-year-old woman had been raped.

A day later, detectives arrested Kurt Roberts – street name Pepe – in Chingford, Essex. His DNA matched that of the Stockwell flat rapist and his fingerprints were found at the Johnson flat. Both Hart and Roberts were picked out of an identity parade by Kirk Johnson.

At the Central Criminal Court (better known as the Old Bailey) in December 1999, Hyrone Hart was found guilty of the murders of Avril Johnson and Patrick Ferguson, two attempted murders, two robberies and two charges of possessing firearms with intent. Kurt Roberts was convicted of the murder of Avril Johnson, two attempted murders, rape and two charges of possessing firearms. There is no doubt that forensic efforts in tracing their footwear at three of the scenes helped convict them.

Sentencing both killers to life imprisonment, the judge, Neil Denison, said: 'I will not waste words on you. Suffice to say your conduct was an affront to civilised society. You were part of what was in effect an execution squad.'

As to why Hart and Roberts picked their particular victims, police could find only two possible connections. The murdered women, Michelle Carby and Avril Johnson, shared a mutual male friend. Carby's phone records further revealed she knew Adrian Francis or 'Prento'.

Police also found a solicitor's letter at Carby's home asking her to appear as a defence witness in a case involving associates of the gang. Apparently, Michelle had refused, which may have signed her death warrant.

Hart and Roberts were under the impression that all of their other victims were cash-rich drug dealers, but it turned out that only Patrick Ferguson had been a known dealer and he'd since turned his back on that part of his life.

In July 2000, Adrian 'Prento' Francis, twenty-two, appeared at the Old Bailey, where he pleaded guilty to the manslaughter of Michelle Carby. On learning that Francis' life was in danger because of the help he'd given police, the judge sentenced him to eighteen months, suspended for two years.

Although I had minimal input in this case, it did at least introduce me and my role to senior investigating officers across the Met Police area. It wouldn't be long before I'd be leading a major murder inquiry from the front and applying forensic science in ways that it had never been used before.

CHAPTER FOUR

OPERATION MAPLE
JULY 2000

People often ask how working on a case like the abduction of eight-year-old Sarah Payne affected me. Of course, I felt shock, disgust and outrage that a little girl could be snatched from the edge of a cornfield in broad daylight. Of course, my heart ached for her parents, Sara and Michael, and her siblings, Lee, Luke and Charlotte. But also, in a strange way, I felt privileged. Because while the rest of the nation wrestled with a collective sense of horrified helplessness, I got to do something about it.

I first found out that Sarah had disappeared courtesy of the Sunday morning TV news on July 2. The previous evening at around 7.40, she'd been playing in a cornfield near Littlehampton, West Sussex, with her three siblings when she vanished. She hadn't been seen since.

Hundreds of police officers and volunteers had scoured the fields of rural Kingston Gorse. When they hadn't found her by lunchtime Sunday, I began to fear the worst. If Sarah had been abducted, then she didn't have long left to live – if she was still alive.

I sat there watching the horror unfold on the BBC's rolling

news channel, willing my pager to buzz. In a child abduction case, every second counts. If Sussex Police were going to draft me in, then the sooner the better. As I paced the room for the umpteenth time, my pager finally convulsed and flashed up a familiar mobile phone number.

'I'm afraid it's not looking good,' reported Nick Craggs, principal SOCO at Sussex Police.

'Has the family been eliminated?' I asked, the case of Billie-Jo Jenkins still fresh in my memory.

'Well, it would have to be a conspiracy between the three generations – grandparents, parents and the three kids – which is unlikely. So far, all their stories are standing up.'

'So, what are we looking at now?'

'Put it this way, Ray, in tandem with the missing persons inquiry, we've unofficially set up a murder incident room.'

I thought this a very smart move. Instead of just looking for Sarah, we needed to be searching for and gathering any and every piece of evidence that might point to whoever had taken her.

If the worst had happened, I needed to know something else.

'Have we obtained suitable samples so that we can obtain a reference DNA profile of Sarah?' I asked.

In the event of a body or even body parts being found, establishing quickly whether or not it was Sarah could prove critical.

'Yes, one of Sarah's teeth fell out at her grandparents' home. Her mum gave it to us. We're also trying to get hold of her toothbrush.'

I found it impossible not to think of her tiny milk tooth, which Sarah would no doubt have placed under her pillow that night for the tooth fairy. I stopped pacing my sitting room, the sheer unbridled innocence of that act when juxtaposed with what we were now investigating stumping me for a few seconds.

'You're working on other identification methods too?' I finally managed.

'Yes, we are going to collect personal items from her home to reconstruct her fingerprints.'

'Good,' I said, 'let's hope we never need any of it.'

'Can you be at Littlehampton police station for the seven-thirty briefing tomorrow morning?'

'I'll be there, Nick,' I said, 'and thanks. I really appreciate it.'

That might sound odd, but I was enormously grateful for the call. First, if Sarah had been abducted, I wanted to help catch whoever did it. Second, I wanted to prove that my role as specialist advisor could make a real difference. It had been three years since Billie-Jo, two since Operation Sturdy. Rumours had been swirling that my bosses were planning to axe the role of SA to save money. That was all they ever seemed to be concerned about. They'd already made the decision to charge police forces a daily rate for using me. In my view, this not only went against the very principle of the SA role, it deterred hard-pressed senior detectives from getting in touch.

Until recently, my greatest challenge had been proving my worth to senior police officers in charge of major criminal investigations. Now, I had to prove it to my own bosses.

MONDAY, JULY 3, 2000 – 36 HOURS AFTER SARAH'S DISAPPEARANCE

Jackie and I had moved from south-east London to rural Headcorn in Kent so, to beat the traffic, I hit the road at 5 a.m. As soon as I arrived at Littlehampton, Nick whisked me into a briefing room already buzzing with dozens of police officers, each one carrying a notebook and pen. It was one of those classic, soulless media briefing spaces with a speakers' table at the top facing fifty or so chairs. Behind the top table, taking centre stage on a large white board, that image of Sarah Payne's angelic face that would become so iconic. Pinned up around it, a timeline of the crime so far and contact numbers for key senior staff.

Amid the hubbub, I caught wind of a major development – they had someone in custody.

That was all I knew as three senior officers trooped in and took their seats at the top table. I recognised detective superintendents Alan Ladley and Peter Kennett right away.

Just a year or so earlier, Alan Ladley and I had worked together solving the killing of a ninety-six-year-old resident of a care home in Bognor Regis. Even earlier than that, soon after becoming SA, I'd been introduced to Peter Kennett. As lead officer for child homicides at Sussex Police, Peter and I had both felt grimly confident that we'd be working together some day. And now, here we were...

The third senior officer – DI Martyn 'Tosh' Underhill – was someone I didn't know. I'd soon discover, however, that he had a deep fascination for forensics and would become a key ally.

At this stage Alan was leading the investigation, and he introduced me to the rest of the team.

'This is Ray Fysh, specialist advisor from the Forensic Science Service. Some of you may already know Ray. He'll be coordinating results from the Forensic Science Service as well as advising the team on forensic matters. I'd ask you all to assist Ray in any way you can.'

And that was it! As SA, I found myself properly on the inside of a major police inquiry for the first time. Now I had to make sure I earned my keep.

We were first reminded of the basic background to Sarah's disappearance on the evening of Saturday, July 1. Earlier that day, her parents Michael and Sara and their four kids had travelled from their home in Hersham, Surrey, to visit Michael's parents, who lived on Peak Lane in Kingston Gorse, on the edge of Littlehampton. At about 6 p.m., the visitors sat down to dinner with grandparents Terry and Lesley. After dinner, all but Lesley made the 600-yard walk to Littlehampton beach.

At about 7.20 p.m., the four children went to play 'dinosaurs' in a cornfield next to their grandparents' home while Terry, Michael and Sara had a quick drink at the nearby Tudor Tavern. At 7.40 p.m., Sarah fell, hurt her knee, became upset and headed off through a gap in the hedge towards her grandparents' home, just 150 yards away along Kingston Lane. At 7.50 p.m., her two older brothers and younger sister got back to their grandparents' home to discover Sarah wasn't there. Lesley sent Lee and Luke out to look for her. At about 8 p.m., Sarah's parents and grandad returned from the pub and – along with concerned neighbours – joined in the hunt.

After more than ninety minutes of fruitless searching, at 9.30 p.m. Sara called the emergency services. Officers had been diverted to Kingston Gorse from their normal Saturday night duties to coordinate the search. But, by nightfall, there was still no sign of Sarah.

At first light, the search had resumed. As news of Sarah's disappearance spread, hundreds of volunteers joined in. But Sarah was still missing.

Mid-morning on Sunday, Sarah's oldest brother Lee, thirteen, made a dramatic revelation to police. On his leaving the cornfield, no more than thirty seconds behind Sarah, a large white van had sped past him in the direction of his grandparents' home. It then turned quickly, wheel-spinning, and set off at speed in the opposite direction. Inside, a scruffy man with grey-flecked hair and a red check shirt waved and smiled at him, revealing yellowing teeth.

Door-to-door enquiries led to a neighbour who also saw a

large, white van speeding out of Kingston Lane at about 7.40 that evening. She described it as a removals-style van with no windows on the side or the rear.

'To those of you who don't know,' explained Alan Ladley, 'this is a remote area with not many homes, one road in and one road out. You'd only go there for a specific reason, especially on a Saturday evening. So, whoever abducted Sarah knows the area well and most likely has connections to it.'

Some detectives had been so convinced of a local connection that, the previous evening, they'd decided to take matters into their own hands. They went knocking on the doors of convicted child sex offenders in the area unannounced, on a so-called welfare visit.

Just before 8 p.m., detective constables Chris Saunders and John Fahy rang the doorbell of a flat on St Augustine Road, just off the seafront in Littlehampton. The inhabitant of the flat, Roy Whiting, had been released from prison less than three years' earlier – in November 1997 – having served thirty-two months for the abduction and indecent assault of a nine-year-old girl in Crawley, West Sussex. The detectives got no reply, so returned at about 9.20 p.m. They rang the doorbell again, repeatedly, but in vain. One of the officers went around to the front of the flat and noticed a window slightly open that hadn't been earlier. He decided to try the flat's landline number. It rang for several minutes before Whiting finally picked up. Reluctantly, he agreed to let them in.

The first thing that struck both officers was how clean and tidy Whiting looked. In previous encounters, he'd always appeared greasy and dishevelled. DC Saunders asked him about his movements the day before. Almost on autopilot, Whiting said he'd spent the day indoors watching speedway and football. Then, at about 7.30 p.m., he went to a funfair in Hove – about twenty miles east of Littlehampton – where he stayed about an hour or so. Whiting said he got home at about 9.30 p.m., had a bath and went to bed.

Whiting didn't ask why the detectives needed to know, so DC Saunders decided to tell him: the previous evening, an eight-year-old girl had been abducted on the outskirts of Littlehampton. Whiting exhibited not one iota of surprise or concern. Then, out of the blue, he said: 'What I put that girl through was terrible. I wouldn't do that again.'

Alan told the briefing how the detectives had left the flat deeply concerned about Whiting. His refusal to answer the door. His clean-cut appearance. His lack of concern for Sarah. His odd statement: 'I wouldn't do that again.' Had he been talking about the case in Crawley for which he'd served time? Or was he referring to Sarah?

Listening to their guts, the enterprising pair decided to sit tight nearby and watch the flat. They called a senior colleague, Detective Sergeant Steve Wagstaff, who joined them.

At about 10 p.m., Whiting exited the flat and walked towards a large, high-sided white Ducato van. From their unmarked police cars, the detectives watched, intrigued.

Whiting rummaged about in the back, before retrieving what looked like a dirty, crumpled T-shirt and returning to the flat. Officers now feared he could be destroying evidence of the crime. Disturbingly, a DVLA check on the van revealed that it wasn't registered in Whiting's name.

At 11 p.m., Whiting emerged again, climbed into the driver's seat and started the engine. Fearing he was planning to get rid of the van, DS Wagstaff drove alongside to block it in. The quick-thinking detective then jumped out, went round to the driver's side and knocked on the glass. When Whiting unwound the window, Wagstaff reached in and grabbed the ignition key.

A murmur of respect radiated from the briefing-room floor. That kind of lightning reaction can't be taught.

DS Wagstaff instructed Whiting to go back to his flat with DCs Saunders and Fahy and show them what he had retrieved from the van. The more senior detective wanted to stay back and give the van a quick search. As Whiting had unwound the window, Wagstaff had spotted a piece of paper dislodging from the dashboard and falling into the footwell. For some reason, that small slip of paper had intrigued him.

He felt around the footwell until his hand finally landed upon it. What he now saw changed the entire course of the investigation: it was a till receipt for £20 worth of petrol from the Buck Barn garage, dated 10 p.m., Saturday, July 1. This receipt was from the night of Sarah's abduction. Whiting had told DCs Saunders and Fahy that he'd been home by 9.30 p.m., having spent the evening at a funfair in Hove. The Buck Barn garage is situated twenty miles north of Littlehampton and Hove.

As Alan Ladley spelled out for the briefing: 'Whiting's alibi is now in tatters. Wagstaff asked him the key question: "Do you know where Sarah Payne is?" Whiting insisted he had no idea so the detectives arrested him and he's currently in custody.'

The room sighed as one. If Whiting did abduct Sarah, at least he wasn't out there on the loose targeting his next victim. And it was barely thirty-six hours since she'd been abducted. There was every chance Sarah could still be alive.

'We've taken DNA, blood and saliva samples, as well as a penile swab and scrapings from his fingernails. We've also seized the clothes he was wearing upon his arrest.'

He looked directly at me: 'Ray, I'd like you to get these to the lab a.s.a.p. and tested for Sarah's DNA.'

I nodded.

'On other forensic fronts, our scenes-of-crimes officers are examining the abduction site, Whiting's home and a Volvo car he owns. More are at the Payne family home in Hersham collecting exhibits like hairbrushes or bands that contained samples of Sarah's hair. But I think our most promising lead has to be Whiting's white Ducato van, which has now been brought to a secure premises.'

Alan Ladley surveyed the briefing room.

'As we know, there are eyewitnesses who saw a van broadly matching the Ducato at the scene of Sarah's disappearance. The bottom line is, if Whiting has committed this offence, Sarah must have been inside that van.'

He turned to me and asked the question on everyone's lips.

'Ray, what are the chances of us finding evidence that Sarah has been inside that van?'

I looked around to see all eyes on me and dry-swallowed. The entire investigation could very well come down to this. I ran it through my mind and began nodding slowly. I then made a declaration that the room needed to hear.

'Every contact leaves a trace,' I said. 'If Whiting abducted Sarah, there will be a trace of her in that van, be it fingerprints, biological fluids like blood or saliva, hair, fibres, DNA material from touching items… there'll be something.'

Alan Ladley and Peter Kennett then made one thing abundantly clear to me. Nothing could be missed in this search. Everything evidential must be recovered from that van. We needed to conduct every possible forensic examination on the vehicle and its contents as speedily but as thoroughly as possible.

It felt so crucial that we got the search of this van right that myself and other key forensic personnel found ourselves holding an impromptu meeting. Along with Nick Craggs and Roger Crowley, principal crime scene coordinator, we drew up an examination strategy document to be signed off by the senior investigating officer. This included: how the van would be examined and in what order things were to be done; a full record of the condition of the van, for example the position of seats, levels of petrol, oil levels, mileage; and what exhibits were to be taken, not only from the inside of the van but from other locations, which could prove critical. Examples included materials from under the wheel arches, the tyres (to be compared against any tyre marks at a deposition site), ashtray contents, any mud or detritus from outside or under the van, control samples of oil and petrol, and seat covers.

The conversation next turned to fingerprints and DNA. If you think about the inside of a van, how many surfaces are actually suitable for fingerprint treatments? What are the best surfaces from which to obtain DNA? We summoned fingerprint and DNA experts from Sussex Police and the lab's Serious Crime Unit to discuss the best techniques to adopt.

The resulting meeting saw us bring something entirely new to the old art of lifting fingerprints. For the first time, we introduced a method that enabled partial prints, insufficient for fingerprint identification, to be DNA-profiled. After all, we needed just a single trace of Sarah Payne inside that van to break this case and it mattered not a jot how or where it came from – so long as it was provable in a court of law.

I arranged for Whiting's clothes to be sent overnight to the lab at FSS HQ and made number one priority. It was very late by the time I got into my car and headed home to Kent. Along the way, the radio reminded me of the sheer scale of the ongoing hunt for Sarah, who – until confirmed otherwise – we had to assume to be still alive.

Two hundred and eighteen trained search officers, seven underwater search unit officers, twenty-six Met and Essex Police dog handlers, the Sussex Police helicopter, West Sussex fire brigade, the Ministry of Defence police, five hundred volunteers and three hundred and sixty-five police officers were all out there, searching roads, sheds, farms and lakes and conducting house-to-house enquiries. Even the RAF had joined in, deploying a hi-tech Jaguar surveillance plane to scan and photograph the Sussex countryside in search of any recently disturbed soil. Calls from the public now numbered thousands.

This was already the single biggest operation in Sussex Police history, dwarfing even the 1984 investigation into the bombing of the Grand Hotel in Brighton when the Provisional IRA had targeted the Thatcher government. Yet there was still no sign of Sarah. And it was beginning to look like we'd have to let the prime suspect for her abduction walk free.

After arresting Whiting on Sunday night, detectives had forty-eight hours to press charges or release him. They were pinning their hopes on trained interrogators opening him up in interview. But, so far, Whiting had been sticking defiantly to a 'no comment' stance – and that forty-eight hours for which they could hold him was running down fast.

TUESDAY, JULY 4 – 3 DAYS AFTER SARAH'S DISAPPEARANCE

Initial results from Whiting's penile swab, nail scrapings and clothes had failed to reveal Sarah's DNA. Officers invited Lee Payne – Sarah's oldest brother – to an identity parade of suspects, which included Whiting. Lee had given a detailed description of the man he'd seen driving the white van from the scene of Sarah's abduction. If Lee could identify Whiting, police would be able to keep him in custody.

Lee Payne failed to pick out Whiting.

With time running out, senior detectives were asking the Crown Prosecution Service (CPS) if they could charge Whiting on the basis of his false alibi and his distinctive modus operandi (MO). After all, his previous known offence five years earlier – for which he'd served a prison sentence – bore startling similarities to the abduction of Sarah.

Back in 1995, he had struck one Saturday afternoon in the town of Crawley, West Sussex, grabbing a nine-year-old girl off the street and throwing her into his red Ford Sierra car. He drove his terrified victim to woodland, climbed into the back and ordered the girl to remove her clothes. The victim stated he used his hands, tongue, mouth and fingers to molest her. He then drove to the car park of Crawley Baptist church, told her to get out and sped off. On the evening of the offence, a neighbour who called in on Whiting expressed surprise at how uncharacteristically clean and well-groomed he'd looked.

But despite the similarities in MO and his discredited alibi, the CPS informed Sussex Police that they hadn't enough to charge Roy Whiting.

Late that Tuesday night, police had no choice but to release the paedophile they strongly suspected of abducting Sarah Payne. On the drive home to Kent, it was impossible not to think the unthinkable. What if he strikes again? How could we ever forgive ourselves?

I racked my brains, desperately trying to think of the quickest way we could prove he did it. I was left with the stark realisation that we had only one chance – we needed to find a trace of Sarah Payne in that Ducato van.

WEDNESDAY, JULY 5 – 4 DAYS AFTER SARAH'S DISAPPEARANCE

Detectives led me inside a cold, echoey hangar that smelled of engine oil and introduced me to a tatty white van that would soon come to dominate my life.

One of the team explained how Whiting had purchased

the white Ducato six days before Sarah's abduction but hadn't registered it. Presumably, he'd planned to use the van to commit an offence, then quickly 'flip' it so no paper trail could connect him to the vehicle.

The seller was a man called Dean Fuller who had used the van for house removals. The detective pointed to the rear doors of the van and asked me if I noticed anything. I remembered how the witness who saw a white van speeding along Kingston Lane on the evening of Sarah's abduction had described it as having no windows on the side or at the back. My heart sank. This van's rear doors had windows.

But then the detective opened the doors, ushered me closer and pointed to some writing.

'The serial numbers on these doors match nothing else in the vehicle,' he said. 'Whiting must have purchased these doors before the abduction, then added them to the van after he'd abducted Sarah to throw police off the scent.'

'And it very nearly worked,' I replied.

Whiting's modifications hadn't ended there. As I peered into the body of the vehicle, detectives explained that a wooden floor, a plywood partition between the cab and the rear of the van as well as plywood panels fitted to protect the interior sides of the van had all been stripped out.

'Why did he get rid of these things? It's not hard to imagine, is it?' said Alan Ladley. 'What a story these objects could tell. We're doing all we can to track them down.'

As I was about to discover, Whiting didn't just buy the van from Dean Fuller. He also bought its contents. A quick inspection revealed that the front and rear were jam-packed with rubbish – clothes, tools, food wrappings, drinks cartons, shoes, bags and dirty, smelly socks. Chillingly, on closer inspection I could see bags of sweets, empty chocolate drink cartons, a dust mask, plastic ties, a knife, soft toys and a bottle of baby oil in a carrier bag.

Alan looked at me anxiously, clearly worried that the sheer volume of junk inside might make our task impossible.

'If Sarah's been in here, we'll find a trace of her... somewhere,' I reassured him once more.

But I quickly qualified this with a cautionary warning.

'What we have to be careful not to do though is overload the lab. If we send in loads of these items, they won't know where to start. We'll have a bottleneck before we've even started.'

Cue the groans, which I'd long since grown accustomed to. The single phrase uttered to me most often during my career as SA came from impatient senior detectives and went like this: 'Just get me some DNA, Ray.'

As I found myself constantly having to explain, with forensic science there are usually several steps we need to take with any one exhibit before we can even get to the part that's exciting the police.

Take, for example, a simple request from a detective to find out whether or not a gun has been fired. This normally involves swabbing the inside of the barrel for firearm discharge residue. But before a ballistics expert can get to that, the weapon has to be checked for DNA, prints, blood, oil. The scientist still has to go through that process, in that order, because you can't afford to miss anything. If you race ahead, you can't then reverse-engineer the tests you skipped and get a credible result. After all that, the scientist may well then find cobwebs inside the gun barrel! It doesn't matter. To be a forensic scientist, you need to be meticulous, conscientious and follow all procedures – no matter what the pressures. It's an immense responsibility that cannot and should not be rushed. The consequences of making assumptions or taking shortcuts can be catastrophic.

Back in that hangar, it felt like the grimmest kind of lottery, trying to pinpoint the items most likely to yield Sarah's DNA. The highly trained and skilled SOCOs began by removing everything of potential evidential value from the van – a total of 302 exhibits. We then narrowed it down to the most promising. A section of rope with two tiny areas of blood. Maybe Sarah's? A reddish tartan shirt. Remember, Lee Payne, Sarah's brother, had described seeing the van driver in a red check shirt. An empty Mars drink bottle. Maybe Whiting had used that to placate Sarah? The plastic ties, knife and soft toys were a given. Having lectured the police about not submitting too many exhibits, I now appreciated just how agonising a challenge it proved to be.

Meanwhile, Ray Chapman – a highly experienced biologist – had been allocated to the case as reporting officer and would ensure everything was done 'by the book'.

For example, each piece of clothing from that van would be studied under a microscope and all visible hairs and fibres removed by tweezers and mounted on an acetate film. All hairs and fibres not visible to the naked eye would then be stripped from each garment, inch by inch, using one-sided Sellotape. One by one, each of these hairs and fibres would be painstakingly mounted on acetate. Next, all stains would be checked and subjected to chemical tests for traces of blood, semen and saliva.

It proved laborious and costly – but it remained our best hope of cracking this case. Almost every day, I attended the early morning briefing in Littlehampton to provide an update on all the forensic work carried out the previous day, including samples submitted for DNA profiling. This allowed lead detectives to assess where we were and to adjust according to their latest intelligence or priorities.

For those first two weeks, I spent my days travelling between my home in Kent, the incident room in Littlehampton and my HQ at the FSS lab in Lambeth, – a round trip of some two hundred miles – either receiving or delivering bad news. One by one, our 'most likely' exhibits came up negative; all the while

Whiting remained free and Sarah's family heartbreakingly dignified and positive.

JULY 17 – 16 DAYS AFTER SARAH'S DISAPPEARANCE

In rural Pulborough, about twenty miles north of Littlehampton, farm labourer Luke Coleman was spending his morning picking noxious ragwort weed from a field next to the A29.

Just inside a ditch flanking the busy road, he saw a shape that he guessed to be a dead deer. As he got closer, he noticed that the ground around it had been interfered with. He took a few more tentative steps. What he now recognised stopped him in his tracks – a tiny human leg with a foot pointing diagonally upwards. He realised he was looking at the dead body of a young, naked girl.

Shocked and dazed, he raced home to call the police.

CHAPTER FIVE

OPERATION MAPLE TWO

DNA confirmed that the body found in a field just off the A29 in Pulborough, West Sussex, was that of eight-year-old Sarah Payne.

Over the sixteen days she'd been missing, we'd come to accept that Sarah was most likely dead. Yet when she was finally found, fly-tipped in a field like a piece of junk, it hit us all hard. The entire nation had been so touched by her family's undimming decency and hopeless optimism. It felt like we all had a stake in getting her back safely. Against all cold, hard logic, we'd hoped for some sort of miracle.

This was no longer a missing persons inquiry or suspected abduction. It was a murder hunt. It was now up to us to put this right and get justice for that poor girl and her devastated family. The entire country was watching and expecting.

By now, we'd exhausted our work at the abduction site, Whiting's home and car, leaving us with just the contents of the Ducato van to scour for a trace of Sarah. However, her makeshift burial site now gave us another shot to forensically connect Sarah to her killer.

An aerial image of the field revealed it offered not one but two locations containing potential forensic evidence. The gateway and rough gravel drive into the field were situated about thirty feet south of where Sarah had been hurriedly buried.

Since Sarah's abduction, it felt like it hadn't stopped raining. Whoever had dumped her here would not have risked driving their vehicle beyond that gravel driveway for fear of sinking into the mud. We'd since discovered that Whiting's van had been leaking oil. We sent SOCOs down to check out that gateway and gravel drive for any signs of a vehicle, be it leaked oil, tyre marks, footwear marks or specks of paintwork.

But the critical site for us forensically had to be her shallow grave. It's always crucial to manage the scene where a body has been found. Things have to be done in a certain order. In this case, there couldn't have been more at stake. The first challenge – how could we ensure that all potential evidence from where her body had been dumped was secured?

In the first instance, we needed to limit the number of people traipsing over that area, otherwise vital clues could be tramped into the quagmire and lost forever. Luckily, it wasn't a place used by dog walkers or ramblers. But we still had to keep the numbers to an absolute limit. In forensic terms, who did we actually need to examine that scene?

An entomologist might be able to assist in establishing time of death. But, to be quite honest, we suspected that Sarah had been killed within a few hours of her abduction, so time of death wasn't relevant to us. Besides, while entomology is one of those exotic disciplines often quoted in newspapers and books and featured in TV dramas, it's an approximate science at best. Especially when a body has been dumped in a field for an indeterminate length of time and subjected to variables such as temperature, moisture and interference by animals. So, we elected not to draft one in.

Similarly, we sometimes use a forensic anthropologist to help establish the sex and age of a body. But, thanks to Sarah's DNA sample, we didn't need any help identifying her. So now we had two fewer specialists churning up the deposition site.

We said yes to a geologist. We wanted to try to link Whiting's van to the scene and we'd already extracted soil samples from the tyres of his van and from his shoes. Soil can be a good discriminator; it is amazing how specific it can be to a certain location.

But our single biggest challenge was still securing the body and all potential forensic evidence from the sodden grave. In days gone by, the SOCOs would send for a few cadets to tackle this unenviable task but, by now, we'd come to realise that the contents of makeshift shallow graves were way too important for a bunch of shovel-wielding squaddies. We needed someone who could bring a fresh level of knowledge and expertise to the job. After all, an object as minuscule as a single hair or a fibre could yet provide the crucial breakthrough in this case.

With this in mind, we took a step I'd repeat many times as SA, which, to my knowledge, had never been done before in forensic science. We looked outside the police and its ancillary services for specialist expertise – and found what we needed in academia. Lucy Sibun is a senior forensic archaeologist more used to excavating ancient burial sites and medieval settlements than fresh crime scenes. But the disciplines she'd learned from preserving challenging scenes and recovering every last piece of potential artefact would, I felt, serve us well in these circumstances.

Lucy reported the grave to be four feet eight inches long, two feet three inches wide and just six to eight inches deep in places – so barely enough to fully submerge Sarah. To compensate, the digger had covered it roughly in soil and turf, which animals had been able to forage through, biting on and pulling at Sarah's bones so that the skeleton wasn't complete.

Lucy calculated that whoever disposed of Sarah could have dug this 'inadequate' grave in less than six minutes. She also spotted something about the spade used – it had a blade tip fourteen centimetres wide, which, as I was to learn, is highly unusual.

Pathologist Vesna Djurovic visited the scene as part of her task to establish cause of death. Sarah's body was then recovered and transported for postmortem. One of the first tasks for the pathologist was to take intimate swabs for any traces of Whiting's semen, saliva or DNA. She also took swabs from parts of Sarah's body likely to have been touched by her abductor and killer – for example, her wrist, ankle and breast – which we could examine for the suspect's DNA.

Vesna reported that the body was in a 'moderately advanced' state of decomposition. Sarah had been dead 'for a number of days'.

This level of decomposition made it impossible to detect internal or external injuries, sexual or otherwise. However, Vesna concluded that 'the possibility that there was some interference cannot be excluded.'

She reported: 'In my opinion, from her appearance and the removal of clothing, her death was the result of sexually motivated homicide' concluding that Sarah had died from compression of the neck or suffocation, possibly a combination of both.

Sitting in my office at the lab's HQ in Lambeth, I realised that one of the exhibits from Whiting's Ducato van still to be tested was a spade, currently covered in polythene and sitting in the exhibits storeroom. I put in a call for the blade of that spade to be measured, just in case.

Within minutes, the call came back: 'The blade of the spade recovered from Whiting's van measures fourteen centimetres.'

My heart raced as I went to take a look at the tool in question. It was a typical jobber's edging spade – old, battered and heavily marked. As any toolmark expert will tell you, even the humble spade has a signature and will leave its distinctive dents and marks in clay it has dug. A cast can be made of the sides of a shallow grave that will mirror all the imperfections on the blade used to dig it. Indeed, the more damaged the blade the better, as it will leave a highly specific signature.

This represented a sudden major breakthrough for us. If we could connect the spade from Whiting's van to Sarah's shallow grave, we'd have him. First, I sent the spade off to be examined for prints, DNA, blood, saliva – anything that might link it to Whiting or to Sarah. I then contacted toolmarks expert Trevor Oliver – an Oxford graduate, keen cricketer and one of the best forensic scientists in the business – who agreed to compare the spade with casts of Sarah's shallow grave.

Meanwhile, the massing of bouquets along the A29 in Pulborough led to more witnesses coming forward – and more sightings connecting a large white van to this crime.

London tube worker Sean Matthews had been driving by this very field on the night of Sarah's abduction when a white van 'shot out from the side' without its headlights on, forcing him to brake. Matthews tailed the van – which he described as being bigger than a Ford Transit – for a few miles until it turned right without indicating. He confirmed that its rear doors had no windows.

A local woman, Jacqueline Hallam, recalled seeing a white van parked along the same section of the A29 earlier that night, 'facing the wrong way', with its headlights off.

Yet again, everything pointed to Whiting's Ducato van. At this stage in the investigation the van, along with the deposition site, had become the main focus of our forensic efforts.

I'd never endured so many negative results in a single case, but I felt convinced that one of these two avenues of investigation would provide the breakthrough we craved. As we continued with testing and examining, again I reminded myself and my team: 'Place Whiting's van at the gateway to that field or match his pockmarked spade to Sarah's shallow grave and we have him.'

I was in the lab when Trevor Oliver came to see me in my office. So much faith had I placed in this spade providing a breakthrough that I'd somehow convinced myself that his personal visit must spell good news. Pointing to photos of Sarah's grave, Trevor highlighted marks that could only have come from a spade with a corner missing. He then showed me a photo of Whiting's spade. All four corners were intact. I couldn't believe it. Neither could the senior officers, who insisted on getting a second opinion – but this merely confirmed Trevor's initial findings.

Casting around for another thread to pursue, I rallied the team. OK then, what about the tests on Sarah's remains? But again, nothing. It turned out that heavy rain had possibly washed all DNA or saliva traces from her body. Internal swabs of various parts of her had revealed no trace of Whiting.

I quizzed myself all the way home that night. Was I making the right choices, doing the right things? Was I doing enough? What was I missing? I found myself confronting the terrifying prospect that we may have developed tunnel vision. What if we'd been targeting the wrong man? What if the real culprit was still out there, free and busy planning his next horrific crime?

I got home late but had one more thing to do before hitting bed. During rare and precious 'down times' in this case, many of my colleagues found it hard to 'switch off'. My failsafe method to relax hasn't changed in forty years. It's an ancient de-stressing technique that also helps me take a step away from the detail and think laterally.

A few beers.

No matter how late I got home, or how frazzled I felt, I always made time for those beers. Somehow, it never failed to help me regain my perspective and recharge my optimism.

I don't know how many beers it took that night. But by the time I got to bed, all I could think about were the tests that we still had to carry out on Sarah's grave and at the gravel entrance to the field. And there were exhibits from Whiting's van that we still hadn't examined. Something would come up. Something *had* to come up.

JULY 19 – 18 DAYS AFTER SARAH'S ABDUCTION

The discovery of Sarah Payne's body in Pulborough and all the resulting publicity didn't just yield potential sightings of Whiting's van. It also led to one of the most critical breakthroughs in this case – in the most roundabout way imaginable.

Local woman Deborah Bray drove a lot around Sussex and Surrey as part of her job. Two days after Sarah's abduction – Monday, July 3 – Deborah spotted something unusual on the B2139. Near a crossroads in the West Sussex village of Coolham, she'd seen a tiny black sandal-like shoe lying in the middle of the road.

She noticed the abandoned shoe on two successive days as passing traffic gradually shunted it to the side of the road. When – over two weeks later – Sarah's body had been discovered close by, Deborah realised the potential significance of the shoe and contacted police. Somewhat bizarrely, an officer asked her to go take a look for it herself.

Next morning, she returned to the spot, rifled through the hedge on the side of the road and – to her amazement – found the black nylon shoe. Forensically aware from watching TV crime shows, Deborah picked it up carefully, gripping the strap between her finger and thumb and placing it in the footwell of her car.

She then drove back to a police control point she'd spotted earlier and handed the shoe to a police officer. PC David Webb sealed the shoe in an evidence bag and asked Deborah to take him to the spot where she'd found it.

A thorough fingertip investigation of the area followed but nothing else of significance found. Now the question was: had this black, right-footed child's size-13 shoe belonged to Sarah Payne? Her mum couldn't say for certain. And we struggled to imagine how it had ended up in the middle of this road on its own. Where was the left shoe? Indeed, none of Sarah's other clothes – a blue Fred Perry-style dress, white socks or underwear – had been found.

But one thing made this shoe potentially invaluable to us – its Velcro strap. Velcro acts like a magnet for fibres and is a gift for forensics. But first we'd have to find a way to prove that it had definitely belonged to Sarah.

JULY 23 – 22 DAYS AFTER SARAH'S ABDUCTION

We trudged into yet another briefing in Littlehampton, braced for yet more evidential dead ends. But Alan Ladley delivered news that silenced our grumbling.

Roy Whiting had been arrested – but not for the kidnap and murder of Sarah Payne.

I now discovered that since his release on July 4, Whiting had been under constant watch by Sussex Police. He had been too scared to move back to his seaside flat in Littlehampton, fearing reprisals from enraged locals. He settled instead at his dad's place in Crawley, but a vigilante attack on that house prompted Whiting to take a drastic step. Armed with a tent and a stove, he set off to live rough in woodland.

Despite Whiting's itinerant lifestyle, detectives still managed to covertly keep tabs on him. The night before this briefing, surveillance officers watched in disbelief as he broke into an E-reg car and drove off. The officers followed and a high-speed pursuit ensued. Whiting had been a rallycross driver, and almost lost them a couple of times. The chase ended with him driving directly at two police cars, forcing them to swerve. He then lost control and crashed into a parked vehicle.

To the elation of everyone gathered for the briefing, Whiting had been remanded in custody. He was off the streets! A court later sentenced him to a hefty twenty-two months for theft and dangerous driving. This changed everything.

'The least he'll serve is a third, so we now have a breathing space of about seven months to prove this case and keep him inside – if he's the offender,' announced Detective Superintendent Peter Kennett.

Addressing me, he added: 'All I ask now is that you continue to take your time and do your work as carefully as possible and make sure you don't miss anything.'

I was still under pressure to find that key piece of forensic evidence to connect Whiting to Sarah Payne. But it was nothing like before, when – delivering bust after bust on an almost daily basis for three whole weeks – I'd felt almost personally responsible for the fact Whiting was still free.

* * *

As the summer of 2000 turned to autumn, we'd still not managed to find that all-important forensic connection to seal the case and I could feel tensions ramping up again. My bosses at the FSS kept asking me why it was taking so long. The morale of my forensic teams – who, by now, had spent months on this case – was starting to sag. It fell on me to keep everyone believing.

We just had to keep pushing.

Fingerprint and DNA testing had failed to prove that the size-13 child's shoe found near the deposition site had belonged to Sarah. Undeterred, we assessed our options. Only one remained open to us. We needed to find fibres on that Velcro strap that could *only* have come from the Payne family home. So, now we were looking for fibres to connect the shoe to Sarah's home and to Whiting's van. Initial tests showed hundreds of fibres on that shoe strap. So, lots to work with.

As I reminded everyone, constantly, there were other grounds for optimism. The police were still hunting hard for missing items: Sarah's dress, her underwear, the other shoe, the spade used to dig her shallow grave, the wooden floor and partitions missing from Whiting's van and its original back doors. Any one of these could yet play a pivotal role in proving the case against Whiting.

All this became almost a mantra – if we keep going, we'll find that nugget of evidence that will prove, beyond doubt, that Whiting abducted and killed Sarah Payne.

But as autumn gave way to winter with still no breakthrough, Nick Craggs and I began to ask ourselves some challenging new questions. Should we be finding something and we're not? If so, why not?

We called a meeting with senior management and launched an independent internal review with our scientists into everything we'd done so far. Sussex Police then drafted in Hampshire Police to perform an external review into our investigations. Some people might feel threatened or undermined by this. I didn't. If something was missed, it hadn't been deliberate. And fresh eyes and minds might just bring fresh ideas. All I wanted was to make sure we were doing everything possible to prove this case. The prospect of failing to pin this on Whiting terrified me far more than the idea of personal criticism.

All the reviews came back with the same question we'd been

constantly asking ourselves. If Sarah Payne had been inside that van, would we expect to find something? The answer remained 'yes'. So, they told us to carry on.

As we entered month five and the run-up to Christmas, the pep talks I found myself regurgitating to my flagging teams became a defence of forensic science itself.

Yes, criminals can take extreme measures to cover their tracks forensically. But you can't stop hair transfer, you can't stop fibre transfer, DNA transfer even. This is going on continuously. And that's what forensic science relies on. It's Locard's principle – every contact leaves a trace. We're seeking needles in haystacks but that's real forensic science! If you don't like it, then you're in the wrong business.

Just days before Christmas, I was making my way to a meeting at the lab when Pat Best – a very experienced assistant who specialised in fibre analysis – stopped me.

Pat had already painstakingly removed 340 fibres from the Velcro strap on that child's shoe. She'd placed them on acetate sheets to be viewed individually under a microscope, and had already isolated several fibres that matched items from inside the Payne family home. It was now beyond dispute that this shoe had been worn by Sarah on the day of her abduction.

Now, on day 170 of this inquiry, she led me into the office of Ray Chapman, the reporting officer. The pair excitedly told me how, on removing a red fibre from the Velcro strap, Pat had remembered seeing its distinctive shade somewhere else among the exhibits. She racked her brain and then it struck her. Among the debris in the front cab of Whiting's van, she'd spotted a bright red sweatshirt.

Microscopic examination showed that the red fibre tweezered from Sarah's shoe was indistinguishable, in terms of size and colour, from fibres from that sweatshirt. This, of course, would put Sarah in the front cab of that van! However, to say for certain they were a match required further testing, including instrumental analysis of composition and dye, which would take a few days to complete.

Next morning, as usual, I attended the briefing down in Littlehampton, where I had to fight an almost overwhelming urge to finally deliver some promising news – but I forced myself to hold back until we were certain. After all, our hopes had been raised and dashed several times already on this case.

A day later, Pat called me on my office phone.

The red fibre extracted from the Velcro strap of Sarah's shoe was an exact match to Whiting's sweatshirt.

My hand shook as I put down the receiver. Sheer, unadulterated relief! The Velcro strap of Sarah's shoe had snagged a thread from Whiting's red sweatshirt in the front of the van after she'd been abducted. This proved, surely, that we were on the right track?

Then, the reality check. Of course, this type of red polyester is relatively common. That would be Whiting's defence. But it gave us fresh belief, which our flagging morale sorely needed. And, as we entered 2001, it gave us a new focus: this development indicated that Sarah had been in the front of the van, so we prioritised exhibits recovered from there.

Meanwhile, Pat Best found another notable fibre on the shoe's Velcro strap. This one was multicoloured, with a very specific mix of man-made and natural dyes. These unusual characteristics made it far more powerful in evidentiary terms. First, though, we had to connect the fibre to what it had originally belonged to.

Tests finally proved that this multicoloured fibre taken from Sarah's shoe matched a very creepy item in Whiting's van – a blue-and-white striped curtain featuring tiny, multicoloured clowns that we'd dubbed the Clown Curtain.

Research into products available on the market failed to come up with anything like it. And this got us really excited. This curtain

RAY FYSH   81

had not been mass-produced; it was rare, meaning the chances of Sarah's shoe having picked up a fibre from another Clown Curtain were very small. So the question now was: where had the Clown Curtain come from?

The BBC agreed to feature the Clown Curtain on its programme *Crimewatch*, and it generated 270 calls from the public. One of these calls – from young mum Trudi Nesbitt – proved vital. Trudi said that, in the late 1980s, a friend of hers had stolen the curtain from a Boots mother and baby store and given it to her. The curtain had hung in her son's bedroom for three years until 1992, when she gave it to her ex-boyfriend to plug a hole in the front seat of his white van. The name of this ex-boyfriend was... Dean Fuller.

Dean was the man who – six days before Sarah's abduction – had sold the Ducato van to Roy Whiting. This had been the break we'd been craving. Surely this would leave any jury member in little doubt that Sarah Payne had been in the front cab of Roy Whiting's van.

But, as I reminded my team, we still had work to do. A court would be expecting us to prove 'beyond all reasonable doubt' that Sarah Payne had been in that van. We were still some way short of that...

The red sweatshirt found in the front cabin of the van had already delivered a fibre connection to Sarah's shoe. We decided to go back and re-examine all the tapings from that garment. Among twenty-four hairs recovered from the sweatshirt, our team found one that was blonde and nine inches long – similar in length and colour to Sarah's.

Time for a deep breath! Hair can provide DNA. If this hair had Sarah's DNA, then its presence on the sweatshirt removed from the cab of Roy Whiting's van would surely be indisputable proof that she'd been in there. But to get DNA from a hair, it needs to have good root material. And the chances of this are fairly remote, as hair tends to fall out because the root is dead.

We submitted this hair for DNA analysis anyway. At that time, we were turning DNA samples around in twenty-four hours, so we promised the detectives we'd have a result by 5 p.m. the following day.

I'd delivered more bad news to this murder team than to any other. I dreaded another bust. I awoke several times that night, wondering how the hell I'd motivate my teams if this hair yielded yet another negative result.

Next day, I tried to get busy with other things and put it to the back of my mind. I couldn't. I found myself appealing to the forensics gods; please go well, please find DNA and please let it be Sarah's.

I was in my lab that evening when Ray Chapman, the reporting officer on this case, walked in.

'We've got Sarah's DNA from that hair,' he stated simply.

I seemed to exhale seven months of pent-up frustration right there and then, deflating madly like a burst balloon. I may even have laughed. And then, in self-preservation mode, I refused to believe it. Ray Chapman assured me he'd double- and treble-checked.

We called the incident room.

Detective Superintendent Peter Kennett responded with disbelief. He tentatively sought reassurance that this was real, that it wouldn't turn out to be some cruel and unusual misinterpretation. We assured him that the DNA people had no idea what they were testing. This hair's DNA matched Sarah Payne's. The chances of it being anyone else's were over one billion to one.

Silence.

Finally, he spoke again: 'Right, I'm off to run naked along Littlehampton beach!'

On February 6, 2001, Roy Whiting was charged with the kidnap and murder of Sarah Payne. It had been seven months and five days since she'd disappeared. For those of us who had worked every single day of the investigation, it felt so much longer. And we weren't finished yet…

We still had to get the case ready for the forthcoming trial. First, we needed to get Whiting's DNA from that red sweatshirt to complete the link to Sarah. Obtaining the DNA of a garment like a sweatshirt involves taking swabs from the places most likely to gather sweat – the collar and cuffs. Both revealed Roy Whiting's DNA.

We still had fibres to examine from Sarah's shallow grave. Tests proved that a brown fibre came from the passenger seat of Whiting's van and a blue polyester fibre matched the driver's seat of the same vehicle. Threads recovered from the improvised grave by forensic archaeologist Lucy Sibun matched a pair of socks found in the back of the van.

To our irritation, despite all the evidence we'd gathered, Whiting wasn't pleading guilty to anything. His murder trial – which I didn't attend – began at Lewes Crown Court, East Sussex, on Wednesday, November 14, 2001. But the kick in the teeth for us arrived several weeks earlier.

During defence examination of exhibits that had taken place before the trial, Whiting's legal team had requested to see two hairbrushes that were retrieved from the Payne family home in Hersham. Each hairbrush had been placed in a typical forensic polythene bag with an adhesive seal. Horror of horrors: in one of these seals, the defence team spotted long blonde hairs, including one about nine inches in length, similar to that found on Whiting's red sweatshirt.

I now learned how defence lawyers operate. The one piece of evidence they were most keen to discredit was the hair belonging to Sarah that we had discovered on Whiting's red sweatshirt. After all, that represented the single piece of DNA evidence of Sarah Payne having been inside that van.

The defence made a big play of the fact that we'd failed to spot Sarah's nine-inch hair on the red sweatshirt when we first examined the garment. We had, in fact, spotted twenty-four hairs on the sweatshirt but didn't think any would have the root material needed to extract DNA. It was only later, when we got desperate, that we decided to take a chance on subjecting the best of these hairs to DNA testing.

The defence pointed out that the polythene bag containing the hairbrush and the rogue hairs in the seal had been sent up to the lab as part of a bundle of fifty-five exhibits. Among the other exhibits was Whiting's red sweatshirt. According to Whiting's lawyers, these fifty-five exhibits had all been placed on an open shelf in a storeroom at the Forensic Science Service prior to examination.

Sally O'Neill QC, defending, said the possibility that one of Sarah's hairs had become attached to the outer edge of the bag containing the sweatshirt and then transferred to the sweatshirt as it was being tested in the lab could not be ruled out. O'Neill put it to Ray Chapman on the stand that finding hairs on the outside of the hairbrush packages would have caused him 'considerable dismay'. She said it raised the possibility that the evidence was contaminated.

'The integrity of the exhibits was compromised,' she said.

Mr Chapman said: 'It opens up the possibility that there may have been a transfer from one to another,' adding that it was, in his opinion, 'unlikely'.

I might have phrased it much more strongly. We had tracked down the SOCO who had bagged that hairbrush. He admitted his mistake in sealing the bag on the carpeted floor of the Payne family's sitting room, where the adhesive label must have picked up the blonde hairs from the carpet. It had been an honest mistake that he'd owned up to right away.

We pointed out that the exhibits from the Payne house were transported in a separate brown sack to those taken from Whiting's van. And that each of these items remained in their own separate evidence bag throughout transport and storage.

What's more, the assistant, Zelda Kemp, who performed the examination of the red sweatshirt in the lab, had insisted that no hairbrush had ever been anywhere near her examination and that it couldn't have happened because the hairbrushes were never examined at all. We knew this because they'd never left the FSS lab storeroom! Besides, when we later tested the hairs stuck to the adhesive label of the evidence bag in question, they turned out to belong not to Sarah but to her youngster sister, Charlotte. So, none of Sarah's hairs had been in that seal in the first place.

But this didn't stop the defence making a big deal out of it over a couple of days. Of course, they didn't have to prove anything. All they had to do was indicate that exhibits weren't looked after properly, that anti-contamination procedures hadn't been strictly adhered to. All they needed to do was suggest that such a thing *may* have happened to plant that seed of doubt in the minds of the jurors.

The implications were massive. If the jury disregarded the DNA evidence, they were left with only fibres connecting Sarah to Whiting's van. No matter how strong that fibre evidence might be, it can never match the extremely strong evidence of DNA. And the jury didn't know about Whiting's previous conviction for the abduction and sexual assault of a nine-year-old girl, which had not been disclosed to the court to ensure he received a fair trial.

On December 12, 2001, the jury returned after nine hours of deliberation to deliver their verdict. We all feared the worst. Had Whiting's defence team undermined all of our painstaking work by calling into question one solitary evidence bag containing an irrelevant exhibit?

Whiting was found guilty of kidnap and murder. The judge sentenced him to life.

The scale of the case remains unparalleled. Police received over 35,000 calls from the public. Eight hundred premises, waterways and agricultural complexes were searched across five counties. More than sixty miles of roads were combed for clues. The case involved 910 police officers and 112 support staff, costing the taxpayer over £2 million. In all, counting everyone involved, 136, 941 hours had been put in – which equates to 5,705 days, or 15.6 years.

And yet Whiting's conviction ultimately came down to the discovery of a few fibres and a single blonde hair. Whenever bean-counters at the Forensic Science Service used to complain about how long it was taking us to crack a case, I would remind them of this.

You can't put a price on a moral imperative like getting justice for Sarah Payne and her family.

CHAPTER SIX

OPERATION GREENFINCH ONE – 2001

We have all heard of the classic 'cold case' from true-crime drama. It's a phrase that has become widely used and accepted in popular culture. It's also a phrase I tried to ban at the Forensic Science Service. I still hate it. For me, it diminishes the humanity of the victim, which seems so insensitive to their loved ones. It also gives the impression that we've gone 'cold' on the investigation, in other words given up. The fact is, murder investigations may go dormant, but they're never abandoned. All police forces conduct a review of unsolved cases every two years. With DNA and other scientific techniques improving all the time, there's always hope.

In a lot of unsolved murder cases, detectives have a firm idea who did it, they've just never been able to find the evidence to press charges. But every now and then, a case comes along that completely confounds police and scientists and makes no sense at all.

Operation Greenfinch was one such case.

Throughout my time as specialist advisor, I kept coming back to this case and trying new things. I don't mind admitting that it got under my skin.

* * *

My introduction to the case came via a statement by Ian Plass, a bus driver in Tunbridge Wells and boyfriend of the first victim, twenty-five-year-old Wendy Knell.

Wendy was the manager of SupaSnaps on Camden Road in the centre of her native Tunbridge Wells. On the evening of June 22, 1987, she left work at 5.30 p.m., dropped some clothes off at a laundrette and headed to the home Ian shared with his mum in Rusthall, a village just west of Tunbridge Wells.

Wendy and Ian spent the evening organising a forthcoming trip to Paris, where they were planning to get engaged. At about 11 p.m., he gave her a lift home on his motorbike. Wendy lived in a basement bedsit – flat 9 – at the rear of 14 Guildford Road in the centre of town. Ian walked Wendy to the front door and kissed her goodnight. As he drove off, she waved from the open front door and he tooted the horn.

Next morning, Wendy did not arrive for work. A colleague called the branch manager and, on her advice, went to Wendy's flat. She rang the doorbell several times but got no answer. Another colleague then contacted Wendy's mother Pamela to check if Wendy was OK. Pamela had no idea so called Ian at work and asked him to pop round to Wendy's flat and find out what was going on.

Ian knocked on Wendy's front door and called her name. When he received no reply, he went to the rear of the property to try the back door.

He later told police: 'There was no movement from inside the flat. I then climbed in through one of the fan light windows. I could see Wendy's head sticking out from the top of the duvet. The rest of her body was covered by the duvet. I lifted her right arm up and pulled one of her eyelids. She didn't move. I couldn't believe she had gone.'

Ian couldn't find Wendy's flat keys, so had to climb back out of the window, before raising the alarm at a nearby fire station.

'I rushed in, I sat down, I cried my eyes out. Not a day goes by when I don't feel guilty about her death. Had I stayed with her that night she would be alive today.'

Police arrived to find Wendy's lifeless body lying on her bed naked, with blood on the pillows, the duvet cover and a towel that had been placed underneath her.

Finding no signs of a forced entry, detectives guessed that her killer had got in through a rear window that couldn't be locked as the latch had been painted over.

A search of the bedsit found that Wendy's keys to the front and back doors were missing. Police launched a murder hunt involving some fifty detectives and, within hours, had a prime suspect.

Neighbours described seeing a man looking through the front windows of 14 Guildford Road the night before Wendy's body was found.

Witness Anthony Len lived at flat 7 and told police he'd seen the same man hanging around the property three times a week for the past five weeks. Neither he nor any other of the residents of 14 Guildford Road knew the man. Nor had they heard any disturbance from Wendy's flat on the night she died.

However, a local taxi driver, Anthony Tate, revealed he had had to brake sharply as a blue hatchback pulled out of Guildford Road at high speed at about 1.10 a.m. that day. Had this been Wendy's killer? If so, he'd spent some two hours at the murder scene with the victim, which seemed highly unusual.

The pathologist's report made for grim reading. Wendy had suffered severe blunt trauma to the back of her skull and bruising to her brain, which suggested her head had been pounded onto a hard surface – such as a carpeted floor.

However, severe bruising to the neck and burst blood vessels in her eyelids, face and the lining of her mouth indicated that she had been strangled. Compression of the neck was cited as her primary cause of death.

Forensics found semen on Wendy's duvet that didn't belong to her boyfriend. With DNA in its infancy, a crude, low-level profile was recovered. Police conducted a mass local DNA screen but no matches were made. SOCOs found other tantalising clues to the identity of the offender. On the towel placed under her body, saliva that didn't match anyone known to her. On a Millets carrier bag stuffed behind the bed's headboard, a partial fingerprint in blood. However, the print was of such poor quality that it couldn't be cross-referenced with databases. On a blouse near her bed, a blood-soaked footwear mark that I believed belonged to her killer and could help convict him.

We just had to find him first…

DECEMBER 15, 1987 – 6 MONTHS AFTER WENDY'S MURDER

A farm worker driving a tractor on the edge of a field in the Romney Marsh area, about forty miles south-east of Tunbridge Wells, spotted a large object in a water-filled dyke. He pulled up, got out and headed over to inspect it. It took a few seconds for him to process what he was looking at – the body of a woman, naked except for a pair of tights.

Detectives identified the woman as twenty-year-old Caroline Pierce, who, three weeks earlier, had vanished from Tunbridge Wells after a night out. Although Caroline hadn't known Wendy Knell, the similarities in their murders seemed uncanny.

Like Wendy, Caroline had lived alone in a ground-floor flat – on Grosvenor Park, less than a mile from Wendy's bedsit. And, like Wendy, Caroline worked on Camden Road, where she managed a restaurant called Buster Brown's.

On the evening of November 24, Caroline had been out with friends and had taken a taxi home at around midnight. Soon after, nearby residents reported hearing two long screams with an 'animal quality' and shouts of 'no'. Caroline had not been seen since.

Just like Wendy Knell, the victim's keys were missing, presumably taken as trophies by her killer. Caroline had complained about a prowler since moving into the property less than two months earlier. Friends and a former boyfriend revealed her horror at discovering that items in her flat had been moved while she'd been out, which prompted her to get window locks fitted. And in another chilling echo of the Wendy Knell case, neighbours reported seeing a man acting suspiciously close to her address in the hours before her disappearance.

A pathologist confirmed that Caroline had been sexually assaulted and strangled. However, as she'd been in water for weeks, nothing of any forensic value could be recovered from her body or the tights she'd been wearing. Despite this, detectives linked the cases. And the primary reason they did this was not revealed to the public or to grieving relatives and friends: the pathologist felt certain that both victims had been sexually assaulted *after* they'd died. Detectives weren't just hunting a killer. They had a serial necrophiliac on the loose.

2001 – 14 YEARS AFTER THE 'BEDSIT MURDERS'

'We're in our seventies now, we just want Wendy's killer to be caught before we die.'

It was impossible not to be moved by the dignity of Wendy's parents, Bill and Pamela Knell, and their quiet determination to keep this case in the public eye. Wendy's murder had destroyed the lives they knew; they were haunted by their grief. It happened on Bill's birthday, which he never celebrated again. As a coping mechanism, he threw himself into work and refused to retire. It was the only way he could stop dwelling on what had happened to Wendy and the fact that her killer remained at large.

Pamela described how, grief-stricken, she cut everything down in their garden 'because it shouldn't be living'. Fourteen years on, she still often found herself in that garden at 3 a.m. crying, with no knowledge of how she'd ended up there. Every day, she still said 'good morning' and 'goodnight' to a picture of Wendy. She felt hurt by the fact that people she used to know now crossed the road to avoid her.

No one wanted to fulfil the dying wish of Bill and Pamela more than Kent Police, who, fourteen years after the murders, asked me to review the case. Reading the file, I felt convinced of a couple of things. First, Wendy and Caroline's killer must have been local. Only someone who lived in the area could have selected and observed these women in the weeks and days before he struck.

I was also convinced that their killer must have built up to these barbaric murders. I've never known a case like this where the offender hasn't got form for violence against women. With a killer or rapist, you can always identify a depressing escalation in their criminal behaviour building up to this ultimate act. It often starts in the home, with domestic violence or sexual abuse. You'll usually then find voyeurism, indecent exposure and sexual assault in their records. I felt certain that this man would be known to police somewhere.

Finally, unless he'd died, emigrated or received a long prison sentence for separate offences, it was a safe bet that he didn't stop offending in 1987. This man had a warped sexual appetite that needed to be sated. Surely he hadn't been getting away with it for the fourteen years since he'd killed Wendy and Caroline?

The obvious first step was to get Wendy's semen-stained duvet back into the lab. By now, we had advanced profiling methods that could extract a more detailed DNA profile. We ran the updated profile through the national database – and got no hits.

At the scene, forensics had recovered a bloodied partial fingerprint on the Millets shopping bag they found. Despite advances in techniques since 1987, we still couldn't extract enough of that poor-quality print to run it through databases.

It shouldn't have mattered. We had his full DNA profile. How, after so many years, had the DNA of a double killer not surfaced on the DNA database? Where the hell had this killer gone and what was he up to? It simply didn't make any sense.

If he was local at the time, he could still be living in Tunbridge Wells, or have family in the town. So, Kent Police conducted a second DNA intelligence-led screen. Again, no matches.

In an effort to trace potential family members of the killer, a number of familial searches of the National DNA Database were performed. How we trace potential relatives of a suspect all comes down to the ten pairs of numbers that make up a person's DNA profile. One half of your DNA profile is inherited from your dad and the other half from your mum. As a result, the DNA profile records of a parent and child – or two siblings – will share a significant proportion of the ten pairs of numbers. Such a search may produce a list of possible relatives, which can then be narrowed down by other intelligence, such as age and geography.

We repeated the exercise several times throughout the 2000s; as soon as you run a familial search, it's already out of date, as more DNA profiles are always being entered into the system.

Again, none of this got us any closer to the killer. It would be another twenty years before we'd find out the grim truth about these murders, and the grotesque way the killer of Wendy and Caroline managed to satisfy his sick sexual urges for decades while remaining under the radar.

CHAPTER SEVEN

OPERATION SWALCLIFFE
ONE FRIDAY, SEPTEMBER 21, 2001

It's just after 4 p.m. when IT consultant Aidan Minter, thirty-two, leaves his office in the City of London to attend a meeting on the South Bank. The capital still feels eerily quiet. It's been ten days since the World Trade Center bombings in New York. Fearing a copycat terror attack, many Londoners are steering clear of the most likely target – the financial centre, known as the Square Mile.

Halfway across Tower Bridge, Aidan glances absently down at the fierce grey river rolling below. He sees, floating towards the bridge, a brown, spherical object moving westward at some speed, caught on the river's strong seasonal tide.

Aidan thinks it must be a beer cask, from one of the many 'disco boats' that ply their trade on the Thames. However, when he sees that the 'beer keg' is wearing orange shorts, he guesses it must be a tailor's mannequin. Intrigued, he makes his way down to the water's edge and waits for the object to float past.

As the current turns, the dummy shifts to reveal severed stumps of bone. Aidan frantically pulls out his mobile and dials 999.

Within minutes, the Thames Marine Police Unit launches a crew towards Tower Bridge. A mile upstream, near the Globe Theatre, a flash of orange in the dark water seizes their attention.

Moments later, an officer hauls the mutilated torso of a small child out of the water. The resulting investigation has been described by one leading officer as the toughest in Met Police history.

MONDAY, SEPTEMBER 24 – 3 DAYS AFTER THE BODY IS DISCOVERED
FORENSIC SCIENCE SERVICE HQ, LAMBETH, SOUTH LONDON

Detective Inspector Will O'Reilly delved into a large brown manila envelope, pulled out a fistful of A5 colour prints and laid them out on the conference room table. The images took some time for my brain to register. Perhaps my brain didn't want to.

These photos showed the body of a young, well-nourished boy minus his head and limbs.

The other officer present, Detective Superintendent Dave Beggs, had called me over the weekend seeking an urgent meeting. I'd dealt with Dave before. A tough south Londoner, his tone had seemed uncharacteristically rattled, and now I knew why.

Over the hum of the overhead fan, Will O'Reilly spoke to the room. 'He was fished out of the Thames late Friday evening. We don't know who the child is, where he is from or what happened to him. We're guessing he's of African or Caribbean extraction.'

As I surveyed the places where the child's head and limbs should be, I heard myself ask, somewhat optimistically: 'And we're sure none of this damage was done by boat propellors?'

Will shook his head glumly.

'A postmortem was conducted by Dr Mike Heath on Saturday. This is what he could tell us:

'The victim is a Black male, aged four to seven years. Death was caused by a violent trauma to the neck. Dr Heath believes the boy was already dead when the head and limbs were cut off, because of the lack of any violent reaction.

'If you take a look at the cut to the neck, it's very precise. A knife had been inserted into the right rear side of the neck and pulled forward in a manner he'd only ever seen in the slaughter of an animal.'

I stopped myself dwelling on the horror of what I was hearing by focusing on the cold, hard facts. It was the only way to cope.

'Dr Heath thinks the knife was then sharpened and used to cut off the arms and then the legs.'

Will allowed some time for the gravity of this to set in.

'Dr Heath believes the boy was placed in the water about twenty-four hours after he was killed. He thinks the orange shorts were put on him just before he went in, as there is minimal traces of blood on them.'

I wondered why they'd dressed him in such an eye-catching colour. Surely whoever had killed and then decapitated this boy didn't want his torso to be spotted floating down the Thames?

Will went on: 'He'd been in the water for up to ten days as the skin is just starting to peel. His genitalia are intact. There's no sign of any sexual interference.

'In your experience, Ray, why would anyone decapitate a child?'

I paused, allowing the shock and violence of what lay before me to sink in. 'Normally, for three reasons,' I began haltingly. 'To disguise the child's identity. You can't check the dental or fingerprint records of a torso. Another reason is for storage. You cut up the body so you can put it into a confined space to either hide or transport. But that doesn't make sense here. This kid is so small, his torso is barely the length of a twelve-inch ruler. They could've stuffed him into a bog-standard holdall and dumped him anywhere. Throwing his torso into one of the world's busiest rivers wearing a pair of bright orange shorts makes no sense at all.'

'And what's the third reason someone dismembers a child?' asked Dave.

'In my experience, mental health issues,' I explained

Will glanced up at me, arching an eyebrow that said 'brace yourself' before speaking:

'Dr Heath believes the body was held horizontally or even upside down after death and drained of blood.' He took a sharp intake of breath before adding: 'He thinks there may have been a ritualistic aspect to this.'

I felt myself shudder. What did ritualistic mean? Black magic? Human sacrifice? How could something like this happen in the centre of London in the twenty-first century? Where did they get this poor boy from? My work over three decades contained a veritable galaxy of horrors, but nothing as singularly disturbing as this.

'What can I do to help?' I asked.

'The first thing we need to do is identify him,' said Will, 'it's the only place to start. Until we've identified him, we're not going to be able to trace his family, the crime scene or the likely offenders. So, use whatever means necessary Ray. Just find out who this poor boy is.'

Our best hope of swiftly identifying this boy was to obtain a DNA profile. But to identify someone using DNA, you need some sort of reference. Needless to say, there was no record of this young boy's DNA profile on the national database. But we figured that there just might be a profile of his parents or relatives.

As DNA is all about genetics and inherited traits, this child's DNA profile would match that of both of his biological parents in certain key areas. These days, tracing people's relatives on the DNA database – a familial search – is commonplace and performed by a computer programme.

In 2001, that wasn't the case.

Back then, our computer systems allowed us to search for a DNA match only. And so, I set about conducting the first ever familial DNA search in the UK in the rather unscientific setting of my sitting room in Kent, using a pen, lots of paper and a couple of spare weekends.

At that time, the National DNA Database held the profiles of about five million people – way too many for one person to trawl through. So how could I narrow that figure down? First, I decided that the crime almost certainly took place in London. It's unlikely you'd decapitate a young boy in, say, Liverpool or Newcastle, then transport the body to the capital to dump into the Thames. If the crime took place in London, the likelihood was that his parents either lived or had once lived in the city. The DNA database records where an offence took place geographically. So, if either parent had been involved in any sort of criminal incident in London, they'd be on that database.

I found another key way to narrow down my search. The victim appeared to be Afro-Caribbean. So his parents would be too. The database contained some 39,000 people of Afro-Caribbean appearance. This slashed the odds of me finding a match from 'impossible' to merely astronomical. From the boy's DNA profile, I worked out sixty-four combinations (from six of the ten loci of the DNA profile) of numbers that his biological mother and father would have in theirs. The National DNA Database cross-referenced these sixty-four combinations with their records, and then manually checked all these profiles against the four other loci in the DNA profile, resulting in thousands of profiles. I then manually checked these results, isolating those that matched closest to the boy.

I was looking for a needle in a haystack, but we had to start somewhere. And so, over the course of those two weekends, my sitting room slowly started to fill with one massive pile of paper – those who couldn't be related to the boy – and one much smaller pile featuring those who just might be related.

It proved tough and the search, fuelled by copious amounts of caffeine, continued day and night. I ended up with thirty-five males and eleven females whom we couldn't exclude from being the boy's parents. I passed on their details to Will O'Reilly, who set detectives the task of checking out these forty-six individuals.

One by one, police eliminated each and every one as a relative of the dead boy. But such is the lot of the forensic scientist: we often deal in painstaking and ultimately fruitless processes of elimination.

Attempts to identify anyone who may have had contact with the boy also proved fruitless: his days spent in water had washed away any traces of blood, saliva, hair, fibres or semen.

Next, we looked at the dismemberment marks on the body and what, if anything, they might reveal about his killers. We brought in an excellent toolmark expert, John Birkett, to examine the cuts. He soaked the relevant bones overnight in an enzyme that stripped them clean of flesh and exposed the very precise wounds. Birkett reported that if police found the knife used in the dismemberment – and it hadn't been damaged since – he felt confident he could match it to the cut marks. Again, it felt like a long shot but, for the remainder of the investigation, police sent us every knife, blade or machete seized in the enquiry, hoping that one would come up trumps.

Finally, toxicology tests on the torso threw up something truly bizarre. The boy's stomach was empty; he clearly hadn't eaten for several hours before his death. But checks on the liver and kidneys uncovered traces of pholcodine, or over-the-counter cough mixture. Before cutting this boy's throat, his guardians had been treating him for a cough. It simply didn't make any sense.

In tandem with our forensic work, police were conducting their own investigations into the crime and the boy's identity. They checked out missing persons registers and immigration records. They contacted 3,000 nurseries and primary schools in London asking if any boys between four and eight years old had disappeared suddenly in recent weeks. They looked for potentially linked cases across the UK and Europe.

The only solid piece of evidence detectives had to work with were the pair of bright orange shorts that had been placed on his torso. The inside label sported the brand name Kids 'n' Co and revealed the shorts to be size 116, for girls aged five to seven. Washing instructions were in German.

Struggling to find out more, detectives featured the shorts on an episode of the BBC's *Crimewatch*. which had become such a key weapon in our investigative armoury. One, and only one, caller phoned in, and claimed that the shorts had a similar label to clothing she had bought in a German store called Woolworths. Detectives discovered that this chain had no connection to the old pick-and-mix Woolworths shops of my youth and were more like Marks & Spencer.

Good old-fashioned police legwork established that the shorts had been one of a batch of 1,000 manufactured in China; and since going on sale in March 2001, 820 size-116 pairs had been sold, across 320 stores in Germany and Austria.

Detectives conducted a feasibility study into tracing every pair of those shorts. But the German economy in those days ran almost entirely on cash – not cards – making such an enterprise virtually impossible.

Another standard tool for investigators is CCTV. As a result of the IRA's terror campaign in the capital since the 1970s, London is awash with CCTV cameras. And that was the problem. Where should police start looking? How could they pinpoint the most likely place along the Thames for the unfortunate boy to have been dropped in? The murder team employed an oceanographer to study the river's tides, in the hope that he could narrow down their hunt to a specific section of the riverbank. The oceanographer's report did the opposite; the boy could've gone in anywhere from Chiswick to the Thames Barrier. The prospect of harvesting and watching CCTV from twenty-one miles of the Thames shoreline, both sides, was swiftly ruled out. However, the oceanographer did furnish us with a far more specific revelation, one that I'd never forget. Two more turns of the tide and we might never have known of the little boy's existence. Had the Thames ebbed twice more, what little remained of this tortured body would have been swept downstream to the sea, forever concealing the unspeakable indignities he'd endured.

Unable to examine activities on the river's shoreline, detectives turned their attention to who was on the river in the ten days leading up to the body's discovery. After all, the boy's body might have been jettisoned from a boat. To our alarm, officers found out that no agency recorded traffic using the river. No one knew what vessels had been travelling up and down the Thames through the very heart of London, or why. Bearing in mind the river passes MI6 HQ, the Houses of Parliament and the City of London as well as the thronged commuter hubs of Victoria, Waterloo, Charing Cross and London Bridge, this seemed an extraordinary gap in the capital's security.

With no leads coming from the shoreline or the surface, detectives decided to dive deeper into the river's murky depths. Searching the foreshore at low tide, officers made a chilling find. Washed up on the southern shoreline near Battersea Power Station, a large white sheet wrapped around seven half-burned candles. A name – Adekoye Jo Fola Adeoye – had been written three times on the sheet and the name Fola Adeoye inscribed on the candles. Could this be the boy's name? Was this proof that he'd been sacrificed in some barbarous ritual?

We examined the sheet and candles for blood, orange fibres – anything that might connect them to the little boy lying on a slab in Wapping mortuary. We found nothing.

Meanwhile, detectives hunted high and low for anyone sharing that name or versions of it, and held a press conference appealing for information. They got no leads.

A detective sergeant on the case, Nick Chalmers, set to work on anagrams of the letters and cross-referenced them with records in the UK and abroad. After weeks of laborious research, he finally found a Foya Adoye, apparently very much alive and well in New York – and aged in his twenties.

Detectives tracked him down, and got to the bottom of their shamanic shoreline find. 'Fola' explained how he'd moved to Manhattan from London a few years earlier. His Nigerian parents, who still lived in London, had made this river offering to the gods in thanks for their son surviving the 9/11 attacks. Yet another bust. A month on from finding this tiny torso, we had nothing.

If, after a month, a suspicious death remains unsolved, the case is subjected to a regulatory review. This is to check that all primary leads have been followed up and to figure out how the investigation can be moved on.

So, where could we go from here?

We had nowhere to start: no one to question, no potential witnesses, no alibis to check, no addresses to visit, no deposition site to search. We had the child's DNA but no one to link it to. We had no fingerprints. We didn't even have a face.

And we had no motive. What could possibly have provoked someone to murder and decapitate an innocent child, dress his mutilated torso in colourful shorts and then throw him into the Thames?

Often, the last resort in a case where we have exhausted all leads is publicity. Sometimes all it takes is a single phone call from the public to crack a case. And this case was a gift to broadsheet and tabloid sensibilities alike. Here we had a headless, limbless child who'd possibly been the subject of some terrifying human sacrifice or black magic ritual in the heart of Britain's capital city. But, in the wake of 9/11 and the invasion of Afghanistan, this case struggled to secure so much as a fleeting column inch. Who cares about the murder of one little boy – however gruesome and mysterious – when the planet is on the precipice? It didn't help that he had no family or community bashing down doors, demanding answers.

With no viable leads and more urgent murder cases coming in thick and fast, the easiest option for the Met Police would've been to have quietly shelved this investigation. They sent the file to the FBI, who advised them to do exactly that. As far as the Americans were concerned, the case was unsolvable and should be consigned to the bin. Will O'Reilly's boss and head of the Met Police's Serious Crime Group, Commander Andy Baker, was in charge of 33 investigation teams, some 1,400 staff, across the Met Police area. The last thing he needed on his heaped plate was an unsolvable case that nobody cared about.

It was now that I gained a unique insight into the human side of the much-maligned Met Police. Will O'Reilly and his boss, Commander Baker, told the investigation team that we would definitely *not* be quietly shelving this inquiry. For starters, there was pride at stake! The message from the FBI had acted like the proverbial red rag to a bull. Who were these Americans to tell us we couldn't solve an inquiry? Commander Baker decided to set up a dedicated 'Gold Group' of specialists to investigate this crime. The group included Andy, Will O'Reilly, Detective Sergeant Nick Chalmers, Kate Campbell, Met Police Press Officer, an advisor on African religions, me and a wonderful man called John Azar, an advisor to the Metropolitan Police who could help us navigate the racial and cultural sensitivities of this investigation.

At our first Gold Group meeting, Andy Baker made a rousing address that left us all in no doubt as to our mission.

'The boy has no community, so we shall be his community,' he said. 'This boy has no family bashing down doors, so we will be this boy's family bashing down those doors. And we will not rest until we've found the people behind his murder.'

Andy Baker and Will O'Reilly decided that, with no photo to use on posters or in appeals, we needed to personalise this boy by at least giving him a name. Perhaps by restoring some small dignity to his soul and reminding people that he was somebody's son, the public would be more likely to engage.

So, what should we call him?

We thought about naming him after the man who first spotted him in the river. But Aidan didn't sound right. We considered the location where he'd been fished out of the water – just yards from the Globe Theatre, synonymous with William Shakespeare. But we didn't want people thinking he'd been named after senior investigation officer Will O'Reilly. Someone came up with Kofi – which, in the Ghanaian language of Twi, means 'born on a Friday', the day the boy had been found. But everyone had heard of the Ghanaian Kofi Annan, then Secretary-General of the United Nations, and we didn't want people to assume that the boy must be from Ghana. The option finally agreed upon is a name that represents all mankind, which we felt fitting: Adam.

* * *

Of course, there were other pressing reasons behind our determination to track down Adam's killers . We needed to ensure that the murder of another innocent Black boy in London didn't go unsolved. For me, this case represented nothing short of a shot at redemption after what I consider my single biggest disappointment during my time as specialist advisor.

A year earlier, in November 2000, ten-year-old Damilola Taylor was found bleeding heavily on a stairwell of the North Peckham Estate in south-east London. Despite the efforts of several passers-by and an ambulance team to save him, Damilola was certified dead at King's College Hospital. A trail of blood from the wound in his leg led to Blakes Road, where police believed he was attacked and stabbed with a broken bottle.

On a human level, Damilola's death shamed us all. So many iconic images from that case still haunt anyone connected with it. That start-of-term school photo of Damilola, smiling and full of hope in his new burgundy school jumper. The harrowing CCTV footage of him leaving the computer club at Peckham Library at 4.51 p.m. The sight of him skipping along with a smile on his face, a boy fresh to London, trying to better himself. Fifteen minutes later, he'd be bleeding to death in a dingy, cold stairwell. The quiet dignity of his parents. His needless death resonates to this day. But it chimed with Commander Andy Baker and me for an altogether more personal reason.

After Damilola's murder, I attended meetings with Andy and learned that two local brothers – Danny and Ricky Preddie, aged twelve and thirteen – were being named locally as the killers. Both were members of the Young Peckham Boys gang, which had been terrorising the neighbourhood for years. Andy Baker's instructions to me were crystal clear. The brothers' clothing and shoes had been seized and sent to the lab. He wanted every thread examined with the proverbial fine-tooth comb for blood. And he wanted a DNA profile taken from any blood sample found.

I got back to the lab and passed these instructions on to the scientist assigned to the task. To my surprise, the scientist responded defensively, basically telling me to stick with liaising with the police and to leave the science side of things to him. In short, keep your nose out of my lab. I felt I couldn't – especially in a case as high-profile and important as this. So, I repeated Andy's instructions in an email to the scientist in question. Little did I know how crucial that email record would later become.

Some weeks later, I reported back to Andy that Damilola's blood had not been found on any of the clothing belonging to the Preddie brothers. The police went on to charge other suspects for Damilola's murder, based on the testimony of a local fourteen-year-old girl known as Witness Bromley. But the trial against these suspects collapsed when it emerged that Witness Bromley had constantly changed her story, had run up a massive hotel bill while in witness protection and had been 'induced' by officers with a reward of £50,000.

A new senior officer was assigned to the Damilola case. One of the first things DCI Nick Ephgrave did was send the clothing seized from the Preddie brothers to a private forensics company for re-examination. Imagine my horror and humiliation when that company found a drop of Damilola's blood on Danny Preddie's trainer and another on a sweatshirt belonging to Ricky Preddie – both exhibits that we at the Forensic Science Service had supposedly painstakingly examined. The news made me feel sick to the pit of my stomach. I honestly believed that a blunder of this magnitude would see the Forensic Science Service scrapping my specialist advisor role at a stroke. If they needed a reason to do so – and fulfil their eternal mantra of saving money – they now had it.

I confronted the scientist who had examined the clothing with the news. His reaction astonished me. He blamed his assistants, to whom he had assigned the work, but he had not checked the clothing for any possible bloodstains that the assistants had failed to locate or detect. My disappointment turned to rage. How could you assign a task of this importance to assistants in the first place? Why can't you just admit you made a mistake and say sorry?

But he never did. He never openly acknowledged the mistake or took any responsibility for it, let alone apologised. But this wouldn't be my first run-in with arrogant boffins at the Forensic Science Service.

I then had to face Commander Andy Baker and confess our mistake. I dreaded it. So much had been at stake in the Damilola investigation. After the Stephen Lawrence tragedy, the Met felt on trial to deliver. And they would have, had we not missed this vital evidence. To me, it was inexcusable. I felt like I had let Andy and the murder squad down. More importantly, I felt like I had failed Damilola's family. Selfishly, I mourned all the trust and respect I had nurtured with senior Met officers over the years.

It was at times like these I learned why certain people are born to lead. Andy took the news stoically, accepted my assurances that vital lessons had been learned, that the mistake wouldn't happen again, and moved on.

Of course, an internal FSS inquiry followed and the scientist in question transferred from the frontline to training. If I hadn't reiterated Commander Baker's specific instructions in that email, I may well have met a similar fate. But that wasn't the main lesson I learned from the Damilola case. From that point on, I became obsessed with checking results. And re-checking results. Anything to ensure that, under my watch as specialist advisor, the FSS wouldn't miss vital evidence again.

Memories of this failure in the Damilola case clearly also weighed heavily on Andy, who made it clear that he wasn't willing to have the unsolved murders of two young Black boys on his record.

* * *

In December 2001 – three months after the discovery of Adam's torso – our Gold Group committed to a pre-Christmas poster campaign, a publicity blitz and a £50,000 reward for information leading to Adam's killers. We also pencilled in a conference about the case at Bramshill police training college, Hampshire, for early in the new year. The idea of the conference was to glean insights from the broadest range of expertise possible, so we invited pathologists, scientists, criminologists, forensic experts and police officers of all ranks, serving and retired.

The only other lead left to explore at this stage was the ritualistic nature of Adam's murder. Decapitation and evidence of bloodletting suggested a ceremonial aspect. Was the manner of his death – and the distinctive orange shorts – a signature of a particular religion or cult that engaged in ritual murder? And could this lead us to Adam's killers?

Dr Hendrik Scholtz was an expert in ritual murders at the University of Witwatersrand in Johannesburg, South Africa. He agreed to perform a second postmortem on Adam and to give his findings at the Bramshill event in early 2002. What Scholtz revealed shocked even the hardened souls gathered for this conference.

He introduced us to the concept of 'muti', which is a Zulu word meaning 'medicine'. It is a traditional form of healing practised by sangomas – witch doctors – and is found in various forms across most of Africa and in the Americas. In the Caribbean it is known as voodoo, and in Latin America santería or candomblé.

Scholtz quoted one report claiming that South Africa alone had 300,000 sangomas, who are consulted by about 80 per cent of the population. Sangomas frequently take out advertisements in newspapers promising to boost salaries, enlarge penises, increase fertility, help people pass exams and win the lottery, and even protect car owners from being hijacked.

Scholtz explained to the gathering that most forms of muti are benign – but not all, as the South African police could attest. Over the previous decade, the country had reportedly seen a sharp rise in the practice of sangomas demanding human body parts to make up their medicines. Some estimates put the number of muti murders in South Africa at more than five hundred per year.

These murders are usually the result of a client approaching a corrupt sangoma with a problem – perhaps a failing business, infertility or serious illness. The sangoma will then hire a killer to provide the specific body parts necessary for the cure. Most of these are often pretty literal; genitals to cure infertility, brains for political power and business success, and so on.

Children's body parts are considered more valuable than those of adults; the younger the child, the purer and therefore more powerful the blood. There is also the idea that each person has a limited supply of luck, which can run out. But very young children have not yet had to use their luck – so it can be transferred to whoever takes the medicine derived from their remains.

According to Scholtz, the bodies of murdered children often indicated that they had been well fed and cared for. Very frequently, indeed preferably, the child victim to be sacrificed was from the client's own family – a son or niece, cousin or sibling. Distraught parents convinced themselves that the child would have a 'better life' with a 'new soul'.

This would certainly explain why no one had claimed Adam or reported him missing.

Of all the body parts used in muti, the one considered most important sits between the neck and the spine. The atlas bone is so named because, in mythology, the giant Atlas bent his neck to hold up the world. Police pathologist Dr Mike Heath, who carried out the first postmortem, had reported that the atlas bone had been severed from Adam's body.

Scholtz confirmed that Adam's body bore all the hallmarks of a ritual killing and that such a human sacrifice would be made when a small group of people needed to obtain supernatural powers to be successful in something like business or politics.

A close examination of the cuts where his head and limbs were sliced from his body showed that they were carried out by an expert using extremely sharp knives specially prepared for the purpose. The process, reminiscent of animal sacrifice, saw the flesh around the limbs and neck cut down to the bones, which were then slashed with a single blow from an implement much like a butcher's meat cleaver. Adam would have been stretched out horizontally or upside down during the sacrifice and kept in position while the blood was drained from his body.

He pointed out that Adam had been circumcised, which suggested he was more likely from West Africa – where the practice occurs shortly after birth – than South Africa, where it is considered a passage to adulthood.

Scholtz told the conference he believed that wealthy Africans based in London had 'imported' Adam from West Africa, probably using a specialist witch doctor for the task. The boy's family may well have sold him in the belief he was being trafficked to a better life – a job waiting in Europe.

Later that day, I faced the task of updating the conference on where we were forensically. In front of such distinguished guests, as ever, I felt nervous approaching the podium. But I knew that, forensically, we'd covered all the conventional bases. The reality I imparted to those assembled was that, in a case as unusual as this, standard forensic tools were not much use. We needed to think of doing something new, and all ideas were welcome.

When I finished, before the entire conference, Commander Andy Baker assigned me one task: try to find out as much as you can about Adam – including his identity – through science.

At first, I reeled. Where could I even start?

But then I felt a real surge of pride. Until now as SA, I'd felt like a bit-part player. In the Billie-Jo Jenkins case, the police had already gathered the evidence, which we then corroborated. In the Sarah Payne case, Roy Whiting had been arrested before I'd got involved. The forensic teams did a great job finding the crucial evidence in Whiting's van but, once again, we were corroborating what they'd already suspected. This time, things really did seem to be the other way around. Whatever you might see on *CSI: Crime Scene Investigation*, the popular television programme, in real life forensic scientists were not usually called on to lead or solve investigations single-handedly.

Now the police were asking me to figure out a way to identify the victim so that they could track down his killers. The detectives needed us scientists to show them the way forward, to drive the investigation. I just had to figure out a way to identify this boy from his tiny, bloodless torso.

I decided to stay overnight at Bramshill and, that evening, met Will and Andy Baker in the rather grand bar, which felt more like a museum of police memorabilia. As we sat, Will pulled out a map of the world, which he unfolded and laid before us.

'So, what we know so far is that Adam is from somewhere here,' he quipped, waving his hand over the whole page. Quite the starting point… We needed to find a way to narrow it down as much as possible.

To say Will and Andy shared my excitement about devising

groundbreaking new techniques to identify Adam would be a rank understatement. A few beers helped us get lateral in our thinking and I found myself furiously jotting down ideas on a piece of paper.

What else could we do with DNA? Could it help narrow down where he was from? What else might reveal where he lived? Parasites in his gut? Fluoride levels in his teeth or bones? Could we do more to trace antibodies or vaccines in his system? What about his lungs? Might traces of pollen tell us if he was from the UK or from Africa? What could his bones tell us? Might they indicate if he was from a rural or an industrial area?

As Andy went to get another round, Will O'Reilly sat back thoughtfully. If his surname didn't already give it away, Will's thick eyebrows, strong face and pale skin were a monument to Irishness. He'd been a formidable rugby player and it showed in his stocky frame and fearless approach to everything. What Will now said stuck with me for the rest of my days as a specialist advisor.

'The trouble with you scientists, Ray, is that you don't speak your minds,' he said. 'You're always hiding behind impartiality and independence. What we need sometimes is your best opinion, without you worrying about how you're going to present it in court.'

I never forgot these words; they became something of a mantra to me. I realised that in forensics we'd got used to being on the periphery of cases, dispassionately examining samples and exhibits, oblivious to the human significance of any result. What we did was black and white, binary and dry.

Now, as forensic science was becoming so critical – not just in proving cases but in helping detectives solve cases – they needed more from us. It was one thing helping the police to 'prove' a case after they'd already done all the hard yards. It was altogether more challenging to help them solve a live, ongoing murder or rape. If we were to be of any real benefit during a live investigation, then we needed to think like detectives, not scientists.

Cops needed us to be more creative and adventurous in our approach, to let our gut instincts lead our brain. If we were going to help them develop and drive fresh leads, we had to take risks and push the science beyond where it had gone before. As the Americans would put it, we had to get out of our comfort zone.

I went to bed late, pumped and a little scared. I couldn't rely on anybody else, because nobody else had done this before. I'd have to plan this route to finding out Adam's identity all by myself.

Andy and Will were expecting results. They'd given me this chance to deliver. I couldn't afford not to.

CHAPTER EIGHT

OPERATION SWALCLIFFE TWO
SPRING 2002 – 6 MONTHS AFTER THE
DISCOVERY OF ADAM'S BODY

My first mission: to delve into Adam's DNA profile to see what, if anything, it might reveal about him or his ancestry. I approached one of the senior biologists at the Forensic Science Service who'd already worked on this case.

I asked: 'What other information might we be able to get from Adam's DNA profile? For example, could it give us clues as to where he comes from or where he lived?'

'It can't be done,' he said abruptly.

'Excuse me?'

'What you're proposing. It can't be done.'

'Right, and you're not willing to even discuss the possibility?' I said, making sure he registered my astonishment.

'You don't want to be wasting my time and the police's money trying to get more out of DNA,' he said.

'It's hardly wasting anyone's time. This is our job! And we are talking about the murder of a child here.'

'Can't be done,' he said, turning his back on me.

'So much for the enquiring scientific mind,' I said, giving the door a good slam on my way out.

* * *

This wasn't the first time I'd clashed with a scientist at the Forensic Science Service. This man was just one of a group who very loudly insisted they didn't need a specialist advisor 'telling them what to do in their own labs'. I was getting used to it. Years earlier, certain scientists at the FSS had objected to me becoming a reporting officer in toxicology because my degree came from a polytechnic and not one of the 'traditional' universities. Such snobbery astounded me, but I could live with it – so long as they did their jobs properly. Alas, some of our more experienced boffins just didn't want to stretch themselves or their science. One we even nicknamed NFA, as in 'No Further Analysis', because that's all he ever seemed to report.

Not Fucking Arsed, more like.

I was far from alone in experiencing this particular biologist's toxic brand of hubris. A senior detective told me how he'd once called him seeking an urgent result. When the scientist failed to return his call, the detective rang again and finally got through. The scientist's response: 'I don't normally start until you've asked for it a third time.'

His frankly offensive dismissal of the idea that DNA could give us more than just a code for someone's identity made me desperate to prove him wrong. I decided to go outside of the FSS and seek expertise in academia. I approached professors from lots of top universities who were publishing papers on the human genome. Some didn't get back to me. Others did and seemed fascinated by what I was hoping to explore, generously hearing me out and giving me the benefit of their wisdom. But no one bit. No one offered to join forces with me to see how far we could push DNA for the benefit of forensic science.

I then remembered a talented and enthusiastic geneticist I'd dealt with over the years at the FSS branch in Birmingham. Andy Urquhart had spoken to me before about his research into using DNA to establish the skin colour of a suspect where there were no witnesses. Andy's endlessly enquiring mind and love for a good pub made him terrific company. I suspected he'd jump at the chance to get involved in something as challenging and unorthodox as this.

I gave him a call and asked him straight: 'Could we work out Adam's ancestry from his DNA profile?'

'There are ways, potentially. But we don't have an international database.'

'So how are we going to go about this?' I asked.

'Well, we're just going to have to build one, Ray!'

As we know, DNA profiles in those days decoded ten areas of DNA. But these ten zones of the genome were selected purely because of their ability to discriminate between people. These numbers do not reveal hereditary detail like eye colour, skin colour, hair colour or shape of nose. So, these DNA profiles have no use for ethnic referencing. But, as Andy explained, there are other zones of DNA that do reveal physical details about a person.

Andy suggested we look at mitochondrial DNA, found in the mitochondria, the cell's energy-producing power plants. Mitochondrial DNA is passed straight from mother to child. You have the same mitochondrial profile as your mother and your maternal grandmother. Furthermore, you have the same maternal profile as your brothers and sisters. Those with this mitochondrial DNA would, somewhere back down the line, share a female ancestor. If, as appeared increasingly likely, Adam had been brought into the country from Africa, it might help tell detectives where to look on the continent.

Andy also suggested investigating Adam's Y chromosome, which is passed down the paternal side. If you are male, you have the same Y chromosome profile as your father, grandfather and so on. However, as you go further back in time, it represents a rapidly diminishing proportion of your total ancestry. For example, you have sixty-four great-great-great-great-grandparents, and share your Y chromosome with just one of these ancestors.

To help our investigation, Andy somehow managed to get hold of DNA profiles from all corners of Africa and set to work. He had no guarantee of success but, refreshingly, wanted to give it a go. Like all great forensic scientists, he wanted to push his discipline as far as it could go.

Only a matter of weeks later, he called me with news.

Adam's mitochondrial DNA and his Y chromosome excluded South Africa and East Africa, linking him to several countries in West Africa, but most specifically Nigeria.

I felt elated. It might not sound like much, but it was our first breakthrough. And it justified the decision to press ahead with the research, which turned out to be a waste of neither our money nor the police's time.

Of course, Adam could've been born and bred in Peckham, south London – as could his parents. London at that time was home to almost 100,000 people of Nigerian origin, so we were still dealing with very long odds. His parents might not even consider themselves African. Their family could've ended up in the Caribbean centuries ago – as so many West Africans did as a result of the slave trade – and come to London from there.

But, thanks to Andy, we had something rare in this case – something we could say for certain. Adam's ancestry was West African.

With apologies to Neil Armstrong, this proved a significant step for our investigation but a giant leap in developing ethnic inferencing from DNA. Eventually an international database of profiles from every corner of the planet was developed. Andy Urquhart died in 2005, but his legacy lives on. Today, you can even find regional variations in mitochondrial DNA on the internet! And a British university is currently building a Y chromosome database that links this genetic information to the other thing a father generally passes on to a son – a surname. As most offenders are male, such a tool could yet prove a game-changer in policing.

* * *

In April 2002, Commander Andy Baker and Will O'Reilly – who by now had been promoted to Detective Chief Inspector – flew 7,000 miles to South Africa, the only country in the world with a specialist occult murder unit.

The first thing they learned was that Adam's murder was most likely not a muti killing as first suspected. Dr Gérard Labuschagne, commander of the South African police's investigative psychology unit, pointed out that when people are killed for muti, their genitalia and vital organs are removed. This had not happened in this case, leading him to conclude that Adam had died in a sacrifice, possibly satanic, not directly connected to African witchcraft.

They also met with Credo Mutwa, one of South Africa's leading sangomas, who delivered a shocking interpretation of the boy's killing. He said the killers would have drunk the boy's blood after his death using a 'skullcap' cut from the severed head.

'His finger joints would've been used as charms or ground into a paste as part of a ritual in order to give these criminals strength. I think this is a human sacrifice to some sort of water deity carried out by a gang of people strengthening themselves to do some very ugly crimes. They have made this sacrifice because they are filled with fear for what they have done or what they are going to do.'

Sangoma Mutwa said the killers were followers of a West African form of witchcraft that practises 'the most horrible form of human sacrifice, usually on a child that has not yet reached puberty'.

Without knowing anything about the other leads already steering the investigation towards West Africa – Andy Urquhart's DNA work and the fact that Adam had been circumcised – Credo Mutwa had pointed us in the same direction. This opened up a significant new lead; if we could identify the West African belief system that practises such rituals, it would bring us into the orbit of Adam's killers.

To help identify the deity to whom the sacrifice was made, senior detectives contacted a criminologist, theologian and lecturer in African religions at Bath Spa university who also happened to be the only multicultural expert on the national police database.

'Identifying the particular god or goddess won't be easy,' he warned. 'There are literally hundreds in the West African pantheon.'

However, as he set to work on the challenge, he acknowledged that the orange shorts and the fact that Adam was deposited in a river may help.

Just a few weeks earlier, I had found myself staring at an empty map of the world, wondering where to even begin. Now, at least we had a place to start – albeit a vast and varied region of 16 countries and over 300 million people. But corroborating a West African connection hadn't been Andy and Will's biggest achievement in South Africa.

It had been our contention since day one that the best chance of catching Adam's killers would be to trace his family. Somehow, we needed to spread the message around the whole continent of Africa: is anyone missing a small boy? Before Andy and Will had left for South Africa, the former had a moment of inspiration.

He asked Scotland Yard press officer Kate Campbell to put in a call to the office of former South African president Nelson Mandela. His personal assistant took the call, listened to what Kate was proposing and immediately passed the phone over to her boss. Within seconds of Kate's explanation, Mandela declared: 'I'll do it. I'll do it.'

What a coup!

Not only did Mandela make a heartfelt appeal for information relating to Adam, he pulled strings to ensure it was broadcast all over the continent and, where necessary, translated into the tribal languages of the most remote regions of jungle, desert and bush. Mandela's interest in Adam didn't end there. Every now and then, he'd personally ring the incident room and politely request an update. We were all simply blown away by the man's humility and utter decency. Small wonder he was revered the world over.

With Adam's ancestry and the nature of his killing pointing to West Africa, Will O'Reilly posed a very interesting question. How did we know Adam had been alive in London? Because if he wasn't alive in London, had a criminal offence even been committed in the UK? Could he have been killed in another country, then his body parts transported to the UK and dumped in the Thames?

How could we find out where Adam had spent his final days? As in previous cases, I returned to archaeology, and discovered how analysis of ingested dust and pollen can deliver answers to this very question. I called a specialist in the field – known as a palynologist – with the very apt name of Nick Branch.

Nick seemed surprised, pointing out that his previous experience studying pollen content in corpses had been on bog bodies found in Cheshire and victims of ritual killings from the Iron Age.

'Do you think you can do it with Adam?' I asked.

'There's no reason why the same principles of detection and analysis can't be applied to modern bodies. I'd certainly love to give it a go.'

How I wished some of my less motivated scientists at the FSS could muster such enthusiasm.

The first thing Nick requested was samples from the pathologist. As nothing had been found in Adam's airways, stomach or upper intestines, his only option was to investigate the contents of the large or lower intestines. You don't go down there to get samples unless you really have to. But there were advantages. Whatever he'd find in the large intestine would've already been digested by the boy, so it couldn't have come from the waters of the River Thames.

A few weeks later, Nick called me at the FSS lab in Lambeth with an update. In Adam's large intestine, he found samples of pollen. Tests revealed the assemblage contained pollen from alder and birch trees, which are found in Europe, but not in West Africa. He also found pollen from grasses and cultivated cereals that can only be found in north-western Europe in September – the month Adam had been fished out of the water.

Branch deduced that the pollen spores might have come from Adam's final meal. If this was the case, he just had to match the pollen to the food in question. Displaying the borderline-insane tenacity of the true forensic scientist, Branch went around supermarkets picking out cereals, breads, crackers and cakes to see whether pollen lived on in them. The answer was no.

The pollen, therefore, had almost certainly been breathed in, hitching a ride on Adam's saliva to end up in his large intestine. As Nick pointed out, this process would've taken up to seventy-two hours. This meant that, in all probability, Adam had been in

Britain for at least three days. We'd answered Will's question – it seemed almost certain Adam had been murdered in the UK.

Sadly, the pollen couldn't tell us if he'd been here any longer than three days. He might still have been born and raised in Peckham, but what seemed more likely was that he'd been trafficked here specifically for the purpose of being sacrificed.

Realising this, I couldn't help wondering what lies the captors had fed him about the purpose of the trip. They'd treated him so well before his killing. At what point did poor Adam realise the horrific truth? I just hoped he'd been oblivious to his terrible fate until the very end.

I reminded myself that the only thing I could do for Adam now was to help find his killers. So, when Nick Branch mentioned he'd found other contents in the boy's large intestine that he couldn't identify, I sent them away for testing. Little did I realise the extraordinary truths these mysterious contents would eventually reveal.

APRIL 2002 – 7 MONTHS AFTER THE DISCOVERY OF ADAM'S BODY

Modelled on a chateau in France's Loire Valley, the Royal Holloway University in Egham, Surrey is just nineteen miles south-west of our grey and brutalist five-storey HQ in Lambeth, south London, but felt a world away.

I parked at the end of the long, sweeping drive, got out and went in search of the office of Ken Pye, the professor of environmental geology.

I'd known Ken, a large man with a jovial disposition, for a few years. He'd frequently assisted detectives and forensic scientists in identifying soil samples. Oddly though, I'd never before worked with him directly. Today I had a proposal for Ken that – if he accepted – would be a world first in forensics. But he might just laugh me out of his office.

In January, at Commander Baker's very public request, I'd agreed to build as detailed a picture of Adam as possible. Our groundbreaking DNA work had proved his West African ancestry. What I wanted to ask Ken Pye today was, is there a way we can establish where Adam had lived for the few short years of his life? Because wherever he lived, his family lived too. He went to school there, had friends. Someone would know *something*.

Part of my role as SA was to try to drive science forward, to do the unthinkable, the unexpected, to try new things. Ever since taking the job, I'd been reading articles and academic papers on subjects like archaeology to see if any developments in that field might help us in ours. I'd discovered that, in universities across the length and breadth of the UK, experts were beavering away, driving new scientific developments that could help us catch killers.

I'd lost count of the number of nights I stayed up late, reading paper after paper trying to understand science outside my specialist field of toxicology. Luckily, my wife Jackie is an avid reader herself and a rock of support, so she'd sit there with me devouring her latest novel. My quest to understand became all-consuming. Sometimes, a scientist would say something and, that night, I'd have to go home and try to make sense of it in a book or online. In effect, I had to become self-taught in all sorts of disciplines like genetics, geology and biology. I had no alternative but to get hold of a book or webpage and learn it.

As the liaison between scientists and detectives, I then had to find a way to communicate complex science into layman's terms – often just so I could understand it myself! But I could see a wealth of possibilities out there in academia, availing ourselves of the very latest scientific developments and adapting them to our ends. After all, forensics has always piggybacked on developments in other scientific disciplines and adapted them for our own purposes. Take DNA for example.

* * *

Back in 1984, geneticist Sir Alec Jeffreys had been examining DNA to try to ascertain why certain racial groups suffer specific medical disorders more than others. Classic examples include sickle cell disease, Creutzfeldt-Jakob disease and the hereditary blood disorder thalassaemia. Assuming it had something to do with their genes, Jeffreys set about trying to establish a method to study a person's DNA. On September 10, 1984 – while looking at the X-ray film image of DNA taken from his technician's family – Jeffreys had his eureka moment. He realised that each person has a unique genetic code.

Three years later, DNA profiling was used for the first time in the prosecution of Colin Pitchfork for the murder of two teenage girls in Leicestershire, exonerating the original prime suspect, Richard Buckland. It is now considered the single most important scientific development in crime fighting. Of course, this had not been what Professor Jeffreys had set out to achieve. But forensic science adopted it anyhow!

The field of archaeology particularly excited me. After all, they too were concerned with the provenance of dead bodies and using evidence found at dig sites to string together a factual picture of events. Late one particular night while reading in my sitting room, I stumbled across an archaeology paper that seemed eerily relevant to Adam's case. It intrigued me that, since the 1970s, archaeologists had been able to determine the geographical origins of ancient bones by studying their chemical make-up. I wanted to know if we could apply this science to identifying murder victims. More specifically, could Adam's bones tell us whether he'd spent his life in London, West Africa or somewhere else?

I delivered the question to Ken and he didn't laugh, which was a good start. In fact, I was relieved to see his eyes visibly light up at the possibilities.

'What do you know about isotopes, Ray?' he said.

'Very little, only what I can remember from my undergraduate days,' I replied.

I was soon to learn a lot more.

All elements, including carbon, nitrogen and oxygen, are made up of individual atoms. Each atom consists of a nucleus, which has a certain number of positively charged particles (protons). The number of protons defines the element: so, six for carbon, seven for nitrogen, eight for oxygen and so on.

Also present in the nucleus are neutrally charged particles called neutrons. These neutrons bind the protons together in the nucleus; without them, the protons would repel each other and the nucleus would fall apart. I liken neutrons to cement that binds the bricks in a wall together. Without the cement, the wall would collapse.

Lastly, to make the atom electrically neutral, the nucleus is orbited by a number of negatively charged particles called electrons. To ensure the atom is electrically neutral, electrons will number the same as the protons.

Isotopes are simply atoms of the element that contain a different number of neutrons. For example, carbon-12 has six protons and six neutrons in the nucleus, carbon-13 has six protons and seven neutrons in the nucleus, whereas carbon-14 (used for carbon dating) has six protons and eight neutrons in the nucleus.

Once I'd digested this, Ken hit me with a fresh query.

'What do you know about strontium?'

'It's a naturally occurring alkaline earth metal element,' I answered, adding, 'and it's relatively abundant in the Earth's crust.'

'Correct. But here's the interesting thing about strontium. It has four major isotopes – 84, 86, 87 and 88. Strontium-87 is formed from the radioactive decay of rubidium-87 at a steady rate since the Earth first formed 4.6 billion years ago. Geologists use the ratio of strontium-87 to strontium-86 to determine its geological period.'

While I found all this fascinating, I struggled to see what it had to do with Adam's ancestry. I didn't have to wait long.

'But here's the *really* interesting thing about strontium isotopes. They remain unchanged in ratio from rock to soil to water to plants,' he explained.

'Animals eat the plants and drink the water. We then eat the plants and animals and these isotopes get passed on to us and stored in our bones in the same ratio. So, basically, the ratio of the strontium isotopes in the soil will be mimicked in our bone chemistry.'

'So,' I said, getting it straight in my mind, 'as the old expression goes, we are what we eat?'

Ken nodded and I felt a surge of excitement at the possibilities this presented.

'So, Adam's bones can tell us where he comes from?'

'In theory, yes,' said Ken.

Ken's use of the word 'theory' told me 'disclaimer incoming'…

'The thing is, Ray, most Western countries have information and databases on strontium levels in rock. I suspect nations in West Africa will have far less. Building a database of this information means basically geologically mapping the entire planet from scratch. It's a massive undertaking.'

I raised my eyebrows in anticipation; was this a 'no can do' or a 'can do, if you give me time'?

'It's going to take us months,' Ken said and I smiled.

'Just think of the possibilities, Ken.'

'I am, Ray. Trust me, I am.'

MAY 2002 – 8 MONTHS AFTER THE DISCOVERY OF ADAM'S BODY

Although Adam's murder had failed to set the news agenda alight in the UK, the case prompted a Europe-wide alert that African ritual killings were being imported into the continent.

The discovery of Adam's torso brought to light a number of other ritual-style killings of young children in Sweden, Germany, Belgium, France and Italy. Although they didn't connect the killings, Europol – the office that coordinates police work across the European Union – in May 2002 called a unique meeting of police chiefs, forensics experts and academics to discuss these cases and pool our knowledge. It was somewhat melodramatically titled The European Ritual Killings Conference, and Commander Andy Baker, DCI O'Reilly, the academic expert in African religions and I were all invited along to the Hague to speak.

While O'Reilly and I glumly relayed our lack of leads and progress over the previous six months, the African faiths expert used the platform to confirm that Adam had been the victim of a human sacrifice and to finger the West African religions he felt most likely responsible.

According to the professor, Adam may have been sacrificed to one of the 400 Orisha or ancestor gods of the Yoruba people, Nigeria's second largest ethnic group. Oshun, a Yoruba river goddess, is associated with orange, which is the colour of the shorts placed on Adam's body before he was offered to the Thames.

The cultural clues certainly fitted neatly with our DNA findings; the Yoruba are found in West Africa, more specifically in Benin, Togo, Cameroon and Ghana as well as Nigeria. By identifying the Yoruba people, the expert in religions had corroborated Andy Urquhart's findings that Adam and his family appeared most likely to have originated in Nigeria.

JULY 2002 – 10 MONTHS AFTER THE
DISCOVERY OF ADAM'S BODY

It's often said that one phone call can crack a case. Whenever I agonise about publicising a crime and giving the media free rein to sensationalise the details, I have to remind myself of this fact. If we get that all-important phone call, then the publicity will have been worthwhile.

Needless to say, the academic's lurid claims at the conference propelled the Adam case onto front pages and news bulletins in Britain and across Europe. A few months later, this surge of publicity paid off spectacularly.

It began in July 2002 with a classic 'it's probably nothing but…' call to the Adam incident room in Catford, south London.

The man who made the call was PC Jim McGlynn, from Strathclyde Police's child protection squad. He'd been sitting at the back of Glasgow Sheriff Court waiting for the next hearing to start when a witness in the current case snagged his interest.

Joyce Osagiede, a West Africa asylum-seeker living in Pollokshaws in the south of the city, was telling the court all sorts of fantastical tales about black magic and dark, unspeakable powers. What really caught his attention, though, were Joyce's claims that her young son had been the victim of a ritual killing.

Kevin Williams, a social worker, testified that Joyce had told him she'd been a member of a cult. And, in her flat, he'd seen all sorts of strange-looking artefacts and colourful bottles containing what looked like alternative remedies.

As far-fetched as it all sounded, PC McGlynn flagged the woman up to detectives in London investigating Adam's murder. He could never have imagined how that single phone call would trigger a remarkable chain of events.

Detectives needed to check out Joyce Osagiede's backstory.

Immigration revealed she'd approached them claiming asylum
with her two daughters, aged six and four, in December 2001 –
three months after the discovery of Adam's body. Exactly how long
she'd been in the UK before that, no one knew for sure.

She told immigration officials that she had originally come
from Sierra Leone and, in the mid-1990s, married a man called
Tony Onus in the Nigerian city of Benin. She described him as a
leading member of a cult called the Black Coat Eyes of the Devil
Guru Maharaj. According to Joyce, this cult had participated in
a number of human sacrifices in which her husband had played
a prominent role. And one of these sacrifices had been that of her
newborn son in 1995.

Joyce claimed she'd fled her marriage and Nigeria because she
feared Tony would sacrifice their daughters as well. As part of their
policy of spreading asylum-seekers around the UK, immigration
sent her to Glasgow, where she secured a flat for herself and the
two girls.

Detective Sergeant Nick Chalmers, telling us the story,
went on:

'Her two daughters were taken into care because there were
suggestions that she had become involved in prostitution once she
arrived in Glasgow. The police went to her house, found the kids
were not being cared for and they were taken to a place of safety.'

Then, on New Year's Eve 2001, Ms Osagiede did a most
peculiar thing. She walked into her local social services department
in Pollokshaws and asked to get her children back. Not, on the face
of it, an entirely unreasonable request from a mother during the
festive holidays. Except, Joyce freely admitted that she wanted to
bring her daughters home so that they could take part in a ritual
ceremony that night. When social workers asked if this ceremony
was connected to the cult she'd fled from in Nigeria, she replied
that it was. That was why social workers had taken Joyce to court:

they were seeking to secure an order banning her from contact with her daughters.

After PC McGlynn's call, detectives travelled up to Glasgow to interview Joyce. Nick Chalmers told me he suspected she knew a great deal more than she was letting on.

'She was not as cooperative as you would expect from someone who was a victim. She wouldn't go into detail about her own son's death. But she did talk in general terms about ritualistic practices and it became quite clear she was familiar with those practices,' he said.

However, police did get one positive lead from the interview. As they were trying to persuade Joyce to take a DNA test, Jo Veale – a sharp-eyed local detective constable – spotted a Blockbuster video card bearing an address in Catford, south London. DC Veale memorised it and passed it on to the London team, who paid it a visit.

A Nigerian woman answered the door and insisted she didn't know anyone by the name of Joyce Osagiede. However, she did recognise Joyce from a photo, claiming that she'd once knocked on her door looking for someone at a nearby address. Importantly, the woman recalled Joyce saying she had lived in Germany prior to coming to England.

This was a critical revelation. Adam's torso had been dressed in a pair of orange shorts that retailed exclusively in Germany and Austria and had gone on sale just a few months before Adam's murder. Everyone wondered the same thing – could Joyce be Adam's mother? The German connection certainly suggested she may be linked somehow to his death. However, a check of German records for all the names given by Joyce – married and maiden – had so far drawn a blank. The decision was made to raid her flat in Glasgow in search of evidence.

During this proposed raid, the detectives wouldn't be alone.

For some months now, a fly-on-the-wall documentary TV crew had been busy filming all the key stages of the Adam investigation, even capturing me in action. When the transmission date of this documentary was eventually announced, I called home to tell my parents.

My dad answered, so I relayed the details of my TV debut to him.

'Oh, well we'll have to tape it,' he said, 'the snooker is on the other side.'

I got the impression my father thought I ran the lifts at the Forensic Science Service! I didn't take it personally. My friends all experienced the same indifference from their dads. It was a generational thing and at least none of us had ever felt under pressure to be successful!

My mum, on the other hand, always wanted to know what I was working on and found the twists and turns of ongoing cases endlessly intriguing.

'I don't know where you got your brains from,' she used to say, but I knew right enough.

Like so many of their generation – especially from our neck of the woods – my parents didn't get much formal education. But they were both intelligent and knowledgeable people. Mum always had her nose in a book and Dad was razor-sharp at maths and anything practical.

They weren't the types to crow about the achievements of their three sons. What mattered to them was that we conducted ourselves in a proper manner and never lost our values. And that included staying humble. I always knew that, no matter what my achievements in life might be, they'd never trump the snooker!

When the time came to raid Joyce's house, the documentary crew was on hand to capture the event. Will O'Reilly, Nick Chalmers and Detective Constable Mark Ham – an outstanding exhibits officer on this case – turned up at the door of her first-floor flat. Chalmers thumped the door loudly, triggering a panicked voice inside. The voice subsided, but the door didn't open. The detectives decided to break it down.

Joyce, who was alone, stood against the far wall. Wearing a brown baggy blouse and blue trousers, she seemed frightened.

Inside a clothes cupboard in a rear room, DC Ham found a number of children's clothes bearing the label Kids 'n' Co – the same brand as Adam's orange shorts that had likely been bought in Germany.

Nick asked: 'Can you explain where you got these clothes, Joyce?'

'I bought them. I was living in Germany. I bought them there.'

'Where would that be in Germany then? What store?'

She looked from one face to the other, as if trying to gauge how much trouble she was in.

'Woolworths,' she said finally.

'Mrs Joyce Osagiede,' Nick said, 'I am arresting you in connection with the murder of a young boy known as Adam in London during September 2001. You do not have to say anything, but it may harm your defence…'

They called me to say a DNA sample from Joyce was being flown down to London. How quickly could I turn it around? I promised to pull the strings required to get a result by the following morning. For the first time in this case – after almost nine long months of graft – I felt like we were finally on the trail of Adam's killers.

The detectives accompanied Joyce on a later flight to London and took her in for questioning. She clammed up but, next morning, spoke more freely. She reiterated what she'd told immigration about moving from Sierra Leone to Nigeria to get married and live in Benin City. However, she now admitted moving to Germany, where her two daughters had been born. She'd lived near Hamburg and bought the Kids 'n' Co clothes in that city. She said she'd never claimed benefits in Germany and had lived there with her husband.

'So, your husband's surname was on your passport?' Nick Chalmers asked. 'What was that name, Joyce? The name you originally had on your passport?'

'Onojhighovie,' she said, looking around nervously.

'I didn't quite catch that, Joyce,' said Nick, 'would you please write it down for us?'

Nick slid across a pad and pencil. She picked up the pencil, toyed with it and finally wrote 'Tony Onus'.

After that, she denied everything. She denied ever mentioning the name Onojhighovie, ever living in Germany, ever talking about clothes or ever engaging in rituals. Just as she'd clammed up, the DNA result came through. How I willed and begged for the news to be positive.

'Joyce Osagiede is in no way related to Adam.'

There was nothing to justify charging her with any offence.

A FEW DAYS LATER...

It was one of those intolerably hot July days in airless central London. But that wasn't the only reason I was sweating.

Ken Pye had something to announce to DCI Will O'Reilly and myself. I turned up ridiculously early in the hope of shaking him down in advance, but he wasn't giving anything away.

It'd been six months now since Commander Andy Baker and DCI Will O'Reilly had laid down the gauntlet: use science to find out all you can about Adam. How I'd boasted that forensics could – and should – do so much more than merely corroborate evidence. Now I had to prove that we could deliver fresh evidence and leads in an ongoing investigation.

So far, science had pinned down Adam's ancestry to West Africa and proved he'd been murdered in the UK. But if we were ever going to trace his family, we needed to find out where he spent his short life. It had been almost four months since Ken Pye had agreed to take on this task. His work on strontium isotopes surely represented our last hope of achieving this.

'Good God, Ray, you look like you've been in a sauna,' quipped Will on arrival.

'It's my Irish skin,' I grumbled. 'I'm not supposed to lie out in that, never mind move.'

With everyone present and correct, Ken opened a paper file in front of him, surveyed the room and started to speak.

'I've analysed samples taken from three sections of Adam's bones,' he began inscrutably.

'One thing we can say straightaway is that Adam wasn't brought up in the UK. The strontium isotope ratios in his bones are a lot higher than those of a child of the same age brought up in south-east England.

'His strontium isotope ratios also don't match anyone brought up in the Caribbean, Asia or the rest of Europe. So, we looked elsewhere. If Adam didn't come from London or the Caribbean, there was a good chance he came from Africa. But Africa is a big place and the isotopic information available is extremely sketchy. The question was, where to look?

'What really helped us was Ray's advice that we focus on West Africa. It turned out that some of the universities there had decent data for us to work with.

'And here's the headline. The West African information matches the geological composition of Adam's bones. There are three specific areas with the same Precambrian rock covering five different countries that match the results very closely indeed.'

He turned a map of West Africa towards us.

'Here, between Kano and Jos; here, in the highlands towards Cameroon and here in the Yorubaland Plateau. The evidence points most vigorously to the last of these.'

I shook my head. This was a genuine eureka moment. I'd checked, and this had never been done before in criminal forensic science. We'd adopted learning from academia, driven it forward and got a result. And that result supported all the evidence gathered so far: from the sangoma in South Africa; from Andy Urquhart's groundbreaking DNA research; from the studies of the deities of Nigeria. It all pointed to the Yorubaland Plateau – a region spreading across northern Nigeria into Togo and Benin.

However, as Ken pointed out, the Yoruba plateau is about the size of Florida state with a population of 50 million people. We still had work to do.

'There is no data for these three areas. But if I could get soil and bone samples from these places, I should be able to determine within a very small radius where Adam spent most of his life. I may even be able to pinpoint it to a specific village.'

As soon as Commander Baker heard this, he decided that Will and I would travel to West Africa and collect everything Ken needed to complete his research.

AUGUST 2002 – 11 MONTHS AFTER THE DISCOVERY OF ADAM'S BODY

The raid on Joyce Osagiede's flat in Glasgow and a trawl through her social services records had thrown up two London addresses with which she had some unspecified connection.

One of the addresses was being rented by a man called Kingsley Ojo, who would later become a major part of the Adam investigation. At the other address, in Lewisham, police found forged travel documents and passports, suggesting an immigration or trafficking racket. One of the passports belonged to Joyce and confirmed she hadn't been born in war-torn Sierra Leone, as she claimed, but in Benin City, Nigeria.

Detectives also found a VHS dated February 1997 and labelled 'Wedding of Joyce to Samuel Onojhighovie'. When detectives watched the video, they discovered that the nuptials included the sacrifice of a live goat. It was time to find out more about Joyce's mysterious husband.

They ran Samuel Onojhighovie's name through the Europol database and got an immediate hit. He was a wanted man in Germany, where he'd lived under another assumed name, Ibrahim Kadade. They called German police, who revealed that – as Ibrahim Kadade – he'd been charged with people-trafficking but had skipped bail. In his absence, the Germans convicted him anyway, sentencing him to seven years.

Joyce, while in Germany, had gone by the name Bintu Kadade. No wonder we had struggled to find records of her there. Records show she had lived in Hamburg with her husband and their two daughters.

At last, we had a former address for Joyce in Germany to check out. Detectives could now find out all about her life there – and whether it involved a little boy matching Adam's description. We felt certain that somebody over there would help us connect the dots and lead us to Adam's family.

CHAPTER NINE

An early autumn summons to Royal Holloway University and Ken Pye's office inevitably meant a fresh break in the case, and boy did we need one. The drive from Kent to Egham gave me a chance to take stock of where we'd got to in the stalled investigation.

This was what we now knew: Adam had been brought up in either Nigeria, Benin or Togo and trafficked to London to be sacrificed; before arriving in London, he'd spent some time in the Hamburg area of Germany, where he most likely encountered Joyce Osagiede.

Our remaining leads consisted of sourcing bones and soils in Nigeria to assist Professor Ken Pye in narrowing down where Adam and his family hailed from, as well as tracing where Joyce Osagiede and her mysterious husband had lived in Germany and what connections – if any – they had to Adam. Another priority was to keep the story in the media spotlight in the hope that somebody out there might call in and provide that all-important break.

On top of that, we had one final lead: identifying the mysterious substances Nick Branch had found alongside the pollen samples in Adam's large intestine. Our hope was that this material had been some sort of 'potion' given to Adam as part of his sacrifice – and that it could provide us with either DNA or a link to a specific location.

All Ken would tell us in advance of this meeting was that his team had 'made breakthroughs' with the contents of Adam's large intestine.

The usual suspects – Will, DC Ham and me – took our seats as Ken Pye stood at the top of the conference room, armed with a laser pointer, a device to flash magnified images up on a screen and, to our intrigue, a knowing smile.

'These are the pellets of clay and alluvial soil found in Adam's large intestine,' he said, pointing to what looked like a blurred splodge. 'In my opinion, this came from a riverbank, a floodplain or a lake margin, and its composition is consistent with a West African origin. We're still working on it, but the mineral make-up of the sand might eventually give us a more precise location as to where it came from, even a specific deposit.

'This dot here is microscopic, about point one of a millimetre in size. Turns out this is quartz. Now I thought maybe this came from the Thames but if it was Thames quartz, it would be much sharper. These soft edges mean it didn't come from the Thames.

'The whole potion or mixture is very high in minerals and metallic particles, including quartz and gold.

'Look at this,' he said teasingly. 'This crossed lattice structure has the chemical signature of calcium and phosphorus. It's bone. I can't tell you yet whether it's animal or human, and it may be too small to get DNA from. We've contacted the office of the Chief Medical Officer in New York. After the 9/11 attacks, they developed a lot of expertise in extracting DNA from tiny pieces of bone. We're hoping they can help us with this.

'So, in summary, we've got alluvial sand that matches West Africa and traces of quartz, gold and bone. But this mixture is high in other minerals. We have traces of carbon that are almost certainly the result of the mixture being burned down in a pot, and that's backed up by traces of tin that we also found. It looks like this concoction had been put in some sort of metal pot, cooked and stirred.

'There's also some plant material but it's too degraded for us to be able to tell what it is. But what can be in no doubt is that this concoction, or its ingredients, were brought into the UK and given to Adam right here, in London.'

'So, just for the record,' Will interjected, 'Adam was given this potion as part of the human sacrifice ritual?'

'There's no question in my mind,' said Ken, 'it would've tasted revolting so it's the only thing that makes sense.'

'We need to identify that vegetation,' said Will, 'it may give us a specific location. Ray, any thoughts on who might be able to help?'

I smiled. 'I know just the woman. She's known as the Miss Marple of Kew Gardens. Her actual name is Dr Hazel Wilkinson. If anyone can identify a degraded smidgeon of vegetation, it's Hazel.' With that, we took some samples to Hazel and so began the nervous wait for results.

OCTOBER 2002 – 13 MONTHS AFTER THE DISCOVERY OF ADAM'S BODY

Commander Andy Baker requested that geneticist Andy Urquhart and myself accompany DCI Will O'Reilly to Nigeria. Our mission: to collect samples that could be used for geo-profiling in order to try and narrow down the area where Adam was born and raised.

These samples included soils, animal bones from local markets, roadkill and – from mortuaries – samples of human bones. A simple shopping list, you might think. The reality of gathering these items proved anything but…

Our travel group of three made one thing very clear from the outset – we wanted to be away for the least amount of time possible. Will and I had other pressing cases. But there was another reason for our haste.

We knew this would be no 'jolly' with opportunities for sightseeing, sunbathing or a spot of shopping. Ahead of us was a hot and gruelling trundle across the dust tracks of a vast, rural Third World backwater collecting dead stuff. We'd work all hours every day to get out of there as soon as possible.

The organisers advised us that the shortest time in which we could complete this exercise was three and a half weeks – beginning with an overnight flight. This was longer than we'd hoped for. But we consoled ourselves that the visit would at least be low-key – just us and a couple of local drivers on a secret 'soil and skeleton' safari.

I can't sleep on planes and, having worked a very long day before take-off, must've looked a complete mess staggering off that flight when it landed in Abuja, Nigeria. We were greeted by High Commission personnel, to whom I made very clear my dual ambitions for the rest of that day – a long shower and an even longer sleep. They had other ideas. Allowing us just enough time to stop off and take a shower, they took us directly to meet the chief of police.

As we were led into the chief's office, we found ourselves getting hosed down by what felt like the flashguns of a hundred stills cameras. Staggering about like blinded chimps, we realised to our horror that the chief had assembled Nigeria's entire media corps to 'welcome his friends from England'. I could only hope that images of me looking like a sack of shit tied up in the middle wouldn't reach the UK. My wife Jackie would kill me!

I had asked for access to a local pathologist throughout the trip, with the aim of picking his or her brains about sacrificial murders We were now informed that a pathologist from Benin City, Dr Wilson Akhiwu, along with Detective Superintendent David Kolo, would be accompanying us for the entire trip. We were in little doubt that they were coming along less to help, more to keep a close eye on us and report back to the chief.

As soon as I got a moment alone with Dr Akhiwu, I asked him if human sacrifices happened in places like his native Benin City.

'Certainly not, Mr Fysh,' he said irritably, clearly offended. I'd have cause to think back on this exchange later.

The plan had been that we'd travel in two jeeps with drivers from the High Commission. Not only did we now have a local cop and pathologist on board, the chief of police added two more jeeps loaded with police armed with AK-47s. Now we were an entourage of four jeeps. Imagine our surprise when, as soon as we visited a new region, local police would add two more jeeps of armed police to the parade. In cities, this procession would be led and followed by blues and twos, all sirens blazing, making us look more like an invading private army than a scientific expedition. All three of us found this mobile battery of close-quarters firepower anything but reassuring. But we did turn it to our advantage in one way, insisting that every guard and cop gave us a sample of DNA.

We pulled up at our first market and watched the translators struggle to explain that these sweaty white men wanted to buy joints of meat, but only needed to keep the bone; the traders could have the meat back. You can just imagine the looks we got. But, like all good market traders, they insisted on charging us full whack anyway.

'I guess they saw us coming,' quipped Will.

We would set off every morning at daybreak, heading to specified locations for soil samples, markets that sold goat meat and to roadside vendors that sold 'bushmeat' like monkeys, rats, snakes and bats. With its mangrove forests and rolling green hills, the Yorubaland Plateau boasts some breathtaking scenery – if we'd been able to breathe in the first place! Makeshift dusty gravel roads, searing midday temperature of up to 90 degrees Fahrenheit and suffocating humidity made our travels a slow-motion torture. But at least we slept soundly. We spent our nights in gated High Commission homes where our hosts went to enormous lengths to make us feel welcome. We'd always find a fridge full of beer and, on one memorable night, we were treated to home-made steak and kidney pie.

Everywhere we went, local fresh-faced kids bursting with life and fun would descend. They seemed so charming, smart, funny and carefree – just how Adam would've been before he was snatched from the world he knew and cast into hell. Perhaps the most sobering thing we learned on this trip was that if Adam had indeed been sold, he would have fetched less cash for his family than an adult goat.

By the second week, and to our increasing alarm, the very appearance of scientist Andy Urquhart in local towns and villages seemed to be triggering a hysteria I can liken only to Beatlemania. Our guards explained why: Andy's flourishing beard gave him more than a passing likeness to Jesus Christ. Enjoying the adoration, Andy cultivated the beard and a genuine love for the Nigerian people. The night before we left, I found him in tears. I guess he was finding the prospect of losing his godlike status hard to swallow.

On another day, Andy and I were deep in the bush collecting soil samples when we suddenly turned to each other and, without saying a word, smiled and shook our heads. We both knew what the other was thinking. All those years of studying and we end up in the middle of nowhere, backs aching, drenched in sweat, shovelling dirt.

About halfway through the trip, we were brought to the Nigerian Forensic Science Lab, and marvelled at the two state-of-the-art DNA processing machines they'd bought from a German company. The only trouble was, they didn't have electricity to run them. Indeed, as our tour guide sombrely informed us, all forensic work had ceased since they'd run out of fingerprint ink, which had been left behind from the days of British colonisation.

Such surreal moments were often overshadowed by horror. We tried to intervene but failed as our guards forcibly removed drivers from their vehicles and beat them with sticks for not getting out of the way of our convoy promptly enough. To ensure we could carry out our research in certain regions, we had to parade before the local leaders, some of whom couldn't wait to show off their obscene wealth and latest prepubescent bride. The low point for me personally had to be taking samples from bones in mortuaries that didn't have refrigeration. No dry-cleaning chemicals can get that out of your clothes. And nothing can expunge it from your memory.

But, we did it! Just shy of a month later, Will, Andy and I returned home with the crucial trophies from our odyssey – 150 samples of soil, bones and rocks gathered from an area of more than 4,000 square miles. We now just had to hope that Ken Pye and his team could narrow that vast area down to Adam's neighbourhood, where someone must know who he was.

* * *

While we were scratching around for bones and soil in Africa, the murder squad had struck gold in Germany.

Detectives travelled to Joyce's suburb in Hamburg and made

a series of critical discoveries. First, they found out that Joyce had been living there until just a few days before she turned up at the immigration service in Croydon in December 2001. Adam's body had been fished out of the Thames three months earlier, so she couldn't have been actively involved in his murder.

German social services confirmed that she had arrived in Hamburg via Italy in 1992 under the alias Bintu Kadade. A year earlier, her partner Ibrahim Kadade had settled in Hamburg. We were in no doubt that 'Ibrahim' was, in fact, Sam Onojhighovie, the people-trafficker on the run and being hunted by German police.

The couple's two children, whom locals knew as Esther and Eseoghen, had been born in 1997 and 1999. Joyce's first child, a son, was reported dead at birth in 1995 – the date, she had told authorities in the UK, her husband had killed him in a human sacrifice.

Esther and Eseoghen had briefly attended a nursery in Hamburg in 2000. A member of staff, Frau Dibbern, revealed that she had fostered the girls for a short period. The last time she saw them was in August or September 2001 – just weeks before Adam's torso was fished out of the Thames. Frau Dibbern, her husband and daughter all vividly remembered this particular sighting of the girls because the eldest, Esther, had been wearing something especially striking that they'd all remarked upon.

A pair of bright orange shorts.

DECEMBER 2002 – 15 MONTHS AFTER THE DISCOVERY OF ADAM'S BODY

Ken Pye kicked off the meeting with a summary of what all present – detectives, a multicultural expert and I – needed to know about isotopes.

'So, let's take Ray,' Ken began. 'He lives in the Weald of Kent. So, his bones will have a Weald of Kent signature. And even if he eats a lot of imported food and drink, the water he drinks and the water his food is cooked in comes from the Weald of Kent, so that will be the overwhelmingly dominant chemical in his bones.

'If Ray decided to move to, say, Birmingham, it would take between six and ten years for his bones to transfer their signature from the Weald of Kent to a Birmingham signature.'

I took a quick scan around the room; I wasn't the only one excited by what bone chemistry could reveal. Every one of Ken's guests had instinctively leaned forward to hang on his every word. After all, this was entirely new to criminal forensic science. But Ken Pye was just warming up.

'So, where are the other places that the body stores elements it can't digest? Teeth. Now your teeth reflect your formative years, basically where you lived after you lost your milk teeth. So, Ray's teeth will have a signature for Belvedere in south-east London.

'Next, hair. The hair on your head grows about 1.5 centimetres a month. So, if someone has hair that hasn't been cut in a few years, you can analyse it to find out where they went on holiday two years ago.

'Finally, your nails contain about a year's worth of data in terms of your travels.'

Ken moved on to the headline: his analysis of three of Adam's bones in comparison to the spoils we'd brought back from our West African odyssey. By cross-referencing traces of Precambrian strontium rock found in Adam's bones, Ken was able to discount 95 per cent of those 4,000 square miles.

Using the strontium isotope ratio alone, the only two areas he could not exclude as Adam's home were Benin City in southern Nigeria and, 175 miles west, the city of Ibadan.

Ken revealed that he didn't just compare strontium isotopes; our bones also have a lead geographical signature. Factors like industrial processes and local petrol pollution are reflected in lead isotopes in our bones. Little did I know how this lead signature would later help us identify the source of bullets in a notorious shooting. Or prove that a terror suspect had spent months in Pakistan at a training camp.

For now, it pinpointed Benin City as the most likely place where Adam was born and raised.

'Somewhere within fifty square miles of Benin City is Adam's home. His family most likely still live there, in either the suburbs of Benin City or one of the numerous small villages on the outskirts.'

Having started with the entire planet as a blank canvas, pinpointing Adam's home as this single patch of Nigeria felt almost miraculous. It couldn't be mere coincidence, surely, that Joyce Osagiede came from Benin City. As did her estranged, people-trafficking husband Sam Onojhighovie. And Kingsley Ojo, Joyce's people-smuggling associate in London.

Will summed up what we were all thinking.

'If we go to Benin City and make an appeal… someone must know something,' he said. 'Somebody there must be wondering where Adam is! The fifty grand reward is a life-changing sum of money. I'm going to start making arrangements to get out there as soon as possible.'

Ken had also roped in Layla Renshaw – a researcher of archaeology at Oxford University – to apply isotopic analysis to one of this case's other burning mysteries. We now knew Adam wasn't from London, but how long had he been in the UK capital before his murder? Again, this information wouldn't convict anyone on its own, but could yet prove crucial to building a case against a suspect.

Normally, Dr Renshaw would examine a subject's hair, teeth and nails to check for geographical changes in diet or pollution. With Adam, of course, this was impossible. Instead, she focused on dietary isotopes like carbon and nitrogen (from animal protein) and hydrogen and oxygen (from water) in Adam's gut, fat and bone. She also analysed his skin, which could retain key signatures relating to diet and air pollution from the last two months of his life.

The good news for Dr Renshaw was that Germany and the UK kept detailed records of isotope values in foodstuffs, which helped her calculate when Adam had spent time in both countries. Her findings suggested that Adam had been brought to London from the city of Hamburg three to four weeks before he was killed – so either late August or early September 2001.

Joyce Osagiede had been living in Hamburg at this time. The evidence that she knew Adam and his eventual fate was mounting. She was married to a known people-trafficker. She had most likely purchased the orange shorts Adam was found in. She had told social services about her links to a murderous cult in the Yoruba area. It was time to take Joyce back in for questioning.

But there was a problem.

By claiming she came from war-torn Sierra Leone as opposed to Nigeria – which would've enhanced her chances of being allowed to stay in the UK – Joyce had lied to immigration. When immigration officials found out, they rejected her bid for asylum and placed her in a detention centre in Northolt, west London. Late in December 2002 – despite protests from the police that she remained a key witness in a live murder investigation – the Home Office decided to deport her back to Nigeria. Indeed, they were in such a hurry to get rid of her that they hired an executive private jet for the purpose. Joyce Osagiede was flown in luxury to Benin City, Nigeria. But she wasn't alone. In a desperate last-gasp bid to get her to open up, Will O'Reilly and Nick Chalmers joined her on board.

Joyce refused to speak. On arrival in Lagos, Will and Nick could only watch as she was led through Nigerian immigration and then disappeared into the throng.

FEBRUARY 2003 – 17 MONTHS AFTER THE DISCOVERY OF ADAM'S BODY

In a blaze of publicity both in the UK and in Nigeria, Will O'Reilly returned to Benin City to seek information about Adam, this time joined by Commander Baker and Detective Constable Mark Ham.

The detectives were at pains to remind everyone about the handsome £50,000 reward on offer for information and took DNA samples from anyone who let them. They also brought loads of Met Police merchandise – iconic 'Bobby' helmets, badges and key rings – to get local kids onside. Surely Adam had siblings, cousins or friends who were wondering what had happened to him?

Meanwhile, attempts by local police to trace Joyce Osagiede post-deportation had proved fruitless. Imagine Will's surprise when he got a call from the High Commission saying Joyce had made an appointment to see them. Imagine Joyce's surprise when she turned up at the High Commission to find three British cops waiting for her.

Joyce had gone to the High Commission to ask about the welfare of her daughters, who were still in Scotland. Instead, she was the one facing the questions – from Will, Baker and Ham. As in previous encounters, 'opening up' Joyce proved challenging. She seemed scared and somewhat unstable.

Eventually, under caution, Joyce admitted being a member of the Guru Maharaj cult from 1994 to 2002, saying she left it because of 'too much evil'. She confirmed that her husband Sam had been some sort of 'high priest' in the cult and repeated the claim that he had been involved in the murder of children. She refused to say any more about the cult, claiming to be too scared of the consequences.

When asked specifically about Adam for the first time, she said: 'I do not know anything about the murder of the child in

London.' But she later admitted: 'I know the child was killed in Lewisham. I don't know where the head and limbs are. I think the boy was sacrificed because his parents were brainwashed by Maharaj Ji's teachings.'

She admitted buying a pair of Kids 'n' Co orange shorts from Woolworths for her elder daughter, Esther. Asked where the shorts were now, she said they were in her old flat in Glasgow. But we'd searched that flat. They weren't there. Joyce then insisted that the shorts must be in her old flat in Germany. But we'd searched that flat too – unlet since Joyce's departure – and no shorts were found. Ultimately, Joyce was unable to offer an explanation as to how an identical pair of orange shorts had ended up on Adam's torso in London.

In her phone, officers found just two names and numbers. One of them was Kingsley Ojo – the suspected people-trafficker who lived in east London.

Despite building a comprehensive picture of Adam's last weeks and days, we were no closer to charging anyone with his murder. Detectives decided to do the next best thing. They targeted the men connected to the case for other crimes.

Scotland Yard's Human Trafficking Surveillance Unit (HTSU) raided the home of Kingsley Ojo in east London. They were met by Ojo, his glamorous girlfriend and an associate with a German/Nigerian passport who promptly jumped out of a window and escaped. Ojo denied any knowledge of Joyce or Adam's murder and nothing was found in the flat to link him to the killing.

However, officers did uncover several items that appeared to be connected to Nigerian juju/voodoo/black magic rituals – call it what you will. These included a cloth bag containing a grotesque animal skull (no one could confirm its identity) pierced with a large metal staple and covered in a heavy, dark, cotton-like twine. One could only assume it was some sort of grotesque death mask.

Ugly, sinister, not to mention potentially cursed... I gave it to an assistant to analyse.

Other bags contained equally peculiar items. Dried dung, strange powders and potions, clay and soil, medicine bottles with wooden crucifixes floating in murky oil-like liquids.

The human trafficking police placed Ojo under surveillance and quickly gathered evidence of him meeting criminal associates and arranging the illegal entry of Nigerians into the UK. It became clear that he'd trafficked hundreds of Nigerians to Europe over the years – some as young as Adam – to work as domestic slaves or in the sex industry or to facilitate benefit fraud. In fact, what surprised surveillance officers most was how cocky and blatant Ojo was in conducting his illicit deals, talking openly on his phone and in public.

Detectives began to suspect Ojo considered himself infallible. One of the supposed 'benefits' of making a human sacrifice to the gods is that it renders the killer 'untouchable'. Could Ojo's confidence have stemmed from Adam's death?

In June 2003, police smashed Ojo's people-smuggling ring, raiding nine London addresses and arresting twenty-one men and women. Two more suspects were lifted a day later. Kingsley, the ringleader, was picked up by a joint force of British and Italian police at an underage brothel in Brescia.

Police traced Joyce's estranged husband and fugitive, Sam Onojhighovie, thirty-seven, to Dublin, where he was arrested and extradited to Germany. A DNA test showed he wasn't related to Adam.

At Southwark Crown Court – on the south bank of the River Thames and within sight of where Adam's body had first been seen bobbing in the water almost three years earlier – Kingsley Ojo was sentenced to four years. Will O'Reilly reminded the media that a young boy's murder remained unpunished.

'This is the trafficking side of the Adam investigation. We have uncovered what we believe is a criminal network involved in people-trafficking, particularly from mainland Africa, through Europe to the UK.'

OCTOBER 2003 – OVER TWO YEARS AFTER THE DISCOVERY OF ADAM'S BODY

From a forensic perspective, we had one solid lead left in this investigation. And I felt real pressure to turn it into hard evidence.

After two years spent building a case, Commander Baker and Will wanted to get a file sent to the Crown Prosecution Service so that charges could be pressed against Joyce, Kingsley Ojo and Sam Onojhighovie, at least in relation to the trafficking of Adam. Maybe more. We learned that Lord Goldsmith, the attorney general, had taken such an interest in the investigation that he'd offered to personally prosecute the case – something an attorney general hadn't done since a spy trial in the 1980s. But we needed to unearth some solid evidence for him to work with. As it stood, much of our case was circumstantial.

The one thing we still hadn't identified was the vegetation found in Adam's large intestine, which had been part of a ceremonial concoction of sediment, quartz, gold and bone fed to him before he was killed. The bone was still with the experts in New York, who were struggling to extract a DNA sample.

Whenever I had a mystery involving plants, there was only one place to go: the world-famous Kew Gardens in south-west London. Once again, my mind instantly went to the wonderful research fellow Dr Hazel Wilkinson, based at Kew. I found out that Hazel had retired years earlier, but still cycled to Kew every day to indulge her lifelong passion for researching rare plants.

I'd given her the magnified images of the mysterious vegetation almost a year earlier but, so far, she'd drawn a blank. I'd reaped so much reward working with academics, but the one key lesson I'd learned is that you can't rush them. Trust me, there's no chivvying along a boffin. They will give it their all – but in their own time.

One day, Hazel called, sounding highly excited.

'I've just had the most extraordinary stroke of luck,' she said.

'We haven't had much of that on this case, Hazel.'

'A few weeks back, I happened to see a poster that details this rare bean. When I realised this bean was found in Nigeria, it occurred to me that it might be the vegetation in the sample you sent. I managed to track down some samples of it, crushed them to simulate it having been digested. I then magnified it using an electron scanning microscope. And do you know what I found?'

'I'm all ears, Hazel.'

'Ray, it's a perfect match!'

'You're certain of this?'

'One hundred per cent certain.'

'And what's this bean called?'

'*Physostigma venenosum*. It's more popularly known as the Calabar bean. But the reason it's significant to this case is because Calabar beans are used in witchcraft in West Africa.'

I asked Hazel to tell me all about it. And later did my own research. What an eye-opener!

The name comes from the town of Calabar, where it was discovered by Europeans in the 1840s. Odourless and tasteless, the Calabar bean looks innocuous, yet the chocolate-coloured pod can cause death within an hour.

It acts like a nerve gas, affecting communication between nerves and muscles. The first sign of Calabar poisoning is copious salivating, seizures and loss of control of the bladder and bowels. The poison then works by slowing the pulse and rapidly raising blood pressure, depressing the central nervous system and causing muscle weakness.

The standard treatment is to pump out the stomach and give the victim an antidote of atropine, derived from plants of the nightshade family.

In Nigeria, the bean is known as esere, 'the ordeal bean', because of its use in testing suspects accused of crimes such as witchcraft. After being forced to ingest the bean, if the accused vomited they were deemed innocent, but if they died it was seen as confirmation of guilt. The bean was also used in a form of duel. Adversaries would both eat half a bean and see who survived. In most cases, neither did.

In the 1840s, Professor Robert Christison, the most famous toxicologist of his time, almost killed himself chewing one-eighth of a Calabar bean to test its effects.

Our Miss Marple at Kew, Hazel, didn't just find one natural sedative in this potion, she also found traces of scopolamine, a chemical that also derives from plants of the nightshade family and, like Rohypnol, can make users submissive and helpless. Notorious in Colombia, where it's known as devil's breath, scopolamine has been linked to thousands of reported 'spiking' cases in bars and nightclubs where victims were later robbed, raped and even murdered. It is also used in kidnappings to sedate the victim.

Both Calabar and scopolamine are very difficult to source in the UK. Like the rest of the contents of the potion, they must have been brought here by the killers from West Africa. Adam would've swallowed the potion within forty-eight hours of him being killed, maybe expertly disguised in a drink.

'This wasn't their first rodeo then?' I said to Hazel.

'It would've taken considerable expertise to administer just the right amount of these drugs to a small child,' she said. 'And that means previous practice, which would inevitably have involved some degree of trial and error.

'The thing is, Ray,' she went on, sounding grave, 'in small doses it paralyses the victim but it doesn't knock them out. Adam would've known what was happening.'

I swallowed hard.

'So, what you're telling me is he was conscious when they cut his throat?'

'I'm afraid so. He would've screamed out and bled. But he wouldn't have been able to struggle or move, even flinch.'

The thought of Adam sitting there in terror, then in excruciating pain, unable to defend himself or understand anything that was going on, filled me with sadness. What a truly vile and inhuman act. How could any right-minded person do this to a small, defenceless child?

I rang Will and told him the news. That soon catapulted me back to harsh reality.

'This proves beyond doubt it was a ritual murder conceived and planned in Benin City,' he said, 'we believe by three suspects who we can show had connections to each other and to Adam. This is the final piece of the jigsaw, Ray. Well done. Write it up and we'll get the file off to the Crown Prosecution Service.'

DECEMBER 2005 – OVER FOUR YEARS AFTER THE DISCOVERY OF ADAM'S BODY

There's no more poignant sight than a child's coffin. We picked a blue one for Adam and had it decorated with teddy bears.

That gloomy December morning – for the last time – the five of us became his family. Will read the eulogy. Andy Baker, Nick Chalmers, Mark Ham and I took turns to throw soil into the unmarked grave and pay our personal respects. I said sorry to

Adam for not doing what I'd promised – finding out his real name. How conspicuous an absence it was from that tiny wooden cross at the head of his unmarked grave, the location of which remains a closely guarded secret to this day. The last thing police wanted was for Adam's final resting place to become a shrine to followers of the belief system that had led to his murder.

We felt we got close; that in Joyce we'd found someone who knew the truth. Confronted with a lengthy jail sentence, she would surely have 'done a deal' and turned crown witness against the others. She was all that we had. But the Crown Prosecution Service felt that Joyce was too unreliable a witness to build a case upon and, to this day, no charges have been brought over Adam's murder.

Will and Andy Baker kept trying to crack the case, right up until their retirements in 2008. It was simply not to be. I'm not a religious person but I drew comfort from the words of the Bishop of Stepney, who compared Adam to the unknown soldier:

'Like the unknown soldier, his death should not be in vain. Some resulting good must be his epitaph.'

All these years on, I can reveal exactly what that resulting good has been.

The groundbreaking DNA techniques pioneered in this case – familial DNA searches, using DNA to identify ancestry, geological mapping to identify where someone has lived – have solved countless crimes across the planet and will continue to do so. Some you'll read about later in this book.

It was all down to Commander Baker and DCI Will O'Reilly, who kept pushing for answers and who refused to listen when anyone said 'it cannot be done.'

Adam's legacy is that he pushed us to be bolder with forensics: to go further, to try harder, to look outside policing for answers. It's because of him that these techniques were developed.

For this, we all owe that little boy an enormous debt of gratitude.

CHAPTER TEN

OPERATION ORB
THURSDAY, NOVEMBER 15, 2001

The Stanhope Estate, south of Ashford, Kent, was one of those post-war social housing experiments that overwhelmingly proved one hypothesis – don't dump the people society least cares about into one grim, ghettoised high-rise council estate.

When it was built in the 1960s, Stanhope was dubbed a 'London overspill' estate – in other words, a dumping ground for 3,000 people the capital wanted rid of. By 2001, Stanhope – dubbed 'No-Hope' by locals – had all the social problems you'd expect of such a misguided project: unemployment, domestic abuse, antisocial behaviour and gangs of feral children terrorising the locals. In one infamous episode, an RSPCA rehoming centre refused to let a Stanhope family adopt a cat because staff feared the kind of environment it would be going to.

However, just like where I grew up in south-east London, really good people lived here too, who never stopped trying to make a difference. Some of these public-spirited locals got together with police to set up a youth club at the heart of the estate on Thursday nights. Of course they had no money, so to advertise the Shuttle Club handwritten posters were erected outside the Ray Allen community centre before every weekly get-together

As the club was wrapping up just after 9 p.m. on November 15, a ten-year-old local girl was sent outside to take down the posters. As she gathered them up, a man standing at the bus stop across the road started telling her to 'hurry up'. She speeded up her work, careful to avoid eye contact with this clearly unhinged character.

All of a sudden, the girl felt herself being lifted off the ground from behind. She couldn't scream because a man had put his left hand over her mouth while his right hand gripped her tightly around the waist.

'If you scream, I'll break your legs or kill you,' he spat in her ear. The girl realised it was the man who'd been heckling her from across the road.

He ran with her across a car park to a cluster of trees behind a floodlit football pitch and dumped her on the ground. He set about sexually assaulting the girl – but the sound of a softball team training on the floodlit pitch on the other side of the trees clearly unsettled him. He grabbed his victim by the wrist and set off running along a tree-lined boundary path south of the school playing fields.

The man stopped at another specific spot along the pathway well screened by trees. He sexually assaulted the girl again. He then dragged her by the wrist past some houses to yet another secluded spot, this time close to some houses. After raping her, he took her t-shirt and ordered her to stare at the ground and count to 500: 'I'll be watching you.'

As soon as she sensed it was clear, the girl stumbled to a nearby house for help.

I learned of the girl's horrific ordeal next morning in a call from the incident room. My feelings of shock and utter disgust eventually gave way to a steely conviction: I can help this girl by finding the sick bastard who did this.

'What can I do to help?' I told the detective. 'Just name it.'

The police had taken the victim to hospital for a medical examination and to get vaginal swabs for evidence. These swabs were now on their way to the lab. Could I make sure they went top of the list for urgent examination?

The biologist detected semen on two swabs that I submitted for an urgent DNA profile. At that time, we could turn a DNA profile around in twenty-four hours, so I'd get the result next morning – a Saturday. With a predatory child rapist on the loose, I'd need the National DNA Database in Birmingham to urgently cross-reference the offender's profile to see if there was a match. If there was, we could arrest the suspect right away and take this maniac off the streets. Trouble was – and you may find this hard to believe – the National DNA Database didn't have staff in on a Saturday.

As I have said before, one of the things I desperately wanted to change was the 9-to-5, 'civil service' culture that dominated the Forensic Science Service and the National DNA Database. I liked the way police approached a major crime. They recognised the importance of 'breaking the back' of the investigation in those crucial early days. Detectives would ring their families to inform them they wouldn't be home for a few days. The team would live on coffee, takeaways and adrenaline until they'd done all they could for a quick win. If forensics wanted to be taken seriously as a partner in cracking major crimes, then we needed to adopt the same proactive, flexible approach. Alas, many of the senior scientists resented the idea of giving up even their precious lunch breaks, never mind weekends. So, despite the fact that a child rapist was on the loose, I had to beg management at the DNA database to get someone in on a Saturday for just an hour.

I felt certain that the man who had raped the ten-year-old would be on the DNA database. Rapists don't start out snatching kids from busy streets. He must have escalated to this.

Word finally came through. This suspect was not on the National DNA Database.

Double and treble checks merely confirmed the fact. I remember groaning loudly down the phone. How could someone capable of such a vile crime have escaped our DNA net? It didn't make sense. More urgently, how the hell would we now go about tracking him down before he struck again?

I reported the bad news to the incident room. Later, I got a call from the senior investigating officer, DCI Colin Murray.

'What worries me, Ray, is that this guy is a risk-taker. He could reoffend at any time. We've got to figure out a way to catch him, and fast.'

Colin wanted to know if I could come into Kent Police headquarters in Maidstone next morning for an urgent debrief. I would've met him that night.

* * *

Nothing beat the feeling of being brought into a major inquiry at the start. It might sound insensitive, but I turned up for that meeting stoked and excited. Five years earlier, when I had taken the role of specialist advisor, there had been no job description. I had to find a way to make myself indispensable to senior officers investigating major crimes. I needed to become their go-to guy. By now – November 2001 – I felt like I'd at least put myself in the shop window. The strenuous forensic efforts I'd nurtured and overseen in the Sarah Payne case had resulted in Roy Whiting going on trial for murder that very month. And we were already pushing science to groundbreaking new limits as part of our quest to identify Adam, the boy in the 'torso in the Thames' case.

Word had clearly got around: I wasn't a spy, a threat, someone coming in with any vested interest. I was just there to help. I could do this in small ways, like expediting results from the FSS or finding the best scientist to perform your tests. Or I could help in a more significant way, offering pioneering new forensic avenues to explore and the best scientists outside the police or FSS to do it. If it went badly, the senior investigating officer (SIO) could blame me. If it went well, he or she could take the credit. After all, I worked very much in the shadows, known only to the senior detectives on the case and my colleagues at the lab.

But there was another reason for me to be optimistic about this case. I'd worked with DCI Colin Murray before and I knew he'd welcome me into his investigation. A slight, olive-skinned man with perfectly quiffed hair and a taste for dapper suits, he reminded me of Al Pacino in the third *Godfather* film. He had the quiet, understated authority of a don, too, and believed in leading by example. Nobody on his team worked harder. Yet he always remained inclusive and open to fresh ideas.

'How's the poor girl doing?' was my first question.

'She's distressed, naturally. Her parents are in bits. It's just such an awful, awful crime. The first thing she told us in her interview was that her favourite Disney character is Eeyore, next thing we find out is that he deliberately injured her so that he could penetrate her. I'm really worried about what this guy might do next. He's clearly a real sicko. And we don't know a bloody thing about him.'

'Where do you want to start?'

He opened a notebook to reveal pages of handwritten notes.

'Let's start with what we actually know,' he said. 'The girl could give us only a very vague description of her attacker. She never got a good look at his face but says he is white, about the same age and height as her dad, so mid-thirties, between five feet five and five feet eight tall, unshaven, brushed-back hair, wearing jeans and trainers. She says he had a soft voice and his breath smelled of alcohol. Officers are getting CCTV from all the local off-licences and pubs.

'We flooded the area with cops last night and questioned everyone. Nobody saw anything, so we're getting CCTV from anywhere we can, including local buses.'

With his usually immaculate attire somewhat crumpled and darkness around his eyes, Colin looked like a man who hadn't slept well. It's not the crime that keeps someone like him awake at night, it's a lack of leads.

'I've spoken to a behavioural scientist, who confirmed lots of things we were already thinking,' he said.

'First, this looks like an opportunistic crime. He approached the victim by crossing a busy road near a bus stop, under a street lamp and in clear view of two houses. He could've picked any number of more secluded locations around Stanhope to have hidden out of sight before pouncing on an unsuspecting child.

'I don't understand why he didn't do that. He clearly knows the area. He dragged the girl directly to a pathway that led all the way to the three locations where he assaulted her. It's as if he preselected those three spots. He knew the path well enough to run in between them in the pitch dark. So, he's either local, has family or friends local, used to live in the area or knows it through his work or a hobby.

'Now to the much longer list of what we don't know.' He sighed.

'We don't know if he was watching the youth club with the specific purpose of targeting a child. Most of the kids had already been picked up by their parents when he struck. This girl may have been the first opportunity he got to snatch someone. Or he could've been waiting for a bus and just acted on the spur of the moment. We've contacted all of the parents, kids and staff who attended the club to find out what they saw. So far, not a lot.

'Another mystery is why he took her T-shirt. He'd used it to wipe himself after the rape, so we initially thought he was being forensically aware. But now we know he made no attempt to clean up the semen from his victim. So, we're thinking it's a trophy. He's storing it somewhere, possibly with other mementoes, so we've put out an appeal through the media about this orange/red T-shirt. Let's hope he's sloppy about storing this stuff, or has a nosy partner.

'Next, where did he go after the attack. Is he local and walked home, or did he leave Stanhope? If so, did he walk, get a bus or had he parked a vehicle somewhere? Like I said, we're getting hold of every shred of CCTV we can.

'Finally, I asked the behavioural scientist what his verbal exchanges with the girl might tell us. He thinks that the suspect's threats to kill and to break her legs indicate he has a criminal past. Here's a thing I didn't know. He tells me that, before turning to sex crime, nine out of ten rapists were already known to police for non-sexual offences. So, he's insisting that this suspect already has a criminal record of some sort. So why isn't he in the database?'

I'd explained this many times before to senior officers – a shocking anomaly that occasionally came back to haunt us.

'The thing is, Colin, when the National DNA Database was set up in '95, the only people added were suspects brought into police stations for an arrestable offence. It wasn't until 1999 that serving prisoners and people being released from prison were automatically sampled and put on the database. So, this suspect may have been released from prison pre-1999 and has not offended since.'

Colin grimaced. 'Or we failed to catch him.'

He went on: 'Just to be on the safe side, we're checking out sexual assault cases that have been discontinued or where the suspect was acquitted.'

He passed over a so-called profile matrix of the rapist drawn up by the behavioural scientist. This calculates the offender's most likely key attributes and criminal past on a sliding scale.

Top of the 'most likely' list: he was a white man aged twenty to thirty-five, five feet five to five feet eight, who lived in Stanhope or South Ashford, was on a database somewhere for familial sexual abuse and had either just come out of prison or was on probation.

'So what are your thoughts about all this, Ray?'

'I agree that the suspect didn't just stumble across Stanhope. It's not the type of place you accidentally end up in. I agree he's local or has local connections. We need to do an intelligence-led screen on current and former residents of Stanhope and South Ashford. We've just conducted one in Sussex that got us a result. So, we need to draw up a list of who to target.'

An intelligence-led screen involves identifying the most likely suspects in an area, taking their DNA and checking it against the profile of our unknown culprit. It's a major undertaking but there are useful shortcuts. The DNA samples taken for a screen don't go through the rigorous testing that samples undergo in a police investigation. There's a quick and simple screening process that can eliminate a batch of thirty people in one go at a fraction of the cost. Not that any of us cared about cost when it came to a ten-year-old victim of rape. But we were conscious that time was a factor. We had to identify this monster before he struck again.

Next, we had to prioritise the people to subject to DNA testing. Sex offenders came top of the list, obviously; but this would prove to be not as straightforward as it sounded. First, we needed to check if these sex offenders were on the National DNA Database. If they were, then we could immediately eliminate them because our suspect wasn't. As I reminded Colin, though, the National DNA Database was set up in 1995 and the Sexual Offenders Register in 1997. Not everyone on the Sexual Offenders Register would be on the DNA database. Detectives needed to be sure to check if locals on the Sexual Offenders Register were also on the database. If not, then their DNA needed to be taken.

Next on the list of people to swab: anyone recently released from prison. We'd then target domestic abuse and child abuse referrals, men on alcohol and drugs-dependency programmes and any male flagged up as sexually violent or violent by the probation service, housing authority and social services in the area.

I advised Colin that any screening process needed a strict identification policy. The notorious rapist Colin Pitchfork, the first man to be convicted using DNA, paid a friend to pretend to be him at a screening, totally wrong-footing the police investigation for months.

Put simply, the bloke has to be who he says he is.

We also needed to stage a press conference to announce the screening. This may lead to tip-offs. Also, if any of our targets for screening suddenly moved out of the area, then they would most likely be guilty of something that their DNA would reveal. To deal with anyone who failed to turn up for screening or refused to give a sample, we agreed on a policy known as TIE – trace, investigate and evaluate or eliminate.

As this exhaustive screening process began, detectives investigated the criminal records of all males who lived or worked on the Stanhope estate and in South Ashford, past and present. They checked out people on the Sex Offenders Register with family living in the area. They checked all outstanding crimes in Kent and across the UK for potential links. They checked the criminal databases at the National Crime and Operations Faculty.

All of this work, including the screening of 3,000 local men, led to nothing.

Colin asked me if there were any other avenues we could

pursue forensically. I had to be honest and say I couldn't see a realistic option. We had no leads left. I lost count of the number of times we sat there racking our brains: have we done everything we can? Is there anything else we should be doing? Anything we may have missed?

To the utter despair of everyone, the investigation had to be scaled down. Colin and a family liaison officer broke the news to the girl and her shattered parents. Yet we all knew he'd strike again. And Colin's big fear was that, next time round, he'd go one step further.

JULY 2002 – 8 MONTHS AFTER THE ATTACK

I answered my mobile phone and was somewhat surprised to hear that the caller was from the National DNA Database in Birmingham. I was even more surprised by what she had to tell me.

'We know you're still looking for a suspect in the case of the ten-year-old girl rape victim in Stanhope. Well, there's been a development.'

I felt my heartbeat quicken. Every morning for the past eight months or so I'd woken with a sense of dread that the suspect would have struck again, ruining the life of another innocent child.

'We've got a partial DNA match to your suspect from a rape in Earlswood, Surrey, on July eleventh.'

The caller supplied a laboratory reference number that allowed me to find out more about this latest victim on the computer. When I clicked on the case management system, I was astonished to discover a very different victim to the ten-year-old girl in the first attack. This time, he'd assaulted a thirty-year-old woman.

'How close is the match?'

'The chances of it being someone else are about one in thirteen million.'

It's got to be him, I thought.

I'd never come across a case before where a suspect raped both children and women. I'm no behavioural scientist, but it struck me as extremely unusual and I wondered if there had been some sort of mistake. I rang Surrey Police to check.

They confirmed that the victim in the DNA-linked rape was a thirty-year-old woman who had been walking her dog in parkland close to her home at around 9.30 a.m. when the rapist struck. In broad daylight, he'd grabbed the woman from behind, dragged her into bushes, tied her hands and pulled her top up so that it covered her eyes.

'If you scratch me, scream or look at me, I will kill you,' he told her.

I've heard officers over the years – male and female – wonder why victims don't fight back or scream their heads off. If you saw the bruises inflicted upon this woman, you'd understand why. Her attacker inflicted fifty-six separate injuries during the course of his vicious assault. This victim felt in no doubt that her attacker was powerful enough to kill her and, had she fought back or glanced at his face even accidentally, would've gone through with it.

Then a twist: the woman explained that, as he pulled down her trousers, she heard the sound of a wrapper.

'Don't worry, I've got a condom,' he told her.

Sure enough, intimate sex swabs failed to reveal any semen. The suspect had become forensically aware. He'd realised from our appeals that we'd got his DNA profile from the semen left at the Stanhope assault. He wasn't going to make that mistake again. But he did make another. During his attack, the rapist engaged in so-called scripting to make it seem like the sex was consensual.

'I want you to fuck me, move back and forward,' he told her. 'Tell me you like it and that I am big and strong.'

So swept along had he been in his delusional state that, at

one point, he licked the victim's left ear. Initial examination of the ear swab using standard DNA profiling had failed to produce a profile. However, a sensitive DNA profiling technique – known as Low Copy Number – revealed the partial profile of male DNA.

This DNA profile provided us with the 13-million-to-one chance of the attacker being someone other than the rapist who had struck eight months earlier in the Stanhope estate. There were other compelling similarities between the attacks. Again, he'd struck in a public place, close to a car park. Any number of people – walkers, runners, people parking their cars, the residents of nearby homes – could've seen him grabbing the victim. Again, this wasn't a public park but a piece of open land at the back of a housing estate known only to those living locally. And again, the victim didn't get to see her attacker's face.

I called Colin Murray right away. Neither of us could understand the change in victim profile, the fact that this attack took place over fifty miles from Stanhope or why he'd taken a break of eight months. Little did we know that, very soon, he'd be making up for lost time.

AUGUST 2002 – 9 MONTHS AFTER THE FIRST ATTACK

Senior officers from Kent, Surrey, Thames Valley and the Met agreed to meet at a hotel near Brand's Hatch racetrack to discuss the rapes in Stanhope and Earlswood – and any possible linked offences in their areas. But they couldn't agree on whether or not to formally link the Stanhope and Earlswood rapes. Commander Bill Griffiths from the Met insisted there was insufficient evidence to say for certain that the same man had committed both offences. Others disagreed. They turned to me, giving me the distinct impression that I had the casting vote.

I knew the risks of linking two offences: it is stating categorically that there is only one offender. The entire investigation would then be calibrated to this as a certainty. If we were mistaken and there were two offenders, then the investigation would have been sent in the wrong direction. What if that resulted in more attacks? We just couldn't get this wrong.

But I had to trust in forensic science. Remembering what Will O'Reilly had said about scientists not speaking their minds, it was time to be decisive. As far as I was concerned, there was one man on the loose who was a danger to women and girls of any age. And he could strike again, anywhere, any time.

The crimes were linked and a cross-border investigation set up. Each senior investigating officer would look into unsolved crimes in their area for possible links to these two cases. Not just DNA and fingerprints but footwear marks, tyre marks, even the modus operandi may be enough for us to connect the offence.

The Met came back that very day with an astonishing revelation.

After committing the vicious rape on the thirty-year-old woman in Earlswood, Surrey, on the morning of July 11, 2002, the rapist struck a second time – that same day.

Just six hours after the first attack, at about 4.30 p.m. in leafy Putney Heath, south-west London, a twenty-six-year-old nurse training for a charity walk was attacked. Again, it was in a very public place, so high-risk, this time along a popular walking route just north of the busy A3 and close to the Telegraph pub. The offender came running up behind the unsuspecting victim before grabbing her in a headlock.

'If you scream, I'll break your neck. I don't want to get caught again,' he told her.

Her rape followed the same grim pattern as the others – she was bound, blindfolded, beaten and threatened with death – though the culprit was clearly growing in confidence.

'You're a nice-looking girl. You smell better than the last one. She stank,' he told her.

'Why are you doing this?' his victim had pleaded.

'Because I'm not getting any sex at home.'

Before raping her, he brazenly lifted her makeshift blindfold just high enough to reveal he was wearing a condom. Several times during the assault, he tried to kiss her on the mouth and engaged in more scripting.

'Tell me you like it, kiss me back.'

When he was finished, he rummaged through her bag and found her mobile phone. Scrolling through her contacts, he found one that said 'Mum' and pressed 'call'.

'Hello Mum,' he said.

'Where's my daughter?' said the startled woman.

'Oh, she's a bit tied up at the moment,' he said, cackling.

This time, the saliva from his attempts to kiss the victim delivered a poor partial DNA match. But we now understood something terrifying – it would be impossible to second-guess his next move. It appeared that the rapist we were looking for randomly picked his spot and waited for whatever unwitting girl or woman had the grave misfortune to come along next.

We had no choice but to go public. A maniac rapist was on the loose who would strike again – and it could be anywhere. No girl or woman was safe. Police weren't just warning women not to go out alone at night, they were warning all females to be on their guard at all times. Somewhat embarrassingly, though, we couldn't provide a photofit or even a description. All we knew so far was that the man spoke with a north-east 'Geordie' accent and reeked of cigarette smoke.

I called Colin Murray in Kent. Inevitably, the ten-year-old victim from Stanhope would now be exposed to the media coverage linking these cases. Last I heard, she'd returned to school and was making good progress.

'It's not good,' he confirmed. 'It's brought it all back. The family liaison officer tells me she can't go to bed on her own and, when she does, she can't sleep. And she can't stand being in the dark. Until we catch him, that poor girl will be forever stuck in limbo.'

CHAPTER ELEVEN

OPERATION ORB TWO

A matter of weeks after raping two women in one day, the suspect struck for a fourth time.

On August 6, 2002, a fifty-two-year-old woman was walking her two Jack Russell dogs on Wimbledon Common in south London when subjected to a 'whirlwind' attack from behind. This time, the victim was threatened with a knife. She called her dogs, who failed dismally to come to her rescue. When she turned to get a look at his face, the suspect smashed her with a fist.

'Are you a virgin?' he asked.

'Hardly, I'm fifty-two,' the ballsy woman replied. 'Are you?'

As he began to fondle her, she pulled away and said, 'You'll have to stab me.'

But the attacker overpowered the woman. He told her he was using a condom but she couldn't be certain. She then made an observation that perhaps gave us an insight into this man's sexual inadequacies.

'His penis felt like a penis but a very small one – small in length,' she told police.

He left with the woman's T-shirt, threatening to slit her throat if she screamed and instructing her not to move for twenty minutes.

A day later, August 7, he launched his most audacious attack yet in Epsom, on the south-western edge of London. He literally dragged a twenty-six-year-old Finnish woman off the pavement into woodland on Epsom Common and raped her. Once again, he tried to kiss the victim and, this time, we managed to retrieve a partial profile from his saliva. The odds of it being another offender were seven million to one.

This was the suspect's fourth rape in less than a month and the fifth since he'd attacked the ten-year-old girl in Stanhope, Kent, the previous November. It would soon become the biggest manhunt since the Yorkshire Ripper almost a quarter of a century earlier, involving five police forces and some 350 officers.

Yet still we didn't have a description of his face. His age had been estimated at anything between thirty-three and sixty. And we still couldn't even begin to guess where he lived. The only two rapes we could geographically link were those on Putney Heath and Wimbledon Common – just a half mile apart in south London. So, we launched an intelligence-led screen of men in that area. But no sooner had we started that process than he struck twelve miles south-west in Epsom.

We were in a tailspin. How was this going to end? Would he take that next step and throttle a victim? For me personally, I'd never known a level of stress and intensity like it. I had work on this case spread across five labs and involving over a hundred scientists and assistants. I knew most of them found me a pain and moaned that I was always demanding results in a hurry. But my argument to them was, 'Don't get involved in work on major crimes if you can't handle the pressure.' I felt my job was to lead scientists, not to manage them. We needed results and we needed them fast; people's safety depended on it. Plus, they got a good pay packet at the end of the month and it was better than stacking shelves!

Also, they weren't the ones in the firing line when the lab got blamed. And we got scapegoated a lot by detectives. The most common complaint was that we were too slow, but I even heard us getting stick for 'failing to get a result' from an exhibit. I had to regularly remind detectives of all ranks that our job was to deliver the scientific facts, not what they wanted to hear.

Managing senior investigating officers from four counties and an officer in overall command (OIOC) didn't help. I liked and respected these men, but they were all used to being *the* boss and expected me to be at their beck and call 24/7. They always wanted a result right away or an exhibit to be urgently tested. This is normally fine, but when you have five senior investigating officers all wanting their numerous exhibits prioritised, it became difficult to organise – especially when, the following week, you had to explain why not all of their requests had been completed.

I'd have to call these five senior officers individually to flag up an idea – there were no group video calls in those days! I'd then have to call each of them back to relate what the others had said. A prime example of this protracted duplicate process occurred when one of them suggested bringing in profilers to identify any links between the crimes that we may have missed. On a regular investigation, with a single senior investigating officer, this would take perhaps two minutes. On this case, I had to set aside two hours. But they did all sign it off – eventually.

The profilers noted that all of the attacks in this case had taken place between Monday and Friday and all but the first – in Stanhope, Kent – had occurred during regular working hours. We deduced that whatever this man did for a living likely took him all over the south of England where he could spot opportunities to launch an attack. Perhaps the Stanhope attack had occurred 'out of hours' because he lived closer to that location?

Our geographical profilers found a couple of other common denominators. The attacks all occurred within easy access of the M25 motorway that orbits London, leading to certain sections of the media dubbing him the 'M25 Rapist'. Most of the attacks had happened close to railway lines, leading to other sections of the media dubbing him the 'Railway Rapist'. And he tended to remove items like clothing from the crime scenes, leading to a splinter group of media outlets referring to him as the 'Trophy Rapist'. Catch him? We couldn't even agree on a moniker.

On Friday, 6 September, 2002 he confounded one of these common denominators by launching an attack on a thirteen-year-old girl in Woking, Surrey – outside of regular work hours. The girl had been cycling through woods off Pyrford Common at about 7 p.m. when a man knocked her off the bike, dragged her into the woods and raped her.

On Friday, October 25, he changed tack again, pouncing on a fourteen-year-old girl north of London, near Stevenage in Hertfordshire. The knifepoint attack followed his by now customary MO except for one key difference: she got a good look at his face.

She described him as between forty and sixty years old, with brown, taut skin and a characteristic that really helped narrow down suspects – striking green eyes. Other details matched those of previous attacks – the Geordie accent, the smell of stale cigarettes, his use of a condom. She helped police draw up a photofit and later confirmed it was 'a good likeness' to her attacker. So good, in fact, that the police decided to feature it on *Crimewatch*, which often had in excess of five million viewers. The appeal resulted in over 5,000 calls from the public.

One of these calls came from a woman in the tiny village of Appledore in Kent, eleven miles south of Stanhope. She suggested that detectives take a look at one of her neighbours who matched the photofit, had a Geordie accent and smoked heavily. Crucially, she provided his address as well as his name: Antoni Imiela.

Of course, Imiela was just another name for the detectives to process at this stage. They finally got round to calling him in November to arrange a buccal (cheek) swab.

Imiela, forty-eight, explained that he was a railway worker currently stationed in Southampton, so there was no point in the officers attending his home.

'We can come down to you then?' suggested the officer.

'No, no you can't come to my place of work,' he protested.

He finally agreed to meet the officers at home on his next day off, November 19. On arrival, the officers were surprised to be quizzed by Imiela about the legality of their request.

'Oh, just give them the sample, Tony,' urged his wife Christine, 'you've got nothing to hide.'

After handing the officers a swab, he asked: 'How long does it take for the result to come back?'

'Between seven and ten days,' said an officer, 'but, like your wife says, I'm sure you've got nothing to worry about.'

Thirteen days later – on Monday morning, December 2 – I got a call from the National DNA Database in Birmingham.

'We've got a match for your M25 Rapist,' the voice said, brightly.

'If you're trying to be funny, pal, then it's not working...'

'I'm serious, Ray. You've got him.'

I called Colin Murray right away. His stunned silence said more than words ever could.

We started to piece together all the information we had on Antoni Imiela – the man we now knew to be the serial attacker known as the M25 Rapist.

Most of the offences had occurred close to rail lines. Imiela worked as a track safety supervisor for Network Rail, in both London and Southampton – hence his frequent use of the M25 motorway. He had clearly used his job inspecting lines to scout out secluded locations where women walked or jogged. When driving between London and the south coast, he'd call on these locations and wait for a victim to come along. His work as a rail supervisor even explained the eight-month gap between his first and second offences; during that period he was being given a lift to and from work by a colleague, so was unable to stake out his preselected haunts for victims.

There was a good reason why we hadn't identified Imiela despite his connection to the railways. Police had checked out railway workers with convictions for sex offences. Imiela didn't have any. But he had been in trouble with the law before, and from a very young age.

Born in 1954 to a Polish soldier and his German wife in Lübeck, in what was then West Germany, Imiela spent the first seven years of his life living in displaced persons' camps. In the early 1960s, the family moved to County Durham for a new life, but neighbours remember his dad being a troubled and unbalanced man who never learned English and frequently thrashed his kids with a belt.

In 1968, when Antoni was fourteen, his mother Elfriede went out for fish and chips and never came back. Imiela went off the rails, turning to burglary and car theft. By sixteen, he was in borstal.

That seemed to straighten him out, at least for a time. He became a plasterer and had a son, Aidan, with his then girlfriend. But, by 1987, he was carrying out armed robberies on post offices across northern England, threatening to 'blow the heads off' terrified staff with a sawn-off shotgun. When police finally identified Imiela and launched an operation to arrest him, he somehow got wind of their plans and fled.

While on the run, Imiela would occasionally put in a taunting phone call to Detective Inspector Arthur Proud, the cop hunting him. Suddenly, about a year later, he handed himself in and was sentenced to sixteen years.

Described as 'a model prisoner', Imiela was released early in 1996. As I'd explained to DCI Colin Murray, it would be another three years before released prisoners were compelled to provide a DNA sample; that's why he wasn't on the National DNA Database. Yet DI Proud – the man who put him away for armed robbery – felt certain that the 'arrogant, smug' offender would strike again.

Imiela sought a fresh start, moving to Rye in East Sussex, where, after a whirlwind romance, he married Christine. He moved into the home she shared in Appledore with her teen daughter Cheryl. Although he never laid a finger on Cheryl, she did describe a disturbing incident when he walked in on her undressing and later asked if she'd 'meant anything by it'. Cheryl told detectives Imiela had 'tried it on' with a female neighbour who later complained about it to Christine. Imiela's loyal wife refused to believe the woman, who later got her revenge by calling Imiela in to *Crimewatch*.

Frustratingly, Appledore had been just a couple of miles outside the intelligence-led screen we'd undertaken after the first rape in Stanhope. Had he been within the screening area, Imiela's previous conviction would've come to light and we would've taken his DNA. We were that close to saving all of those subsequent rape victims.

As soon as we got the DNA result matching him to the rapes, we needed to arrest Imiela before he struck again. His wife revealed he'd left home at 5 a.m. that day – December 2 – to make the long drive to work in Southampton. She was expecting him back that night. A plan was hatched to track his movements using his mobile phone and to arrest him as soon as he drove back into Kent that evening.

Later that day, we learned of a horrific twist that cranked up the pressure on us making this arrest. A few weeks earlier, when Imiela had provided officers with a swab, he'd asked how long it would be before they got the result. Of course, Imiela knew that this swab would unmask him as the M25 Rapist – that his days of freedom were numbered. In a sickening display of defiance, he decided to make the most of those final days as a free man.

Two days after providing the swab, he called his wife saying his car had broken down in Oxford and he needed to stay overnight. In reality, he was driving to Birmingham to randomly target another young victim. He spotted the ten-year-old girl walking along a street and asked her to get into his car. She refused. He followed her, told her he had a knife and that he'd kill her if she didn't get in. That was the start of a five-hour ordeal for the girl, during which time he sexually assaulted her on eight separate occasions. The final assault on the back seat of his Citroën Xantia lasted ten agonising minutes. Before throwing her out on the street, he told her: 'You're OK, you've got your whole life ahead of you. Mine's over.'

The full scale of Imiela's horrific crimes in Birmingham only came to light that evening, just as he set off from Southampton on the four-hour drive home. He must have known that we either had or would very soon be getting the results of his swab. We suddenly realised he had nothing left to lose. Our biggest fear at this point was that he'd make a diversion off the M3 motorway to target some random young girl, one last time.

As they observed his progress up the M3 via 'pings' from his mobile phone, DCI Murray and his team felt as if they were in an invisible car behind Imiela. In case of any technical hitch, police surveillance teams from Hampshire and Kent were on standby to take over. Murray had considered deploying these teams to shadow Imiela's car. However, he guessed that the suspect would be on a state of high alert. There was a risk he'd sniff out the police trap and escape, just as he had back in the 1980s when he'd remained on the run for a year. They couldn't afford to let that happen again.

All of a sudden, the 'pings' changed direction.

Imagine the horror of DCI Murray and the observing detectives when Imiela suddenly turned off the M3. They realised he was heading towards the town of Eastleigh. Terrified that he was intent on committing one last atrocity on some unsuspecting child before his inevitable capture, DCI Murray dispatched the Hampshire surveillance team to locate him.

He just had to hope they'd get to him in time. How would it look if a serial rapist was to strike under the very noses of police following his every move? The pings stopped in Eastleigh. What the hell was Imiela doing now?

The minutes ground past as Murray and his team waited for a confirmed sighting of Imiela from the Hampshire unit. Next thing, Imiela's car returned to the M3. What had he been up to in Eastleigh?

They could do nothing now but watch his progress up the M3 and around the M25, before he finally turned off for Kent and the M20. DCI Murray called in the strike. A waiting police traffic team carried out a Tactical Pursuit and Containment (TPAC) manoeuvre to box in his car and arrest him.

The first thing arresting officers demanded to know was what Imiela had been doing in Eastleigh. To the intense relief of all involved, Imiela had merely stopped off for fish and chips, his last supper as a free man. I asked them to seize his car, as one of the finest scenes-of-crimes sleuths I'd worked with – Maureen 'Mo' Hughes – was on hand to examine it. As the offence in Birmingham had been just over a week ago, I was hoping Mo would find something in that car to forensically connect Imiela to his ten-year-old victim.

Next morning, I got a call from the incident room. We needed to process an evidential swab to corroborate the cheek swab taken from Imiela at his home on November 19. And it needed to be turned around quickly so that they could charge him with the rapes. I was then invited to a case management meeting the next morning to thrash out where we'd take the prosecution from here.

Meanwhile, Mo Hughes found two hairs on the back seat of Imiela's car that belonged to the ten-year-old he'd abducted in Birmingham. That plucky girl not only came down to positively identify his car, she also picked Imiela out of an identity parade. Detectives promised her that Imiela would never see the light of day again as a free man.

If only I could've made her the same promise. In truth, we were a long way from being able to prosecute Imiela for most of the rapes he'd carried out. This case's biggest challenge in forensic terms still lay ahead.

The case management meeting was boisterous, with lots of back-slapping and an overwhelming sense of relief; the man who had been terrorising southern England for twelve months was safely behind bars. The police had done their job and apprehended the suspect. Time for me to play party pooper.

We were focusing on eight of the attacks that Imiela had carried out: the girl aged ten in Stanhope, Kent; the thirty-year-old in Earlswood, Surrey; the twenty-six-year-old nurse in Putney Heath; the fifty-two-year-old dog walker on Wimbledon Common; the Finnish girl, twenty-six, on Epsom Common; the thirteen-year-old bike rider in Woking, Surrey; the fourteen-year-old in Stevenage who'd got a look at his face; and, finally, the girl he had most recently abducted in Birmingham, just days before his arrest. Because of his use of condoms, we had DNA evidence in only four of those cases: Stanhope, Kent; Earlswood, Surrey; Epsom Common; and Birmingham.

What about the other attacks? Apart from MO and details

like his accent and personal odour, we didn't have any forensic evidence connecting him to these rapes. It was absolutely imperative that we didn't let him get away with any of his crimes; that each and every one of his victims would get justice for what they had been put through. But how could we connect Imiela to these other attacks? I was told to come up with a proposal and present it in a week's time.

Without DNA, we had to find other ways to link him to all eight rapes. Imiela's mobile phone activity and bank cards corresponded with the times and locations of all eight attacks. That was a good start. It was also the end of all conventional investigatory methods we could use. And we were still falling well short in the four non-DNA cases. We needed to come up with something new and different. Something that perhaps hadn't been done before.

We had early on dismissed fibres as a source of evidence. None of the victims had even seen what Imiela was wearing when they were attacked, so checking their clothes for fibres belonging to their attacker had seemed redundant. Chances were he'd destroyed the clothes he wore during the attacks anyway, to ensure they wouldn't trip him up later. If he hadn't, then someone as forensically aware as he was would've at least put them through a very hot wash, maybe more than once.

But fibres were all we had left, so I had to think of something or someone who could help. I contacted Sue Cheshire, a fibres specialist, and arranged to meet her in the lab for an urgent conflab.

After a long discussion, she suggested that we analyse the clothes of all the victims to see if they shared any common extraneous fibres. If any of these fibres were distinct in colour or chemical make-up, we might be able to match them to a specific garment owned and worn by Imiela.

'But of course, it would have to be a very uncommon fibre for this to be convincing,' she pointed out, 'and you'd have to prove that it came from something that he had worn or been in contact with on the day of the offence.'

I decided that this was a good idea, largely because it was our only idea. In truth, it felt like an outlandish, last-gasp 'Hail Mary' throw of the dice. Imiela looked like a man who wore the kind of casual clothes that would be hanging in the wardrobes of half the male population of England. And even if we did find a distinctive and unusual fibre on a victim, how on earth could we connect it to him on the specific day of the assault?

But we needed a result from somewhere. And, I had to deliver something to the upcoming case management meeting.

My five bosses looked as unimpressed by my fibres proposal as I had felt delivering it. But, finally grasping the desperation of the situation we were in, they gave it the green light anyway. We started with clothes from the cases where we didn't have DNA – Putney Heath, Wimbledon Common, Woking and Stevenage. A couple of days later, I got a call from Sue Cheshire asking me to pop down to her lab.

'I've found something on a couple of these victims that is certainly distinctive,' she said, inviting me to look through her microscope.

The fibre looked to be a gaudy dark pink.

'It's polyester,' Sue pointed out, 'there's also some acrylic ones of the same garish hue.'

'It's not a colour I'd wear,' I said.

'That's what I thought. If Imiela has something of this colour, well, it'll stand out because it won't be like anything else in his wardrobe.'

I decided to meet Sue Cheshire and Mo Hughes at Imiela's home in Appledore, to look for anything inside that might match these pink fibres.

Inside the house, framed photographs of Imiela in various

loving embraces with his wife Christine loomed from every wall. On closer inspection, only one of them appeared besotted, and it wasn't Antoni.

I marched upstairs to the master bedroom to inspect his wardrobe. Just minutes later, I found myself coming back down, bitterly disappointed. I'd seen more colour in a Charlie Chaplin movie.

'Come here a sec, Ray,' Mo called from the sitting room.

I walked in wondering why she was standing with her back to some curtains and wearing a massive grin. Then the penny dropped; the curtains were a migraine-inducing pink colour and a ringer for the fibres Sue had viewed through that microscope. But how would a fibre from a household curtain in deepest Kent wind up at a crime scene in south London?

I decided to worry about that later, obtained a taping for a sample and called the incident room. I knew that detectives were in the process of interviewing Christine because I'd heard a few comments about the poor woman's 'Mills & Boon' take on her love affair with 'Tony'. He was quite the romantic, according to her, frequently surprising her with little gifts and spontaneous gestures.

'Looks like he saved his biggest surprise till last,' one of her interrogators had quipped.

I told him to ask Christine about their morning and night-time routines, with specific reference to who opened and closed the curtains to the patio doors.

They got back quickly. Christine had waxed lyrical about how 'Tony' was always first up and did little jobs around the house before he left, including making her a cup of tea, turning on the hot water and – the one we needed – opening all the curtains downstairs.

Now we just had to prove that the pink fibres found on three of the victims had come from the curtains in Imiela's home. While we waited for the result, I had someone call the curtain manufacturers.

On the plus side, they confirmed that the curtains were made of polyester and acrylic. On the downside, they'd sold thousands of sets in that shade.

Finally, the call came through: 'Those fibres found on the women are a match to the curtains in Imiela's home.'

This was strong, but we needed more.

We broadened the search for these pink fibres to the cases where we had Imiela's DNA – and found them on the clothes of those victims. More evidence, but still not enough for a 'beyond all reasonable doubt' jury decision.

My fibre sleuths went back to the victims' clothes in search of other alien or unique-looking threads. To my amazement, they came back with more.

They reported finding minuscule bright yellow and orange polyester fibres on many of the victims. None of these women had been wearing anything of either colour or would've had cause to in their day-to-day lives. But why would Antoni Imiela have worn yellow and orange clothes when carrying out his attacks? Surely the last thing he wanted was to be easily spotted?

And then we twigged. As a worker on the railways, Imiela would wear luminous orange and yellow jackets and bibs when on duty. We've all seen those track workers because they're probably visible from Mars! When he planned to launch an attack, he most likely took off his hi-vis jacket and left it in the car. But all contact leaves a trace; these jackets deposited orange and yellow threads on his underclothes so distinctive that they shine in the dark! When he attacked these women, he unwittingly passed these telltale luminous fibres on to them.

Once he got back to his car after an attack, he no doubt put the hi-vis jacket straight back on so that he'd melt into the background. After all, the irony of hi-vis is that you never really notice the people wearing it. And no one would suspect someone in a hi-vis to have just carried out a rape in a public place. It was perfect cover – except for those clingy loose fibres.

We sent an officer to the Southampton rail depot to seize Imiela's safety jackets, and got them straight into the lab. Tests revealed that fibres found on the clothes of seven of our rape victims were a direct match to either one of these jackets or the curtains from his home.

We had him!

However, determined to put his victims through the ignominy of describing their ordeals in court – while facing him – Imiela pleaded not guilty. Many commentators said it was his last sick attempt to control and humiliate those victims.

Everything I saw during his trial at Maidstone Crown Court in March 2004 bore out the exact opposite: every victim who gave evidence exhibited a moral courage, dignity and quiet rage that electrified the courtroom. It felt as if, by telling their stories, the victims were exorcising his power over them and reclaiming the narrative and their own selves. The only person I saw weeping during the trial was Imiela himself, the epitome of the cornered, snivelling rat. He tried everything to wriggle out of it, claiming that the police had framed him and that he was a homosexual.

I wasn't there for the verdict but saw it on TV. He was convicted to seven life sentences for each of the rapes. He got a further twenty-nine years for the kidnap, attempted rape and indecent assault of the ten-year-old girl in Birmingham.

But that wasn't the end of the Imiela case. Nobody could have foreseen the twists that lay ahead.

As ever, there was no party or piss-up in the pub afterwards; by the time trials came along we were inevitably knee-deep in some other calamity. But, months later, I was invited to a function and presented with a commendation for my work on this case. It felt good seeing all these people without the shadow of a serial rapist hanging over us.

I was particularly pleased for Colin Murray, who had been hunting this suspect from the beginning. He told me that the ten-year-old victim of that first attack on the Stanhope estate had been making really positive strides since the trial. Catching Imiela had freed that girl from her own personal limbo of terror. I dearly hoped it was the same for all of his victims – that they could get on with rebuilding their shattered lives now Imiela had been sentenced to life in prison.

Little did we know how hard the police would have to work to keep him there.

Incredibly, Imiela had to serve a minimum of just eight years before he could apply for parole. We guessed he'd never be granted parole, but the police didn't want to take any chances. One thing still confounded detectives and psychologists about this case. When police catch a rapist, they can normally detect an escalation in his behaviour that culminated in rape. A rapist typically starts out as a flasher or a peeping Tom and will have minor convictions for such offences. Or social services records will show suspected domestic abuse or sexual abuse in the home. The point is, rapists don't start out snatching ten-year-old girls off the street. Police felt convinced that Imiela must have committed other sexual offences prior to his spree between 2001 and 2002.

The Met started looking at unsolved rape cases that had materials still on file that forensics could profile. One thing we found over the years was that, long before the emergence of DNA profiling, many biologists used to cut out pieces of semen-stained clothing and literally clip them to the case file. They also retained any slides containing the 'heads' of the semen 'tadpoles'. Maybe they had a premonition that some new tech would come along one day capable of exploiting this evidence. Maybe they saw DNA profiling coming! I salute their foresight but also their common sense. They must have known that, had they sent this material into police storage, it would've inevitably been thrown out whenever they were low on space.

One such progressive scientist had done exactly this in a case dating back to Christmas Eve 1987. Mum of two Sheila Jankowitz, thirty-one, and her husband were on their way home from a pub in Sydenham, south London, late on Christmas Eve when they quarrelled. She stormed off, eventually getting back to their nearby flat to find her husband not there. She went out to look for him and was grabbed, dragged into bushes, threatened with a brick, severely beaten and raped.

In March 2012 – eight years after his convictions for the serial rapes – Imiela appeared at the Old Bailey charged with the rape of Sheila. The court heard that, at the time of the attack in 1987, Imiela was on the run for armed robbery. Two weeks later, he handed himself in, admitted to his part in the armed robberies and was jailed for fourteen years. As the rape offence pre-dated DNA profiling, police failed to connect Imiela to the attack in Sydenham.

Almost a quarter of a century on, a minute trace left at the scene of Sheila's rape had matched Imiela's DNA profile. He pleaded not guilty, insisting the sex had been consensual. As a result, Sheila's former husband and daughter had to give evidence in court, reliving their ordeals all these years on.

We heard how the attack had taken a terrible toll on Sheila; relatives said she never got over it. Her marriage had ended and she had moved to South Africa, where, in 2006, she was murdered. Uniquely, she now gave evidence against Imiela from beyond the grave, courtesy of her written statements from the time.

Of course, Imiela's claim that the sex had been consensual was as preposterous as it was insulting to Sheila's memory. Sentencing him to twelve years, Judge John Bevan QC told him,

'I find this case saddening, not only because Sheila Jankowitz's life was blighted from at least 1990 onwards by mental illness until her murder in 2006, but I also find your approach saddening, surprising as it may seem.

'I disagree with the prosecution's suggestion that you hate women. From what I have heard in this trial, you seem to me to have a dislike of humanity in general.'

He went on: 'You are wholly unrepentant about your life of guns, rape and general violence and, despite having served eight years of your life sentence, you have not expressed one jot of remorse.'

We thought the proverbial key had been thrown away this time, but we were wrong. In January 2018, I was flabbergasted to read that Imiela, now sixty-three, was once again being considered for parole. He died two months later at Wakefield Prison, before the decision could be made.

It was one of the few times in my life that I thought to myself: 'Maybe there is a God, after all.'

CHAPTER TWELVE

OPERATION THESEUS
JULY 7, 2005

All Londoners remember exactly where they were when they heard the news. I was sat in a meeting at Dartford police station in Kent. What exactly this meeting had been about I can't quite recall. All of a sudden, it didn't really matter.

We located a TV and watched the rolling news unfold; the first explosion was reported at 8.51 a.m. on the Hammersmith and City Line at Aldgate station on the edge of the financial centre, the City. A second just five minutes later on the Piccadilly Line, Russell Square, in the bustling West End.

Anyone who'd ever ridden London's tube system could envisage the carnage. All those people, all that metal and heat, in such a confined, dark space.

A blunt pager message from FSS HQ in Lambeth: 'Ray, get back to the lab right away.'

On the drive back, news of a third explosion on the Circle Line at Edgware Road Station, just a half mile north of Marble Arch. Then a fourth on a bus at Tavistock Square near Euston. The thing we'd been fearing most since 9/11 four years earlier had finally come to pass – suicide bombers in the heart of London.

'It isn't a matter of if there are fatalities, but how many,' reported the news.

Terrorist bombs weren't new to the UK. Irish Republican groups first targeted the capital with dynamite in the 1880s. Almost a century later, the Provisional IRA regularly targeted London's most iconic buildings – and it wasn't all that difficult. Back then, you could park your car virtually anywhere. In March 1973, I was at work on the tenth floor of the Met Lab in Holborn when I heard and felt an almighty, ground-shaking boom. I looked out of the window to see smoke over the Old Bailey. An IRA terrorist had simply parked a car containing a bomb outside the grand old building and walked away.

Word came in that we were next. Anti-terrorist police received intelligence that the IRA had parked a car bomb outside our building. After all, we'd helped put several of their operatives away. Weirdly, we were so used to bomb threats in those days that no one panicked; we just calmly evacuated the building.

It turned out the Met Lab hadn't been targeted. But the bomb squad defused two more car bombs in central London that day, one of them outside the glass-fronted Scotland Yard HQ in Victoria. The only thing that worried us? These defused bombs were often brought directly to Holborn for storage before being transferred to the explosives lab, then based at Woolwich Arsenal. We knew only too well how skilled the IRA had become in booby-trapping such devices.

Fears that we'd be targeted by the IRA weren't assuaged by the move to our new HQ in Lambeth – south of the river – in 1974. With a railway line passing above to the commuter hub of Waterloo station, a big tunnel underneath and free parking all around, we couldn't help thinking there could be no more ideal building for a terror group to target.

But it was an IRA bomb in London's West End in 1981 that affected me most. Back then, we were known as the Met Lab and took immense pride in being a part of the capital's police force. When one of ours got killed in the line of duty, we all felt it. On Monday, October 26, the Met's bomb disposal unit was called to a Wimpy burger bar on Oxford Street – London's busiest commercial thoroughfare – where a device had been found in a basement toilet. Despite knowing it was probably fully loaded, bomb disposal specialist Ken Howorth went in to defuse the device. The bomb detonated moments later, killing him instantly.

The Met set up an annual six-a-side cricket tournament in his honour, with every civilian department competing for the annual Ken Howorth trophy. I even managed to be on the lab's successful winning side on one occasion. What a privilege it felt to receive the trophy from Ken's widow, Ann, and the Met commissioner, Peter Imbert.

After the IRA ceasefire of the mid-1990s, London enjoyed nineteen years without a lethal terror bomb. But in July 2005 all that changed, and we found ourselves confronted by an unthinkable new nemesis – religious extremists detonating bombs on their own person, also known as suicide bombers.

The heaviest casualties of this coordinated, four-pronged attack on July 7 had been on the Piccadilly Line. The train had been in a tunnel, so there was nowhere for the force of the explosion to go except through the carriages. Tragically, 27 people died and 344 were injured.

The other two trains, at Aldgate and Edgware Road, were in ventilated sections of the network, so the impact had been marginally less; eight people dead and ninety injured at Aldgate, seven dead and 185 injured at Edgware Road.

Meanwhile, at Tavistock Square, the bomb on the double-decker bus killed fourteen and injured seventy-four. Had the roof of the bus not peeled off like the lid on a tin of tuna, God knows how many more might have perished.

In total, the four bombs killed fifty-six innocent commuters and the event remains second only to the Lockerbie air disaster as the worst terror atrocity ever committed on British soil.

The Met Police's SO13 anti-terrorist branch and its specialist forensic management team (FMT) would lead the hunt for the masterminds behind these attacks. Whereas crime scenes had civilian SOCOs, the FMT was made up of police officers specially trained to handle the aftermath of terror attacks. Often ex-military, these FMT officers could work in the worst imaginable conditions and were considered the best in the business.

All exhibits from these four terror attacks would be coming to us at the FSS. I immediately identified two fundamental problems with this.

First, me.

Back in 1996, two fellow senior scientists and I were appointed as specialist advisors for London and the south-east. We carved up responsibilities and regions between us; I took south-east London, Kent and Sussex. Dr Ann Priston took west London and the anti-terrorist branch known as SO13 – a unit that relied heavily on expert forensic science.

Provisional IRA volunteers had become so forensically aware and difficult to identify that SO13 needed to find a new method to catch them. Ann Priston's expertise in fibres became their secret weapon. Ann's ability to link suspects to bomb factories and safe houses on the basis of mere threads had secured several convictions against IRA operatives. Thanks to Ann, fibres had proved the IRA's Achilles heel; SO13 loved Ann's work and they loved Ann.

Earlier in 2005, Ann had retired, and left me responsible for handling the exhibits from the 7/7 attacks.

Since taking over Ann's role, I had found SO13 and the FMT

tricky. Just trying to get a meeting with them proved a challenge. I had to keep asking them not to leave me out of anything important and insisting that I could help. They were civil and professional, but I could sense their suspicions about me and my motives. Were the FSS trying to take over an investigation? Or take over the FMT's role at terror scenes?

During our rare face-to-face meetings, I reassured them that I had no interest in the power struggles of warring department chiefs, that I was only here to help. In the months since, I'd facilitated a couple of submissions into the lab on their behalf, nothing more. As things stood, they clearly preferred and trusted their own expertise. So, when 7/7 came along, this was it. This was my chance to get SO13 and the FMT onside, to prove our worth and win their trust. If we couldn't win them over with an atrocity like this, then we were never going to get anywhere with the anti-terrorist branch.

This dilemma segued neatly into the second problem 7/7 presented to the FSS. How would we cope with the sheer magnitude of this task? How could we process such a large volume of exhibits with the speed and precision that SO13 and the FMT would expect and demand? After all, when a terror incident happens, their teams work every hour they physically and mentally can. Either they break the back of the investigation, or the investigation breaks them. We at the FSS couldn't continue as we were, with labs empty evenings and weekends while exhibits lay unchecked on people's desks. Not while FMT officers were painstakingly sifting through the blood and gore of underground bomb scenes 24/7.

For some time, I'd felt that we needed a wholesale cultural shift at the FSS. Now 7/7 gave me a chance to impose it. I presented my vision for a major crime team to my boss, Alan Bailey. Alan and I had bonded right away when, on his first day in charge, I advised him of his primary function as my boss: 'You've got one job and

one job only, Alan, and that's to keep management off my back.'
Alan did just that and we got along famously.

He immediately bought into the concept of a major crime team.
We then used the urgency of the 7/7 terror attack investigation to
sell it to FSS management. We needed to be fit and ready to handle
anything of this magnitude at all times. To our astonishment, they
signed it off. I'd grown up hearing about London's legendary
'Blitz Spirit' as bombs rained down during World War Two. I was
now experiencing a little bit of this war-ready 'can do, will do'
resourcefulness for myself.

So, how would this major crime team work? First, we'd have
a lead scientist for each discipline: biology, trace chemistry,
fingerprint development (serious crimes unit), firearms, toxicology
and so on. With almost a decade under my belt as SA, I knew
which scientists would be up for it and those not to bother asking.

A number of junior reporting officers would work under these
lead scientists. Next came teams of lead assistants, assistants and
technicians, who'd carry out the bulk of the physical work. Although
lead scientists would deal with the major analytical strategies, there
would always be a reporting officer in each lab dealing with results
and anything else that cropped up.

We identified the staff we considered willing and capable of
committing to twelve-hour shifts so that the lab could run 24/7,
seven days a week, at least until we'd broken the back of the
7/7 investigation. To my relief and delight, most FSS employees
were up for it. They too had come to realise that forensic science
needed to keep up with major investigations, that we had to be
and do more.

Over a hundred of them signed up to the plan.

Meanwhile, Alan Bailey took care of the pastoral side. Most
of the volunteers lived in the suburbs or outside London, so he
laid on taxis at night and – for those burning the midnight oil –

accommodation at the nearby Army & Navy Club in Waterloo. Food could be ordered to the building at any time, on account. In short, there were no excuses.

Bombs were going off in London. It was the least we could do.

In return, I promised staff a detailed daily briefing as to where we were in the investigation. Everyone would know as much as I knew. I would be available 24/7. I would manage the overarching review of the work to ensure nothing was missed or overlooked. I had always been a devotee of the spreadsheet; this case became my personal spreadsheet heaven.

I was now able to offer this guarantee to SO13 and the FMT: any exhibit you deliver to us on any given day, we'll turn around and have the results for you by eight the following morning – even DNA profiles. In other words, they'd have the results they needed before their morning briefings. We would be part of the investigation, helping to drive specific lines of enquiry.

But this came with one proviso. SO13 and the FMT had already hired a massive industrial unit in London to house the exhibits from this terror attack. It was top secret – so secret that we were told not to go there in marked cars, uniforms or even wearing ties. Inside already were thousands of exhibits from these terror attacks. If they overburdened us with exhibits at the lab, the system would break down. They had to prioritise what they needed testing, and I could help them do that.

I felt nervous as hell making this commitment. But I had to believe in my team. And I had found over the years one sure-fire cure for anxiety: throwing myself into the job.

The next ten days or so were the busiest of my entire life. My wife Jackie insisted I came home every night. I think she worried that I wouldn't stop working at all otherwise! But calls and pager messages at 3 a.m. became the norm. Especially if the FMT had located something vital, like a suspect's mobile phone. Of course, detectives would be pushing to download and analyse all the calls, messages and contacts. But in the forensics world, everything has to be done in the correct order. So, before anyone can download anything, we had to test that phone for DNA, prints, blood and other traces. Something like that shouldn't have to wait until I got up in the morning.

The downside of course was that the buzz of a pager in the wee small hours usually translated into me working all night and until late the next day. This I could handle. But what started to grind me down was my inability to switch off at the end of a shift like this. Even my trusty quota of beers failed to cure my burgeoning insomnia. Thankfully, a guardian angel was on hand.

Pretty soon, I realised someone was making all these decisions for me. The lead biologist Bridget March had bought into the major crime team concept from the start, and before long, she was running the entire day-to-day operation at the labs. She was feisty enough to manage the expectations of SO13, the FMT and even me! She also really looked after the welfare of the team and stood up for junior staff when it was needed. It was Bridget who first coined the phrase 'quick wins' – which means identifying those exhibits that are most likely to give us the evidence we are looking for. And this came in especially handy when we were presented with our first task – to help identify the 7/7 suicide bombers.

This turned out to be a less challenging task than we'd expected. After all, the four suspects had wanted to die as martyrs so had made no effort to disguise their identities. Each had been found with personal effects stating who they were; we just needed to prove it.

First, we had to confirm that the dead suspect Germaine Lindsay, nineteen, from Aylesbury, Buckinghamshire had detonated the device on the tube train near Russell Square station. Quick win one: we took a razor from his home and tested it for DNA that matched his. A toothbrush is the best domestic object from which to get a DNA sample – provided it's been used only by the suspect – but a razor comes a close second. After all, it actually scrapes and gathers skin cells.

We'd confirmed Lindsay's identity. But we still needed to prove he'd been part of this plot. Through CCTV, detectives had pieced together the movements of the four suspects. Three of them had travelled down from Leeds by train. They got off the train at Luton station, about thirty miles north of London, where they met Lindsay. The four then took a Thameslink train into London's King's Cross station. In the car park at Luton, detectives identified a red Fiat Brava registered in Lindsay's name. Quick win two: a gun hidden in the car had his DNA on it.

Proving the identities of the other three was even more straightforward.

The bus bomber was Hasib Hussain, eighteen, from Leeds. Forensics officers found his driving licence and credit cards at the scene. After the bombs went off, Hussein's parents had filed a missing persons report, saying they hadn't heard from him since he'd left home for London at about three that morning.

CCTV at King's Cross station showed Hussain exiting the Northern Line. This had been his intended target, but the line had been suspended that morning. Mobile phone records showed he tried to call the other suspects, but their devices had already gone off. He then boarded the number 30 bus, detonating the bomb at Tavistock Square.

Shehzad Tanweer, twenty-two, from Leeds, detonated his device near Aldgate station. His DNA was already on the national database for a previous offence.

Thirty-year-old Mohammad Sidique Khan, a father of one from Leeds, was identified as the Edgware Road train bomber through DNA samples taken from his parents.

That had been the easy part. Terror investigations differ from most others because it's not enough just to identify who committed the offence. As I was about to find out, the scope is much broader. For a start, we needed to find out who made the bombs and where. We had to confront the unthinkable – that another batch sat ready and waiting for the next terror team targeting London or another UK city. And how did these devices work? The Forensics Explosives Lab in Fort Halstead, Kent, had never encountered crude home-made devices like this before.

The detonator consisted of a battery powering a lightbulb that had been smashed to expose the filament. The heat of the filament ignited an explosive compound called TATP, which had been stuffed into a cardboard tube.

The detonator's job was to set off the main bulk explosive, which consisted of ground pepper and hydrogen peroxide. Except this wasn't the 9 per cent peroxide you can buy at the pharmacy or the 18 per cent you find in a hairdressing salon. The hydrogen peroxide in these devices wasn't like anything you can buy, even for industrial purposes, and was thought to be closer to 70 per cent – in other words, just 30 per cent water and 70 per cent pure hydrogen peroxide. If hydrogen peroxide at this concentration is mixed with a carbohydrate fuel – such as ground pepper – when detonated, it will explode with primary explosives such as TATP or HMTD.

How the makers created hydrogen peroxide this deadly only became clear when – through intelligence sources – we traced their bomb factory to a small block of flats in Burley, Leeds. Had anyone been paying attention, the signs that something bad was brewing inside 18 Alexandra Grove were plain to see: in the garden, all the vegetation was either dead or dying. Inside, paint peeled from the radiators.

This was caused by fumes, most of which emanated from a stove where 9 per cent hydrogen peroxide had been constantly boiled down in pots and pans to boost its concentration by evaporating the water. Also at the property was all the paraphernalia you'd expect for a bomb-making lab – save for any safety precautions. For example, we found lots of cigarette ends. Nothing like a smoke when you're cooking up some explosive hydrogen peroxide! Bridget's 'quick wins' that linked the bombers to the lab included these smoked cigarettes and food and drink containers, as well as kit used to build the devices: pepper packets, peroxide bowls, masking tape and saucepans.

In all, just shy of 1,350 exhibits were seized from this flat. Detectives weren't going to stop at just connecting the bombers to the property. They hoped that DNA and prints might reveal some of their fellow conspiracists in the plot who were still alive to tell the tale.

Clearly, the four bombers didn't do this all on their own. Their phones revealed links to Pakistan, but they must have had support in the UK too – both financial and logistical – to pull off an operation of this scale. These people were still alive and – most likely – also radicalised and capable of doing the same.

Then everything changed again.

JULY 21 – TWO WEEKS AFTER 7/7

Once again, I happened to be at Dartford police station in Kent. I'd even made a quip: 'Last time I was here, all hell broke loose.'

Talk about tempting fate…

At 12.26 p.m., as I sat in a meeting room, reports came through of an explosion on a tube train on the Hammersmith and City Line near Shepherds Bush station, west London. Four minutes later, another on a tube train at Oval station in south London. This time, I didn't wait for a message to get back to the lab in Lambeth. In the car, I learned of a third explosion at Warren Street station in

London's West End. Then, in a chilling echo of 7/7, reports of an explosion on the top deck of a bus, this time in Bethnal Green, east London. I don't mind admitting I felt a sickening, rising panic at this news.

As soon as I got back to the lab in Lambeth, I discovered that miraculously, in all four cases, only the detonators had gone off. Somehow, these detonators had failed to trigger the bulk explosives. All four suspects had fled the scenes on foot. In a bitter-sweet twist, we now had four failed suicide bombers on the loose in London.

Despite working closely together for the past fortnight, I felt that SO13 and the FMT were still keeping us at arm's-length. They were cordial and polite, but we felt more like clients than colleagues. That morning, I took a call from someone senior at the FMT whom I can't name for security reasons. He had a simple request: could we keep Bridget March and the rest of the 7/7 team on board, but refocus their efforts to this urgent 'live' case known as 21/7?

I said I'd ask, while working hard to rein in my relief. We – or rather Bridget – had broken the ice with the anti-terrorist branch! Despite having endured two sleepless weeks, Bridget immediately agreed to this new plan. Like most of us, she felt this latest attack must've been connected to 7/7, and by now she considered 7/7 *her* case. I knew if Bridget came on board, she'd bring the rest of the team with her.

Again, identifying the bombers became priority number one. By day two of the investigation – July 22 – police had released images of the four suspects to the media. As all of them had lived in London for many years, calls identifying the men came flooding in.

Meanwhile, at each of the four scenes, forensics discovered virtually identical devices still bubbling away. Each suspect had carried their bomb in a five-litre bucket inside their rucksack. Rather than black pepper, the fuel this time had been some sort of white powder. However, post-detonation, this white powder had reacted with the hydrogen peroxide in each device, a sizzling chemical mix that had reduced to virtually nothing. Working out exactly what this powder was would have to wait until later; we had four would-be suicide bombers to catch.

Just as in 7/7, the suspects had left clues to their identities at the scenes. At Shepherds Bush, forensics found a gym bag belonging to Hussein Osman, twenty-seven, complete with a gym membership card with a photo matching the suspect caught on CCTV. The card also gave his address as a block of flats in Stockwell, south London. Detectives established Osman lived there with his wife and kids and immediately placed it under surveillance.

Next morning, July 22, officers saw Osman leave the building with a rucksack and catch a bus. They followed him as he disembarked and entered Stockwell tube station just before 10 a.m.

It's important to remember that, at this moment, thousands of police officers patrolled tube stations and the streets in fear of another terror attack. Many of these officers were armed and the whole transport system was on high alert. Just that morning, Met Police commissioner Sir Ian Blair had said it was very possible that 'those at large will strike again' or that another terror cell might do so. Referring to the 21/7 attack, he warned: 'This is not the B-team. These were not the amateurs. They only made one mistake [in failing to detonate the bombs] and we're very, very lucky.'

It was in this atmosphere that armed officers followed Hussein Osman down the escalator at Stockwell tube station and onto a train. Seconds later, marksmen shot him seven times in the head. But the man they killed wasn't Osman, it was innocent Brazilian electrician Jean Charles de Menezes, also twenty-seven.

This deadly blunder cranked up the pressure on police not to just trace these radicalised bombers, but to ensure no other innocent party got hurt in the process. The eyes of the world were on the Met Police. We needed to deliver. And we still didn't have a suspect in custody.

Releasing CCTV images of the four suspects did, however, provide an early break. The parents of Muktar Said Ibrahim realised that the alleged bus bomber was their son. The twenty-seven-year-old British Eritrean shared a flat in New Southgate, north London, with another suspect: Yassin Hassan Omar, twenty-two, a Somalian-British citizen suspected of attempting to blow up the train at Warren Street.

No one knew the whereabouts of either suspect. But CCTV revealed how six-foot-two Yassin Omar had escaped London on a National Express bus wearing a full-length black dress and a burka and carrying a white handbag. They tracked him to a property in Birmingham. Armed police stormed the house. To their horror, the suspect confronted them wearing a massive rucksack.

Fearing he was carrying live explosives, officers tried to wrestle the rucksack from his back. During the ensuing struggle, one of the cops managed to taser Omar. As he fell backwards onto the floor like a great oak, how everyone inside that property must have winced…

Nothing went bang.

Omar was arrested and his rucksack searched; it contained an empty grey bucket. The suspect refused to speak to detectives, let alone reveal the whereabouts of the other suspects.

As we slaved away in the lab, a combination of briefings by anti-terrorist police and the FMT along with rolling news kept us up to date with developments in this case. Two days after the failed 21/7 attack, police discovered that this terror cell had wanted to go one better than 7/7. A fifth device had been found dumped in undergrowth at the north end of Little Wormwood Scrubs, west London. As in all the other cases, CCTV had captured images of the suspect with the device. But suspect Manfo Asiedu, thirty-two, didn't wait to be found. He walked into a police station, insisting he had no idea that the device had been a bomb, that he'd never met Muktar Said Ibrahim or Yassin Omar and had never handled hydrogen peroxide.

Two down, three to go.

On Friday, July 29 – eight days after the failed bombing – detectives received a tip-off about another of the wanted men. The caller said he'd seen Muktar Said Ibrahim in a fourth-floor flat of block K on the Peabody estate in Dalgarno Gardens, North Kensington.

After a tense stand-off with police – all captured on video by a neighbour and beamed around the world – at 1.33 p.m., two men slowly emerged from the flat naked but for their underpants, their eyes streaming from the effects of CS gas. One was Muktar Said Ibrahim; the other was Ramzi Mohammed, caught on CCTV running away from Oval tube station after his rucksack bomb apparently failed to go off. They had both expected glorious death on 21/7. Instead, they now stood humiliated in front of a live global audience, stripped of both clothes and the air of satanic glamour lent to them by those chilling CCTV grabs. They were ordinary-looking, and they were captured in an ordinary place, still living among us.

However, what police found inside the flat provided a stark reminder of their murderous intent. A ripped-up suicide note written by Mohammed told his family not to cry for him; what he had done had been for the sake of Allah. They also found a mobile phone in a pot of water – presumably an attempt to destroy it – and two improvised spears.

The final drama that Friday afternoon happened several thousand miles away in Rome. Hussein Osman – the failed Shepherds Bush bomber – was using a mobile phone that belonged to his brother, the owner of an internet cafe close to the main railway station in the Italian capital. As the days went by, investigators working with Italian phone companies were able to listen to conversations between Hussein and his brother and follow the electronic trail of the mobile from London to Brighton, where he lay low for three days. The trail then went back to London Waterloo station and on to Paris via Eurostar, then Milan, before finally stopping in Rome.

Hussein was apparently holding the bugged telephone when forty Italian officers stormed a two-bedroom flat in the Tor Pignattara area of southern Rome. He was brought out of the flat with a black hood over his head. Computers and software were taken from this address as well as from his brother's internet cafe at Termini station.

All five would-be bombers had been apprehended. By now, the operation had cost more than £4.5 million. The police had followed up 5,000 tip-offs from members of the public, taking 1,800 witness statements and examining 15,000 CCTV tapes. There were at least twenty-nine arrests, in southern England and the Midlands. And yet the investigation was far from done.

Now it was up to us at the FSS and the Forensic Explosives Lab (FEL) to forensically prove that this gang had plotted a terror attack on London – something that proved far trickier than any of us had expected.

CHAPTER THIRTEEN

OPERATION VIVACE

Once again, I found the scientists spending all hours at HQ driving our work into connecting suspects to a terror attack – in this case the bloodless 21/7 suicide bombing mission in which five devices had failed to properly go off.

We started with Hussein Osman. As well as his gym membership card, he had left a Reebok baseball cap at the Shepherds Bush scene, from which we got his DNA. We found more of his DNA on a comb in his gym bag, and his fingerprint on the back of a family photo.

On the bus at Bethnal Green, we found Muktar Said Ibrahim's DNA in the failed device's battery terminal.

The front clip on a rucksack left at Warren Street station provided a DNA match to Yassin Omar. We also found his fingerprint on a bottle of aftershave inside the bag. All five suspects had brought along beauty products to look and smell their best for those vestal virgins waiting for them in paradise. As my dear late dad quipped at the time: 'All them vestal virgins... there can't be many of them left by now!'

I remember watching the chilling CCTV footage of the failed attack at Oval. It captures Ramzi Mohammed, in the tube carriage, wearing a distinctive polo shirt bearing the words 'New York', presumably in some sick reference to 9/11. He leans nonchalantly against a horizontal rail handle. Then, as the train approaches the detonation site of Oval station, he turns his body so that his rucksack containing the explosives is directed towards a young mum and her nine-month-old baby. He detonates the device but it just fizzes and smokes. Panic erupts. The carriage empties save for one heroic young man who demands to know what's in the rucksack.

'It's nothing, it's just bread,' says Mohammed, who then flees the train.

Members of the public chase him up the escalator. He's next seen on CCTV running out of Oval underground station towards Brixton Road, a game flower-stallholder in hot pursuit.

An eagle-eyed local spotted Mohammed turning left into Mostyn Road and the labyrinth of a Brixton housing estate. Later, forensics found his 'New York' top, wires and batteries dumped in various places around the estate, from which they extracted Mohammed's DNA. We also found his fingerprints on the horizontal handrail of the tube carriage in which he'd travelled.

Lastly, although CCTV captured Manfo Asiedu with the device later dumped at Little Wormwood Scrubs, we couldn't find any trace of him on the rucksack or its contents. We needed more evidence to prove he'd been an active participant in the plot, and hoped to get it from the gang's bomb factory in north London at Yassin Omar's ninth-floor flat at number 58 Curtis House, New Southgate.

Thanks to the information provided by Ibrahim's parents, police had found the bomb factory on day two of the investigation. Had this been an IRA operation, that flat would've been cleaned of all traces of the suspects. That's why fibres had become so critical in convicting IRA bombers – it was often the only forensic trace they unwittingly left at a scene. However, these suspects had clearly expected to die and so had made no effort to disguise their bomb-making activities.

Although the anti-terrorist branch's forensic management team would deal with the scene, the exhibits were coming directly to us at the FSS HQ in Lambeth and the Forensics Explosives Lab (FEL) at Fort Halstead. From the kitchen, the FEL found evidence of an explosive substance in one saucepan and concentrated peroxide in another. The FEL uncovered traces of TATP on three sets of rubber gloves. The front of the oven and a microwave exhibited signs of corrosion from peroxide fumes. A piece of paper with a rota detailing the progress of boiling down hydrogen peroxide over a two-week period was found ripped up in a bin, alongside another sheet of paper tracking the density of the explosive material.

From the lounge, the inside of a sideboard revealed the remnants of an explosive mixture. Meanwhile, at the factory, the FMT found extremist videos, batteries, wiring, bottles of hydrogen peroxide and bottles of nail varnish remover, which contains acetone, which may be used to make TATP.

In the rubbish bins, they found masses of empty hydrogen peroxide containers – 140 one-litre and 52 four-litre bottles. On these bottles, we found the prints of all five suspects, including Asiedu – so much for his claims that he didn't know the other suspects and had never handled hydrogen peroxide.

Police also found receipts for these bottles from local hardware stores and a hairdressing salon dating from late April and early May – well in advance of the 7/7 attack. CCTV from a hardware store showed Asiedu purchasing several containers of hydrogen peroxide; he'd told staff he needed them for his painting and decorating business.

We took notebooks and sheets found at the scene to the Forensic

Science Service's documents section for examination. They use an electrostatic detection device known as ESDA, which can reveal words up to six layers below the top sheet. ESDA had played a key role in overturning several convictions in the UK where it showed police statements had been altered or signed in reverse order to the main notes.

It works like this: you cover the document with an acetate sheet, sprinkle it with iron filings and run an electrostatic charge over it. Filings go into any indentations on the sheet. The acetate sheet is then tipped to shed all loose filings and reveal the impressions on the paper. The beauty of this old-school science is it doesn't damage the document in any way, so it can subsequently be retained as evidence or subjected to further forensic tests. What ESDA found on one notebook in the bomb factory was references to 70 per cent – the desired percentage level for hydrogen peroxide in an explosive device.

In summary, we had forensics linking the five suspects to the bomb factory and four of them to the scenes where the bombs had failed to go off. We had CCTV of four of the suspects fleeing the scenes and Asiedu carrying a device in Little Wormwood Scrubs, close to where it was later found dumped. Phone records revealed contact between the five suspects on the morning of July 21.

All five were charged with conspiracy to murder. I'd like to say that those of us who'd slaved away on this had a celebratory drink, but the only thing we could collectively feel was exhausted relief and validation.

We felt that, surely, we'd covered all the angles and their convictions were a foregone conclusion. Little did I suspect the twist that came next and how it would prove one of my most daunting challenges as SA.

DECEMBER 15, 2005
NEW SCOTLAND YARD HQ, CENTRAL LONDON

Along with many of the key figures involved in the 7/7 and 21/7 investigations, I was invited along for what I thought were Christmas drinks at New Scotland Yard. Anticipating an evening of mulled wine and mutual back-slapping, I took the train into town. As I strolled past the iconic revolving Scotland Yard sign, I couldn't help feeling a little chuffed with what we'd achieved over the previous epic five months. A little acknowledgement tonight felt like the least we deserved.

But instead of strolling into a soirée, I found myself marched into a meeting room. Just as well I had the case notes in my bag.

Around the table sat the 21/7 senior investigating officer, Detective Superintendent Doug McKenna and his team; the top dogs from SO13 and the FMT and their teams; Clifford Todd, chief scientist at the Forensic Explosives Lab, and his team; the case prosecutor Nigel Sweeney QC and his team.

And little old me.

Not that I felt remotely intimidated. Everyone agreed that the FSS had risen to the grim occasions of 7/7 and 21/7.

And then Nigel Sweeney QC posed a simple question to the FEL that set off a bomb, for want of a better phrase, under the entire investigation…

'What was the actual composition of these devices?'

The FEL had established that the 21/7 devices contained hydrogen peroxide, explosive TATP and, to act as fuel, a polysaccharide or starch foodstuff, which they described as some sort of flour. These bomb mixtures had been stashed in five-kilo plastic buckets that – by the time the FEL had got to them – only had a few grammes of the explosive material remaining. At the time, their explosives officers had no idea what these substances were. Fearing some sort of atomic or biological hazard, they took the safety-first option and destroyed most of the material, retaining just samples. So, with the limited analysis performed by the FEL, we didn't know the precise ingredients that made up these devices, or their ratios. Neither, did the FEL have any idea how they could identify the chemical composition of the devices or the concentration of each component. It was the first time they had encountered an explosive mechanism like this and, as yet, had not developed methods to analyse them.

'Well, this means we have a major problem,' Sweeney snapped.

We all looked at each other in confusion. The evidence we'd gathered against the five suspects had been little short of overwhelming. We could connect them to the bomb factory, the bombs, the locations where they'd failed to detonate. Why did we need to work out the exact contents of these devices?

'Hussein Osman is fighting extradition from Italy,' said Sweeney with a sigh. 'The grounds he's fighting it on give us a good indication of the defence they are all going to adopt. When you think about it, it's the only defence they can adopt.'

I tried not to look lost.

'Osman is claiming that these devices were never supposed to explode. That the whole operation had been an elaborate hoax to protest against the invasion of Iraq. According to Osman, the passengers on those trains and that bus were only supposed to get covered in flour and go home laughing.'

I may have said 'shit' out loud at this juncture.

Sweeney went on: 'Osman and the other defendants will be claiming these were not viable explosive devices. If we don't know what was in these devices and the quantities, we can't prove that they were viable devices. Like I said, this is a massive problem.'

The representatives from the FEL explained that they'd never encountered devices like this before; they can't test something that no longer exists! As it was so unconventional, they wouldn't know where to start.

Everyone turned to me. I gulped.

'The Forensic Science Service doesn't deal with explosives,' I croaked.

I left there with this handwritten brief:

Tasks [as of December 15, 2005]:

Identify exact composition/make-up of each mixture [including concentration of components].

Compare each device – are they from a common source?

Any evidence of evaporation of hydrogen peroxide?

Were all prepared at Curtis House [or individually made up at different addresses]?

Any other useful scientific evidence.

Sweeney's parting words went something like this: 'Find some experts who really know about these things.'

I looked over at the people from the FEL and scowled. Why wasn't it their Christmas holidays that just got cancelled?

I needed a drink. And I needed a think. Alone.

That meant I couldn't risk any of the pubs closest to Scotland Yard; I'd be bound to bump into *someone*. Perhaps fittingly, as this brief felt like the blackest of surreal comedies, I headed to the Grafton Arms on Strutton Ground – the pub where the Goons famously worked on their scripts.

I sat at a table towards the rear of its suitably gloomy, dark wood interior, nursing a pint and a conundrum: 'Where do I go with this?'

Composing myself, I thought: 'I've got to treat this as an academic exercise. I've got to cut it down into manageable chunks and try to prove one thing at a time.'

As a Christmas office party whooped and hollered next to me, I started thinking about hydrogen peroxide. Well, someone had to.

I knew it broke down into oxygen and water, but that wouldn't help us; the oxygen would have dissipated and you couldn't differentiate the water that resulted from the peroxide from any other water present.

So how could we work out how much hydrogen peroxide had been in these devices and its concentration? I thought about impurities and remembered how, because hydrogen peroxide is such an aggressive chemical, the manufacturers put stabilisers into it. One of them is sodium stannate, a tin-based salt, and the other one is sodium salicylate, which is basically aspirin. I started thinking: could we analyse the scene residue for impurities instead? We could test that residue for sodium, tin and for salicylate if necessary. From the quantities present, we could extrapolate the amount of hydrogen peroxide used and its purity. Well, this felt like a starting point at least, and something I could credibly propose to an outside academic.

The other thing we could do was properly analyse the polysaccharide in the device and trace its origins. I reminded myself that, as specialist advisor, I'd gone outside the Forensic Science Service before and, in cases like Adam, it had led to significant breakthroughs. I could do this again. I just needed to find the best person for the job.

The white powder in the devices was clearly plant-based and there was only one place to go when it came to all plant-based science: Kew Gardens. Also, a bonus of using Kew was that outside the Jodrell lab was a little gate into the glorious gardens themselves, meaning that I always brought Jackie along so she could enjoy Kew's beauty while I tapped their expertise.

I had one other expert in mind for this. Throughout the Adam investigation, I had heard about Dr Stuart Black's work in isotope analysis of materials from archaeological digs. I found out that, as well as being a senior lecturer in environmental radioactivity at University of Reading, he did some excellent work identifying suspect powder from Pakistan for the anti-terrorist branch – and I now knew what hardasses they could be.

I'd asked his advice on the phone several times and liked his laid-back, personable approach. For a genius, he wasn't remotely intimidating. I also got to know through speaking to him that he had access to a vast array of complex instrumental analytical techniques, and experts who knew how to drive these machines. In truth, his department made the FSS look a very amateur organisation indeed, when it came to the identification and quantification of chemical compounds!

In the past, I've had to call several academics before finding one who was a) willing and b) available to help. It's a bit of a chore running through the entire backstory of a case over and over so, in the call to Stuart, I got straight to the point.

'You know the devices from 21/7 that didn't go off? Well, the suspects are claiming they weren't supposed to go off. I've been told to prove they were and, to do so, I've got to identify what was in them. Can you help?'

He went quiet for a few moments.

'After all that London has been through this year,' he said finally, 'I think it's the least I can do.'

I set up an urgent meeting for December 27 at Kew Gardens between their staff, Dr Stuart Black, Detective Constable Steve Barnett from SO13 and myself. How odd it felt that crisp and clear morning, striding past gambolling families filled with festive spirits to hunker down in a lab for a briefing about terrorist bombs. As it was the holidays, Stuart Black didn't have his usual lecturing duties at the University of Reading – yet he still managed to be late. This, I soon learned, was something I'd have to get used to!

The purpose of the meeting was to gauge what both parties could offer and to agree on a route forward. I also wanted to check out Stuart's personality. Carrying out scientific work that will later be challenged in court by top QCs requires a particular type of character. Anyone who takes this on has to be especially fastidious. They have to immediately grasp the importance of ensuring all the checks and balances are in place so that the results are fireproof. Leave a single gap and the lawyers will gleefully drive a coach and horses through it.

I'd grown wary of gung-ho experts who instantly want all the exhibits delivered to them and make declarations such as: 'Just leave it to me!' Every stage of these processes needs to be formulated and discussed in advance. I'm delighted to report that Stuart 'got it' right away. Within weeks, we'd agreed on our plan, which was supported by the experts at Kew.

Now, to the science… To identify the starch, we subjected it to X-ray diffraction analysis, which transfers an image of its crystalline structure onto photographic film. This method can distinguish between different pulses and grains like chickpea, lentil and plantain. We found that the starch in the devices and at the bomb factory – 58 Curtis House – appeared to be wheat-based flour.

X-ray diffraction also revealed the presence of the stabilisers sodium stannate and sodium salicylate in the remains of the device from Warren Street, which matched the brands of liquid peroxide that had been found in the bins at Curtis House, called Technique Basics and Pro-oxide.

Next, we moved on to Stuart's area of expertise – isotopes. Every element has known isotopic forms, which are like non-identical twins. Take a carbon isotope. It has the same number of protons in the nucleus – six – but a different number of neutrons. Almost the same, but not quite…

Carbon has three isotopes – carbon-12, carbon-13 and

carbon-14. Carbon isotope analysis measures the ratio between carbon-13 and carbon-12 against a known standard. Photosynthesis is the method by which carbon dioxide from the atmosphere is converted into carbohydrates in plants. It occurs through three major pathways (C3, C4 and CAM). The C3 plants (wheat, rye, rice, cotton) are grown in temperate climates and have a carbon isotope ratio of approximately -25 per cent. Whereas C4 plants (sugar cane, corn) are grown in more tropical climates and have a carbon isotope ratio of approximately -10 per cent. Stuart's department had a chart that revealed the carbon isotopic ratios of key crops around the world, ranging from rice to sugar cane.

Our sample closely matched wheat. The absence of sodium bicarbonate meant it wasn't a self-raising flour. So, what kind of flour was it? We sent SO13 out shopping! Their mission – to pick up every type of flour they could lay their hands on within the M25 orbital.

We now moved on to a different isotope – lead. We tested each flour sample's lead isotopic signature, in the hope that one would match the flour found in the failed bombs. Bingo! The flour found at the scenes and in Curtis House shared a lead isotope ratio with a very specific imported brand – Fudco chapatti flour. We could now test this flour and determine its exact composition, which could help us work out the volume and concentration of the hydrogen peroxide that had been mixed with it in the devices.

And it all comes back to my initial idea that December night in the Grafton Arms – measuring impurities.

Chapatti flour contains a high level of calcium. Hydrogen peroxide has none. By measuring the level of calcium in the bomb residue, we could work out how much the flour had been diluted. The calcium level was only 20 per cent what it should've been. In other words, the flour had been watered down by four-fifths. Bearing in mind that each of the devices came in a five-kilo bucket, this meant that about one kilo of the total volume had been chapatti flour.

Similarly, in the hydrogen peroxide residue from the scenes, the levels of tin – from the stabiliser sodium stannate – and sodium – from the stabilisers sodium salicylate and sodium stannate – allowed us to work out the concentration of the hydrogen peroxide used in the devices.

Through numerous experiments of slowly evaporating 18 per cent hydrogen peroxide over a period of time and measuring the concentration of the resultant solution, what we worked out was this: the suspects boosted the proof of commercial-grade 18 per cent hydrogen peroxide to between 58 and 72 per cent; they mixed 21 to 22 litres of this more concentrated hydrogen peroxide (evaporated from 378 to 405 litres of 18 per cent hydrogen peroxide) with the Fudco chapatti flour in a ratio of approximately 70:30.

So, starting with just a few grammes of residue, we managed to calculate the composition of the devices that targeted London on 21/7.

Our next challenge – had all the devices been mixed and made at Curtis House? We could scientifically link the pans used for boiling down the hydrogen peroxide at Curtis House to each of the scenes. The devices were made up of the same types of buckets, adhesive tape and shrapnel (screws, nuts and washers added to cause injury), suggesting they had been made at the same time. Masking tape, red wires and battery connectors recovered from devices matched the brands found at Curtis House.

In short, and thanks to Stuart, we had worked out the component parts of each device and the ratios and strengths of ingredients used, and proved that they had all been constructed at Curtis House. I reported these findings to the investigation team and waited for a thank you. Instead, I got an invite to the Wiltshire countryside and Britain's most secretive and controversial military research facility.

* * *

Porton Down commands 7,000 acres of the Wiltshire countryside near Salisbury and looks every bit as daunting and intimidating as it sounds. Thankfully, some hotshots from SO13 were on hand to waft me through the rigid security.

Once Stuart and I had delivered our results to the investigation team, they decided there was only one thing for it: they commissioned the Forensic Explosives Lab to build a device to the exact specifications we'd reported.

Over the next few weeks, a group of engineers and scientists were hard at work creating, then tweaking and fine-tuning the device. After an agonising wait, at last it was ready. This eerily impressive device now sat in a bunker behind a small gap that we found ourselves gawping through. I took a quick look around, and winced. Prosecution and defence lawyers were present, along with an alphabet soup of interested parties – the MoD, the FEL, the FMT and SO13. The pressure was on – this device had to behave exactly like we said it would, or it would have all been for nothing and we would be back to square one in trying to prove the bombers' guilt.

As I stood there in the dark room waiting for the last-minute checks, I was lost in thought. I'd often wondered how the 21/7 bombers felt when their devices fizzed and failed: surely, deep down, they can't have been disappointed? Or were they so convinced that paradise awaited that they had genuinely wanted to die? Now, in a surreal perversion of events, here I was willing this device to go off. There was no paradise waiting for me, just the hell of humiliation and shame if it failed. As Nigel Sweeney QC had made abundantly clear that December evening at New Scotland Yard, the entire prosecution depended on this thing going bang.

As the signal was given for the device to be activated, the room around me fell still. Collectively, we held our breaths, waiting.

Just to shred my last remaining nerve, the explosives team insisted on a Hollywood movie-style countdown.

5-4-3-2-1...

'Fucking hell,' I felt myself mouthing.

In this black, spartan cavern, the powerful explosion looked momentarily breathtakingly beautiful; shards of the bomb and its insides flew in arcs in the contained space. But almost instantly, my mind was transported back to a tube carriage, and I felt sick to the pit of my stomach. I thought of that young mum and her nine-month-old baby on the underground train near Oval. That child will, thankfully, grow up not knowing how close they came to oblivion.

After a few long exhales I escaped into the fresh air and rang Stuart. Like me, his overriding emotion was one of relief.

These devices weren't props or toys. They were bombs. The only reason they didn't go off was because the hydrogen peroxide had been mixing with the flour since the devices were put together – probably the day or evening before July 21. Over the course of the night and the six hours it took to transport them to their destinations, the hydrogen peroxide's proof had slipped below that required to explode.

Now we just had to convince a jury.

JANUARY 15, 2007 – WOOLWICH CROWN COURT, EAST LONDON

In my specialist advisor role, I was invited to sit in and observe the trial of the 21/7 suspects and to assist whenever an issue surrounding forensic evidence cropped up. I turned up at south-east London's Woolwich Crown Court to find a new, modern and sparse building with rigorous, state-of-the-art security. The Woolwich courthouse was constructed specifically to deal with terror suspects being held at the adjoining Belmarsh Prison, which has a 48-single-cell high-security unit considered the most secure in the UK. In fact, the prison is connected to the court by tunnel, eliminating the security-risk prison vans.

The trial of Muktar Said Ibrahim, Manfo Asiedu, Hussein Osman, Yassin Omar, Ramzi Mohammed and an associate called Adel Yahya began at Woolwich Crown Court on January 15, 2007. Although Yahya wasn't involved in the attack, evidence suggested he'd helped purchase hydrogen peroxide and had full knowledge of the plot. All six denied conspiracy to murder and causing explosions.

The defence called Professor Hans Michels from Imperial College London as an expert witness. A specialist in chemical engineering, he'd been recruited to look into the probability of these devices going off. While on the stand, Professor Michels produced a series of probability diagrams to assist the jury in understanding his points. From what I could read from their faces, they didn't.

And neither did I.

If you want to be an effective expert witness, there is one golden rule – make sure the jury members understand what you're telling them. A classic example is when a forensic scientist in the witness box is asked the very straightforward question: 'What is DNA?'

So often, an expert witness's reply will begin: 'DNA is a complex molecule…'

I've seen jury members visibly switching off at the term 'complex molecule'. This is the definition of DNA that I offer to a jury:

'DNA is a substance that, when decoded, varies from person to person. So, your DNA is different from mine. Therefore, it's got the ability to differentiate between persons.'

That's all they need to know about DNA. The role of the expert witness is to explain science so that it's understandable to the ordinary man or woman in the street. But some scientists either can't do this, or they like to look really clever, so they won't. Like Professor Michels.

Using a scale of zero to one, he argued that the fact the four devices had failed to go off meant the probability of them exploding was less than 0.5. In short, he was using the fact that the devices didn't go off to argue that they wouldn't have gone off!

His next finding was that the proof or strength of the hydrogen peroxide would have *increased* when it was in the device mixing with the flour, on account of the evaporation of water. For some reason he hadn't included flour in his experiment, which, under the circumstances, seemed a glaring omission.

The professor produced a graph showing hydrogen peroxide in water to illustrate his point. When Nigel Sweeney QC challenged him, Professor Michels opened his bag and started producing results from other experiments he'd conducted. The eminent QC looked around in horrified disbelief as urgent murmurings filled the court. By law, evidence like this has to be disclosed before the trial. And we were in danger of disappearing down a black hole of complex chemistry that could befuddle a jury already stretched by the science in this case.

On Thursday, April 12 the judge, Justice Fulford QC, declared, 'We can't go on like this' and called a halt to the trial. The judge instructed me and DC Steve Barnett to go to Professor Michels's lab that evening, interrogate his instruments and the results of his experiments and report back to court the next day.

DC Steve Barnett ran the gauntlet of rush-hour London traffic that evening to get me and the prof to his lab at Imperial College. When we finally entered his lab, I said:

'Right, where's your machine?'

'There,' he said.

'Great, can you open up the data system?'

'I don't know how to use the machine. I'll have to fetch a technician.'

I rang Jackie. It was going to be a late night.

By the time we got back to pick up my car from Woolwich Crown Court, the place was shuttered and my car locked in. Steve kindly dropped me off at my parents' in nearby Belvedere, where I borrowed my dad's car to get back to Kent. I returned it the following morning and Dad dropped me back at court.

We spent the next day in chambers analysing the professor's results. On Monday, Nigel Sweeney QC showed no mercy as he set about the professor and his findings. Stuart Black and I had met Professor Michels before the trial and had tried to warn him about what to expect. But he wouldn't listen. And that's something I've found over the years. Beware of the retired professor getting involved in court proceedings. All through their careers, students have hung on their every word. It's not like that in court. Every pronouncement you make will be scrutinised and challenged. You need to be able to back up your statements in a very clear way that a jury of regular people can grasp.

After the Professor Michels saga, the supposed ringleader of the 21/7 plot, Muktar Said Ibrahim, took the stand. The anti-terrorist branch had uncovered evidence that Ibrahim had been in Pakistan nine months earlier, in November 2004 – at the same time as two of the deceased 7/7 bombers. Ibrahim denied ever meeting the 7/7 bombers or attending a jihadi camp in Pakistan to learn how to build a hydrogen peroxide bomb. Instead, he insisted that he was self-taught from the internet. The message to the jury was clear, though – you don't go all the way to Pakistan to learn how to make a hoax bomb.

Ibrahim admitted making the devices for 21/7 but claimed that, as soon as the hydrogen peroxide hit 70 per cent proof, he added the same volume of water to weaken it down to 35 per cent. After all, he didn't want to hurt anyone.

Happily, our work in establishing the precise contents of these devices – and then detonating the mix to such spectacular effect at Porton Down – made a mockery of these claims.

On July 9 2007, after a trial lasting five and a half months, a jury found Muktar Said Ibrahim, Yassin Omar, Hussein Osman and Ramzi Mohammed guilty of conspiracy to murder and cause explosives. The judge sentenced them each to forty years.

Later, Manfo Asiedu pleaded guilty to a lesser charge of conspiracy to cause explosions and was sentenced to thirty-three years. Adel Yahya, of Tottenham, admitted a lesser charge of collecting information useful to a person committing or preparing an act of terrorism and was sentenced to six years and nine months.

Both Stuart Black and I received commendations for 21/7. I got another for 7/7. I accepted both on behalf of my FSS team. They were the ones who really deserved the awards, for stepping up and delivering under the most intense and relentless pressure imaginable.

I look back at 2005 as the year the FSS grew up and turned pro. We showed those doubters in SO13, the FMT and within our own organisation that we could respond to a national emergency like 7/7 and, just fourteen days later, service the country's biggest ever manhunt. The major crime team model had been implemented and proved itself ready for anything. Not bad for a bunch of civil servants!

Anti-terrorist cops and the FMT aren't the type to send you a 'thank you' card. But, a few years later, Bridget March, scientists Karen Taylor, Rob Ballance and I received something much better from them – an invite to a tube train bombing rehearsal at an explosives testing site in Buxton, Derbyshire. Finally, the FMT had accepted us as legitimate and equal partners in the job of catching and convicting terrorists.

CHAPTER FOURTEEN

OPERATION CATHEDRAL TWO
NOVEMBER 2004 TO FEBRUARY 2006

As I thundered west along the A27 towards Brighton in morning rush-hour traffic, a sign for Hastings gave me a sudden flashback. Had it really been seven and a half years since my first 'live' murder investigation as SA? It felt far longer ago than that, almost like another lifetime. So much had changed.

Turning up to a murder scene or an incident room, I no longer felt like an imposter. And thanks to my role in investigations into the cases of Sarah Payne, Adam and the M25 Rapist, nor was I treated like one. I had grown in confidence and, as a result, the SA role had expanded in scale. I felt now that I was helping forensics to drive investigations and we at the Forensic Science Service were always on the front foot.

But were my achievements as SA about to be overshadowed by that first murder case?

I had never thought for one second that the Billie-Jo Jenkins murder investigation would come back. However, just a few months earlier, in July 2004, the Appeal Court had quashed the murder conviction of her foster father Siôn Jenkins and ordered a retrial.

And it all came down to our forensics work.

Biologist Adrian Wain had found 158 tiny spots of Billie-Jo's blood on the trousers, jacket and shoes of Siôn Jenkins. In Adrian's esteemed professional view, the nature of this aerosol-like fine spatter was what he'd expect to find following an impact onto a surface wet with blood. Invisible to the naked eye, these minuscule spots indicated to Adrian that the force of these impacts had been 'considerable' and that whoever had worn these clothes had been close to Billie-Jo at the time of the attack.

'The overall distribution of spattered blood is consistent with that which I would expect to find on the clothing of Billie-Jo Jenkins's attacker,' he had reported.

Adrian observed similar blood patterns on Billie-Jo's leggings that, he said, had also come from the 'fine impact spray' of the vicious assault. His conclusions had been corroborated by an independent biologist, the highly respected Russell Stockdale. All agreed that the weapon used to batter Billie-Jo to death had been a heavy, eighteen-inch metal tent peg found at the scene. The prosecution case had been that Siôn Jenkins – provoked by a day of constant frustrations – had picked up the tent peg in a moment of blind rage and battered Billie-Jo across the skull. According to his estranged wife Lois, Siôn had serious anger management issues and was capable of sudden explosions of violent temper that, later, he didn't seem to even remember. On July 2, 1998, Siôn Jenkins was convicted of Billie-Jo's murder.

Siôn's defence team had since wheeled in retired professor David Denison, an expert in respiratory physiology from Imperial College London, who had done a lot of work on deep sea diving and the condition known as the bends. He was assisted by Professor Robert Schroter, an expert in bioengineering.

At Siôn Jenkins's original appeal in late 1999, one of the first things Professor Denison did was criticise the experiment biologists

Adrian Wain and Russell Stockdale had conducted using a pig's head, blood and a tent peg to demonstrate blood spatter. To counter their argument, Professor Denison employed a football, a sponge and a wig to double as Billie-Jo's skull.

In Professor Denison's view, Billie-Jo could have exhaled the droplets of blood onto Siôn's clothes as he tended to her after the assault. His argument was that a blockage in her upper airways – such as blood in her mouth or nose – had built up pressure in her already hyperinflated lungs. Siôn described pulling on Billie-Jo's shoulder at one point as she lay on the patio. According to Denison, a movement like this may have temporarily released the blockage and resulted in an exhalation of blood-borne air through one of Billie-Jo's nostrils, which landed on Siôn's clothes.

Using a tube and a three-litre syringe to represent Billie-Jo's upper airways and a nozzle to act as her nose, he showed how relatively low pressure could project three droplets of blood fully a metre away. If the nozzle was angled thirty degrees upwards towards a white screen, the droplets reached a height of eighty-five centimetres above ground level at a distance of half a metre. Denison's overall conclusion was that the blood spattering found on Siôn's clothing could have been caused by 'a brief passive or transiently active expiration from Billie-Jo' as Siôn had crouched over her prone body.

However, at the appeal hearing, pathologist Dr Ian Hill, who carried out the postmortem on Billie-Jo, said he found no evidence of any obstruction of the upper airways, and nothing to suggest a sudden removal of a blockage so as to allow a brief exhalation.

Our biologist Adrian Wain also weighed in on Denison's hypothesis. He pointed out that when he placed a female volunteer in the position Billie-Jo had been found in – on her front with the left side of her face pressed against the patio tiles – neither pulling nor pushing her shoulder had raised the head significantly above the floor. His tests found that the distance between the nose of the volunteer and the ground had been no more than ten centimetres or four inches, a third of the height quoted by Denison in his experiment.

Siôn Jenkins's appeal was dismissed on the following grounds: after her body had been found, no one – not her sisters, the neighbour Denise Lancaster or the paramedics – had claimed to have seen any sign of Billie-Jo breathing. The clothing of others who had tended to Billie-Jo – such as Denise Lancaster and the paramedics – had not been similarly spattered. The court further found that Billie-Jo's nostril would've needed to be twenty centimetres or eight inches off the ground and angled at between thirty and forty-five degrees to have projected the blood spatter found on the upper part of Siôn Jenkins's fleece jacket. This they ruled implausible.

And that, I thought, would be that.

But Professor Denison and Siôn Jenkins remained undeterred. Supported by the wealth of a friend of Siôn's father, a former chief executive of Kwik Fit, they took their arguments to the Criminal Cases Review Board and, in June 2004, won a second appeal. When I learned of this, I must admit assuming that Siôn and his team were going through the motions, contesting legal technicalities.

I was wrong.

They were still contesting the source of this 'fine spray' of Billie-Jo's blood on Siôn's clothing. Professor Denison told this second appeal that a histology examination of Billie-Jo's lung tissue – histology being the study of the microscopic structure of tissues – revealed that she'd suffered from a condition known as pulmonary interstitial emphysema (PIE). This is where extreme pressure inside the lungs leads to tissue being ripped or split. Professor Denison argued that pressure of this intensity could only have been generated by a blockage in her upper airways and questioned why pathologist Dr Ian Hill hadn't carried out histological or microscopic examination of her lungs as part of the postmortem.

Dr Hill explained that he'd preserved specimens from each of the lungs, from which a few slides had been prepared. He did not consider it necessary to conduct histological examination of that material, and neither at the time did Dr Richard Shepherd, the pathologist instructed on behalf of Siôn Jenkins.

Denison found something else in the histology slides to support their narrative. He claimed that Billie-Jo had developed atelectasis, a condition in which the airways and air sacs in the lung collapse or do not expand properly. He argued that this partial collapse of the lung is generally caused by an obstruction of the upper airways and, in order for this to have developed, Billie-Jo would have been alive for many minutes after the blockage had occurred. Denison told the appeal that the most likely cause of this blockage was a spasm in the larynx triggered by her swallowing blood. Alternatively, it could've been a blood clot, or Billie-Jo had swallowed her tongue sufficiently to have caused an upper-airway blockage. Whatever the cause of the blockage, he contended that the movement of Billie-Jo's body when Siôn pulled on her shoulder may have temporarily released this obstruction, causing a sudden release of built-up air through her nostril that sprayed those droplets of blood onto Siôn Jenkins's clothing.

Dr Ian Hill accepted the presence of PIE in Billie-Jo's lungs. He also accepted that, at some stage during the attack on Billie-Jo, she must have suffered a substantial blockage in her upper airway. He agreed with Denison that the most likely cause of this had been spasms of the larynx. That was enough 'reasonable doubt' for the court of appeal, which ruled that a fresh jury must be made aware of this alternative scenario. They set a retrial for April 2005.

Siôn Jenkins walked out of prison on bail, his murder conviction quashed.

Had we really got it wrong?

If Billie-Jo had exhaled with sufficient strength to spray blood on Siôn Jenkins, he would've noticed it. After all, he told a 999 operator that she was unconscious minutes before this allegedly happened. He never mentioned a sudden wheeze or breath to anyone, including the paramedics on the scene.

There is no doubt that the work of biologist Adrian Wain had been pivotal in securing Jenkins's conviction. That was why his defence team had been so determined to find a way to undermine it. We, on the other hand, were scientists who just wanted to get to the truth of what had taken place in the Jenkins's back garden that afternoon.

We'd have to find stronger evidence to prove our hypothesis to a fresh jury. And that would be a hell of a job, because this jury would be aware from all of the publicity that the Siôn Jenkins case was coming back from the court of appeal. It felt critical to me that we stood by our scientists and our science and fought this with all we had. After all, we felt, our reputation at the Forensic Science Service was at stake here.

So, when I got an invitation from Detective Chief Inspector Steve Dennis from Sussex Police to assist the prosecution case in the retrial, I jumped at the chance. I'd already worked with Steve on a couple of high-profile cases in Brighton and had liked his cultured style, both professionally and personally. Long before the actor John Thaw had embodied melancholy TV detective Inspector Morse, Steve had driven a red MK 3 Jag and enjoyed the finer things in life like classical music, dapper clothes, golf and haute cuisine. In fact, before following in his father's footsteps and becoming a cop, Steve had trained as a Cordon Bleu chef in Europe, and it showed. He was open-minded and willing to try new approaches; he liked to mix things up a bit.

Steve told me Dr Ian Hill was retiring and asked if I could recommend a pathologist with expertise in lungs. I knew just the man. Dr Nat Cary had been a Home Office forensic pathologist since 1992 and was already making a name for himself on high-profile cases such as those of the Soham murders and Victoria Climbié. He always came across as fastidious, fearless and quite brilliant. And, having worked as a consultant pathologist at Papworth Hospital in Cambridgeshire from 1989 to 1998, he had become a specialist in lung pathology. And lung pathology had now seemingly become pivotal to this case.

Nat agreed to travel to Brighton to meet Steve and me. Had he expected to see the city's iconic beach, piers and pavilion, Nat would've been sorely disappointed. The major crime teams were based at Sussex House on the Hollingbury industrial estate, just off the A27 and opposite an Asda superstore.

With his frizzy hair, moustache and glasses, Nat looked every inch the archetypal professor, which I found immediately reassuring. He oozed confidence and got straight down to business. He started by addressing the defence's claim that Billie-Jo had pulmonary interstitial emphysema or PIE – that her lungs had been split by air pressure, usually caused by a blockage in the upper airways.

'The lungs have split in places,' he conceded. 'That's why they will have thought this. What they clearly don't know is that lungs splitting is common as an artefact in the preparation of the lung tissue for histology examination. It happens all the time.'

An artefact is something that – rather than being naturally present – has been caused by the preparation or the examination technique applied. When lung tissue is prepared for analysis, it is frozen and thinly sliced, which can cause it to bubble. So, in Nat's view, the defence were misinterpreting this bubbling as evidence of Billie-Jo suffering from PIE. On top of that, Nat said he could find no evidence of bleeding into the spaces produced by the splitting, which he'd expect to find had this splitting occurred while Billie-Jo was still alive. This, he said, suggested that the lung tissue had split *after* her death.

'The thing is, it is notoriously easy to overdiagnose PIE because of artefacts inadvertently caused during the preparation of the lung tissue for histology examination. Postmortem lung histology, by its very nature, involves the examination of lung tissue in a suboptimal state. The splitting of the tissues is common. The rule is you never start with lung histology as your first proof. But Professor Denison doesn't specialise in lung histology of postmortem specimens so he wouldn't necessarily be aware of this.'

Both Steve and I felt he was building to a conclusion, and instinctively leaned forward.

'So…?' I ventured.

'I'm not saying that Billie-Jo couldn't have exhaled blood onto Siôn Jenkins's clothes,' he said, 'but I do think it is very unlikely.'

This was just what we'd wanted to hear. And Nat delivered it with such conviction that it seemed to banish all of our gloom. Here we had a Home Office pathologist declaring that the defence theory was 'very unlikely'. How could any juror buy into Denison's hypothesis after that?

Of course, I was keeping Adrian Wain abreast of all developments. I could sense his relief on learning of Nat Cary's 'very unlikely' dismissal of the defence's take on those blood spots. But he was able to trump my news with an intriguing discovery of his own.

Ever conscientious, Adrian had asked to re-examine the clothing of Siôn Jenkins and Billie-Jo for the retrial. The exhibits arrived that morning and, on laying them out, he spotted something within the very tiny blood spots that had now dried out.

'There are these white inclusions, Ray. I have no idea what they are.'

'Well, let's try to find out,' I said.

Most microscopes show objects between forty and eighty times their size. The white inclusions Adrian wanted to examine within those microscopic spatters of blood would require something far more powerful. I knew just the thing! I'd seen it in action at Dr Stuart Black's lab at the University of Reading. A scanning electron microscope (SEM), as the name suggests, uses not light but electrons, and can magnify an object up to a mind-boggling 10,000 times its size.

We had a couple of these instruments at the London lab of the FSS, but they were currently being used for gunshot residue. I needed someone with immediate access to an SEM and specific expertise in blood spatter to jump on this right now. So I gave Nat Cary a call. He recommended Dr Jeremy Skepper, a physiologist and expert in microscopy at University of Cambridge.

Meanwhile, we sent four pieces of Billie-Jo's lung tissue to another pathologist for that all-important 'second opinion'. Dr Alison Cluroe had papers published on histology and is considered one of the pre-eminent UK experts in the field.

'It is not possible to confidently diagnose pulmonary interstitial emphysema,' she wrote in her report. 'The changes seen here could equally well be explained by tissue artefact.'

In February 2005 – two months before the retrial was due to start – Dr Skepper got back to us. He had results from his analysis of the white particles in the blood spatter found on the clothes of Siôn and Billie-Jo Jenkins. Skepper reported that, in his opinion, these white inclusions 'are composed of a mixture of cells from the superficial layer of skin, the keratinised epithelium and the lower fibroelastic layer of the dermis or its deeper connective tissues.'

I gave Skepper a call. I needed this in plain English.

'There are samples of what I believe to be skin in blood on Siôn's trousers and jacket as well as on Billie-Jo's leggings,' he explained.

Dr Cary later picked up the thread: 'These particles were deposited as part of the spatter itself, which we believe came from the blows to Billie-Jo's scalp; in other words, scalp tissue that has been forcibly impacted.

'Now, it's hard to see how skin from Billie-Jo's scalp could've ended up on Siôn unless he was the attacker. But I'd contend that the presence of skin on the front of Billie-Jo's leggings is just as significant.'

'How so?' I asked.

'Siôn Jenkins said he found Billie-Jo lying on her front. So, the deposits of blood and skin must have been deposited when she was face up, in other words, lying the opposite way to when she was discovered.

'The thing is, Ray, the spatter on her leggings is similar to the spatter on his clothes – same particles of blood, same tissue fragments. I'd argue that they had to come from the same action, which is from the blows that killed her.'

Skepper's results came just in time for our first case conference with the prosecuting lawyer Nicholas Hilliard QC. I attended that meeting feeling confident. We could contest the defence's claim that the splitting in Billie-Jo's lungs had been pulmonary interstitial emphysema, caused by a blockage in her upper airway. We could reveal that fragments of Billie-Jo's skin were found in the blood spatter on Siôn Jenkins's clothes. We could reveal that Siôn and Billie-Jo both had similar blood and skin spatter on their clothes, suggesting that they'd both been present when she was assaulted.

However, the prosecuting QC felt he didn't need to rely on our forensic work. Nicholas Hilliard told the case conference he'd settle for a 'scoreless draw' on the science – because he felt he had enough alternative evidence to sway the jury. His secret weapon? Lois Jenkins. Siôn's estranged wife hadn't given evidence in the original murder trial. Now she was flying in from her new life in

Tasmania to lift the lid on Siôn's sudden and violent outbursts by describing to the jury several incidents in which he beat her and the children. I had to admit, this felt about as damning as testimony could get.

The retrial began in April 2005 and Hilliard was right about one thing: the science didn't fly. Rather it got bogged down in counter-arguments and complexity, which seemed to suit the defence just fine. Siôn Jenkins's team countered our discovery of skin in the blood spatter by insisting that this material must have come from the inside of Billie-Jo's damaged nose.

Pathologist Dr Ian Hill told the court that Billie-Jo had not suffered internal injuries to her nose. The defence asked to see the note he'd made of this observation during the postmortem. Hill responded by saying he hadn't made a note of it because there was nothing to report. The defence insisted that, without a contemporaneous written note to back him up, Hill's testimony was compromised. And this basically summed up the endless scientific 'ding-dong' between the prosecution and defence that, in the end, prompted the following remarks from the presiding judge, Justice Anne Rafferty:

'I'm very perturbed about what the jury is making of this,' she said, 'We may be asking the jury to referee at a very high level.'

This wasn't our only setback. Lois Jenkins's testimony about Siôn's sudden violent rages was ruled inadmissible. The jury saw only the 'other' side to Siôn Jenkins when he took the stand, coming across as a meek, quietly spoken and lost soul. One of the prosecution team noted two female jurors dabbing tears from their eyes as he described the pain of losing contact with his beloved biological daughters through this 'ordeal'.

On Friday, July 8, after five days of deliberation, the jury still hadn't reached a verdict on Siôn's guilt. Justice Rafferty told them she'd accept a 10–2 majority decision. By the end of play on

Monday, they were still at loggerheads. Justice Rafferty said she had no choice but to discharge the jury and order a retrial. After the original murder trial, two appeals and a further trial, a date was set for murder trial number three for Siôn Jenkins. Fittingly for this ongoing horror show, it would start on October 31, 2005.

Despite Nicholas Hilliard's continued confidence in the prosecution case against Siôn Jenkins, we felt that the only sure-fire way to convince a jury of his guilt lay, as ever, in forensic science. However, no matter what avenues we explored, we kept coming back to the one irrefutable piece of evidence against Siôn Jenkins – those 158 tiny droplets of Billie-Jo's blood on his clothing, and the matching spatter on her leggings. Thanks to Dr Skepper's scanning electron microscope, we had identified minute pieces of Billie-Jo's skin within these spots. That hadn't been enough to convince the jury, but it was enough to convince us to give it another go.

I asked Dr Skepper to look at further inclusions in the blood spatter to establish whether or not any more information could be gleaned. For Dr Skepper, this meant going back over some of the 158 blood spots to perform complex and intense examinations. Bearing in mind he worked full time as a lecturer and just months remained until the next retrial, we knew we were pushing his capacity to the limits. But if we wanted to get to the truth of what happened in that garden, this felt like the only way.

In another unwelcome twist, the inconclusive first retrial had ended just a few days after the 7/7 bombings. The unprecedented workloads generated by this and 21/7 pretty much took us out of commission until September, when we regrouped for Siôn Jenkins's third murder trial. Dr Skepper reported that he had found some fresh alien objects in nine of the blood spots he had examined, but was struggling to identify what they were. The previous two trials had been postponed for a few weeks because of similar deadline pressures. I felt that, if we were on the brink of finding something definitive and game-changing, the quest for truth in this long-running legal saga would surely trump court schedules.

As weeks until murder trial three became days, Dr Skepper kept promising me his full report, but it kept not arriving. I knew he was giving it his all and making dramatic breakthroughs. I couldn't ask him to work any harder. If what he'd been finding was as significant as he'd hinted, I felt sure it'd be worth all the frayed nerves and stressed-out calls.

Dr Skepper's report finally arrived on the morning of the third trial. What it contained felt, at least to me, nothing short of sensational.

The report focused on nine of the droplets of Billie-Jo's blood found on Siôn Jenkins's clothing. On Jenkins's trousers, within a single sample of blood splatter, Skepper found one small droplet of white paint containing titanium, which is from rutile, a component of white paint. Billie-Jo had been painting the French doors with white paint. Dried white paint had been found in her hair. What the discovery of white paint in this blood spot on Siôn's trousers implied was that tiny particles of white paint in her hair had got transferred to his trousers along with the blood from the impact of the assault on her skull.

Another of the blood spots on Siôn's trousers was found to contain the elements calcium, oxygen and phosphorus – which together make up calcium phosphate, the main ingredient in bone.

Skepper had identified other strange inclusions in these nine key blood drops that appeared, at least to me, even more incriminating for Siôn Jenkins.

Inside another spot of dried blood, he found a small metallic fragment containing iron and chromium. The metal tent peg had been made of iron and painted in green paint that could have contained chromium. Chromium oxide is a green pigment used in paints. The same spot of dried blood contained another fragment of white paint.

In another blood spot on Siôn's trousers, he found a large fragment of a very dense material containing iron and chromium. We had sent the tent peg to Dr Robin Keeley at the FSS to confirm if the green paint on the tent peg contained chromium oxide.

In short, somehow, microscopic blood drops had been transferred from Billie-Jo Jenkins to the clothes of Siôn Jenkins – most likely from her skull. These blood spots were initially found to contain skin belonging to Billie-Jo. In the recent retrial, Siôn's defence had insisted that these skin samples had come from the inside of her injured nose when she'd exhaled on Siôn as he'd tended to her. But now, we'd found traces of bone and white paint that surely didn't come from the inside of her nose but from her head hair, as well as chromium and iron that may well have come from the murder weapon.

As far as I was concerned, this appeared to be powerful and critical new evidence.

On the first morning of Siôn Jenkins's third trial for murder, we presented the report to the judge, Justice David Clarke – and all hell broke loose.

Christopher Sallon QC, defending Siôn Jenkins, applied to have them ruled inadmissible because they had been served on his team too late.

In submissions in the absence of the jury, Sallon argued: 'The crown are proposing a further series of tests of an unknown nature by unknown experts employing unknown protocols that are to be reported some time in the future.'

He added: 'The consequences for the defence are very real. How do we cross-examine Dr Skepper? How do we present our case properly without further exploring the issue with different experts?'

Despite the seemingly profound implications of these latest findings, Justice Clarke was in no mood for revisiting his busy diary.

'All this has come extremely late,' he said. 'It is material that has been served very, very late without any warning that it was coming.'

He ruled on the admission of Skepper's report: 'I have very much in mind the impact in this exceptional case that a further significant delay will have. Having regard to the extreme lateness of what is now sought, I have decided to refuse.'

At this very moment, I knew deep down that Siôn Jenkins would walk. It didn't matter how much his character was trashed. It didn't matter how suspicious his behaviour had been before and after Billie-Jo's murder. Only one thing would put him away – irrefutable forensic evidence.

Perversely – at least to me – this third trial chugged on for three months, during which time the same old arguments and debates were trotted out before yet another jury. In my mind, the only thing that mattered was the new forensic science that the jury would only find out about once the proceedings were over. That and the small matter of evidence of Siôn Jenkins's history of domestic abuse against his wife and children, again ruled inadmissible by Justice Clarke. I couldn't understand how the judges in both retrials had been allowed to rule out this evidence when the Criminal Justice Act 2003 specifically permits the admission of relevant 'bad character' evidence in a trial. Again, one for the lawyers.

After a mammoth thirty-nine hours and ten minutes deliberating, the jurors told the judge that they were not going to agree on a verdict. Shortly afterwards, the Crown Prosecution Service said Siôn Jenkins would not face another trial.

I can only imagine how Lois Jenkins and Billie-Jo's relatives felt when, on February 9, 2006, Siôn Jenkins walked out of the

Old Bailey a free man, hand in hand with his new wife, the millionairess Christina Ferneyhough, whom he'd wed in secret in February 2005.

In a prepared statement, he couldn't resist a dig at the police:

'Billie-Jo's murderer has escaped detection because of the dreadful errors in the police investigation and their single-minded and desperate determination to convict me at all costs.

'The police who have been in charge of the inquiry have been wilfully blind and incompetent. The murder investigation must be reopened immediately with a new police team who will put all their energies into finding Billie-Jo's killer. Thank you.'

Again, I tormented myself with questions: did we do enough? Did I do enough? What else could or should we have done to prove this case?

I hadn't felt this low since the Damilola Taylor case, when the lab had failed to spot a critical piece of evidence on some clothing.

I reassured myself that we hadn't actually missed anything forensically in this case. It wasn't the people in forensics who had let Billie-Jo down. We had done our very best.

CHAPTER FIFTEEN

In my role as specialist advisor at the Forensic Science Service, there were certain callers to my pager that I responded to immediately, no matter what. One of them was DS Mike Jolly from the counter-terrorism command (SO15).

'Ray, what do you know about thallium poisoning?'

'Try me!' I replied.

'We've got a Russian defector under armed guard at University College Hospital, in a critical condition,' he said. 'They're pretty certain he's been poisoned. He's ex-KGB and a very public critic of Putin. He's been ill for about two weeks. It started with vomiting and diarrhoea, after a couple of days his hair started falling out in clumps…'

'That sounds like thallium,' I said.

'Here's the thing though, Ray. They started treating him for thallium poisoning last week. He rallied for a few days. But now he's deteriorating fast, his bone marrow is failing, his organs are shutting down.'

'I've never heard of thallium doing that,' I said, 'what are the levels in his urine?'

Mike knew I'd grill him and had the answer to hand.

'That's not really high enough for poisoning,' I said. 'Someone who eats a lot of seafood could have that much thallium in their system. What about his peripheral neuropathy?'

'Eh?'

'Any numbness or tingling at the ends of his fingers or toes?'

He rifled through his paperwork.

'Nothing saying that here, Ray.'

'Look, I don't want to jump the gun, but this really doesn't sound like thallium poisoning to me.'

'We're now thinking the same. We really need to dig into this. I'm scheduling a meeting at the lab Monday morning. It'll be us and our forensic management team, and some poison experts we've used.'

'Is the victim conscious and talking?' I asked.

'Yes, Detective Inspector Brent Hyatt is interviewing him today, or at least getting information from him whenever he has the strength to talk. He's very ill.'

In fact, Brent later said to me it was the first time he'd ever interviewed a murder victim.

* * *

Back in the early seventies, thallium changed my life, in a manner of speaking. When I saw first-hand the trailblazing and critical work the lab did in exposing serial poisoner Graham Young, I knew I wanted a piece of that action.

I joined the toxicology department and had some amazing mentors, chief among them the department head, John Jackson. Despite having no formal scientific degree, Jackson became a global giant in the field and, in 1963, a founder member of TIAFT,

The International Association of Forensic Toxicologists. Just as influential was John Taylor, who, from day one, took me under his wing and involved me in all of his work.

By 1979, I'd got my degree in chemistry and was promoted to the role of reporting officer – which meant preparing cases for court and, when required, giving evidence. Around that time, we realised there was no definitive guide as to how to test for poisons. John Taylor and I spent eighteen months putting together and internally publishing *The Poisons Screen* – a booklet detailing how to test for as many poisons as we could find. In 1983, I presented the work to the International Association for Toxicologists' annual conference in Seville, Spain. Over a quarter of a century later, I was rather flattered when toxicologists at a private forensic company begged me to let them photocopy it!

The Poisons Screen included tests for thallium, a tasteless, odourless and colourless metal discovered by Sir William Crookes in 1861 after burning dust from a sulphuric acid industrial plant. Thallium is used as a rat-killer and, in humans, causes gastrointestinal upset accompanied by nausea, vomiting and acute pain. In more severe cases it attacks the nervous system, causing peripheral neuropathies (tingling sensations in the extremities), and triggering convulsions and coma, before fatal respiratory failure or cardiac arrest. It's easy to see why medics initially suspected thallium was the substance used to poison this man.

It also causes hair loss – something the CIA had wanted to turn to their advantage in one of their more hare-brained schemes. Classified papers made public in the 1990s revealed a plan to plant thallium salts in the shoes of Cuban leader Fidel Castro to cause his beard to fall out, which, they hoped, would undermine his godlike status among his people.

I had my own encounter with the stuff in the 1990s. Special Branch brought me a sample of mysterious white powder and

asked me to identify it. I suddenly remembered an incident early
in my career when John Jackson had asked me: 'What is the first
thing you do when you get an exhibit to test?' I came out with all
these elaborate and fantastic tests, trying to look clever. Jackson
shook his head.

'No, Ray, the first thing you do is pick up the phone and speak
to the investigating officer and find out all that you can about the
case. It's all about context.'

These Special Branch officers refused to answer a single question
about this mystery white powder and they weren't for budging.
Tests confirmed it to be deadly thallium acetate. I later learned that
it had been part of Saddam Hussein's personal stash at one of his
many palaces in Iraq.

Another key early lesson I'd learned in toxicology is that, when
it comes to poisonings, the one consistency is symptoms. Each
poison triggers a specific set of reactions, depending on the amount
used. And that's why I doubted that the man DS Mike Jolly called
me about had fallen victim to thallium poisoning: he suffered only
some of the documented symptoms, not all of them. What's more,
he had other symptoms that are simply not synonymous with
thallium ingestion. I felt certain he'd been targeted with another
type of poison. But quite what, how and by whom we'd have to
figure out.

* * *

Next morning's Sunday papers at least answered the question as to
why this man had been targeted.

Alexander Litvinenko, forty-three, had in 1988 been recruited
from military college to the KGB, which, after the fall of
communism, became the Federal Security Service or the FSB, led
by a certain Vladimir Putin. In 1998, Litvinenko started blowing
the whistle on links between the FSB and organised crime. Arrested

on trumped-up charges, in 2000 he fled Russia for the UK, where he continued to make allegations against Putin and provided intelligence to MI6. The authorities clearly valued his information because, weeks earlier, he'd been granted British citizenship. He lived with his partner Marina in a house in Muswell Hill, north London, owned by another Russian defector and enemy of Putin, oligarch Boris Berezovsky.

On the day of his poisoning – Wednesday, November 1, 2006 – he'd met a journalist contact at an Itsu restaurant in Piccadilly, central London at about 3 p.m., then went on to a business meeting at the Millennium Hotel in Grosvenor Square.

What the papers didn't know at this point was that Litvinenko was busy solving the case from his hospital bed. He'd already identified his killers to DI Brent Hyatt. They were the two men he'd met at the Pine Bar in the Millennium Hotel – Andrei Lugovoi and Dmitry Kovtun.

Litvinenko had first met Lugovoi in Russia in the 1990s when both were part of Boris Berezovsky's entourage. In 2005, Lugovoi re-contacted Litvinenko in the UK and suggested they work together, advising Western firms wanting to invest in Russia. He arrived in London on October 31 with members of his family, ostensibly to attend a Champions League soccer match between CSKA Moscow and Arsenal at the Emirates Stadium the following evening.

At 11.41 a.m. on the day of the poisoning Lugovoi called Litvinenko on his mobile. He suggested a meeting. Why didn't Litvinenko join him later that day at the Millennium Hotel? Litvinenko said yes; the plot was on.

Litvinenko told DI Hyatt how he'd taken a bus from Muswell Hill and then a tube to Oxford Circus to meet an associate, Italian lawyer Mario Scaramella, at Itsu. In between, he fielded several calls from Lugovoi, who was becoming increasingly impatient. Lugovoi called Litvinenko again at 3.40 p.m. and told him to 'hurry up' if he wanted to catch him before he headed off to the football.

Just after 4 p.m., Litvinenko arrived at the Millennium Hotel and called Lugovoi from reception. Lugovoi met him in the foyer and led him into the Pine Bar and a table in the far corner. As the police would soon discover, the Pine Bar had no CCTV – something a surveillance expert like Lugovoi would no doubt have clocked. While the pair sat chatting, they were joined by Dmitry Kovtun, a man Litvinenko had met just a few times and didn't trust.

From his deathbed, Litvinenko said: 'There were a few mugs on the table and there was also a teapot. Straight away a waiter came up to us. I could not see him because he came up from the back. He asked "Are you going to have anything?" I think Andrei [Lugovoi] asked, "Would you like anything?" I said, "I don't want anything," and he said, "OK, well we're going to leave now anyway so there is still some tea left here. If you want, you can have some." And then the waiter went away or I think Andrei asked for a clean cup, and he brought it. He left and when there was a cup I poured some tea out of the teapot, although there was only a little left on the bottom and it made just half a cup. Maybe about fifty grammes. I swallowed several times but it was green tea with no sugar and it was already cold. Maybe, in total, I swallowed three or four times, I haven't even finished that cup.'

That evening – to mark the sixth anniversary of his arrival in the UK – Litvinenko's wife Marina made a meal for him at home in north London, which he ate with a healthy appetite. But he was already a dead man.

Whatever was in that teapot at the Millennium Pine Bar would most likely kill Litvinenko. Now we just had to work out what it was.

On Monday morning, November 20, DS Mike Jolly's appointed guests gathered in a space very familiar and handy to me – the world's most generic conference room at the FSS HQ in Lambeth, south London. Mick opened by running through Litvinenko's medical woes since his ill-fated late-afternoon tea on November 1.

He began vomiting that night and couldn't stop. Next day, Marina telephoned a doctor, who recommended that he take salt and mineral solutions. However, Litvinenko couldn't even keep those down and on November 3, she called an ambulance. The paramedics examined him and said he was probably suffering from a flu or bug and advised him to stay at home.

Later that day, Litvinenko complained of extreme abdominal pain and passing blood. A doctor said – again – he must be suffering from food poisoning or an infection, but this time sent him to Barnet General Hospital.

During my years in toxicology, I'd found that doctors simply can't diagnose poisonings. This is because, almost without exception, the symptoms of poisoning mimic those of well-known illnesses and diseases. And what medics are trained to do is diagnose illnesses and diseases – not to detect foul play. As a result, poisonings slip through the net, even when there's a fatality. Once a death has been ruled 'not suspicious', there's no postmortem or investigation. It is simply written off. God knows how many murders by poison have been missed over the years.

On November 4 – three days after he was poisoned – medics put Litvinenko on a course of ciprofloxacin, a relatively strong, broad-spectrum antibiotic, and conducted blood tests. Over the following days, doctors observed that the red and white cell counts in his blood had fallen to a subnormal level, as well as his blood platelet count, which controls clotting. On or around November 9, Marina Litvinenko asked the consultants if her husband's infection could have been the result of poisoning.

Dr Andres Virchis, a haematologist, contacted the Poisons Unit at Guy's Hospital. They came back with a diagnosis: that Litvinenko's condition should be regarded as 'suspicious thallium poisoning' and treated with Prussian blue. This drug – taken in pill form – binds to thallium in the intestines, which then leaves the body through stools, thereby preventing the thallium being absorbed into the general circulation.

On November 17, Litvinenko was transferred to University College Hospital, where his condition was reported to be improving. The next day, Professor John Henry, an internationally renowned toxicologist hired by Litvinenko's family, examined the patient and publicly expressed his support for the diagnosis and the treatment.

However, by the time we met on the Monday morning, November 20, Litvinenko's condition had once again deteriorated: he'd been vomiting blood and medics were considering transplanting his failing bone marrow. Those iconic photos of him in intensive care looking hairless, emaciated and pale were taken that very morning and released via the media to a horrified world. After all, here was a man who'd just become a British citizen, poisoned in his adopted homeland. The counter-terrorism command was now officially in charge of the case.

As we discussed his symptoms at the meeting, I reiterated my belief that thallium poisoning simply didn't fit. At this point, a man I'd never met before – Dr Nick Gent of Public Health England – made an astute observation. Gent had an immense amount of experience with poisoning, its diagnosis and treatment, including work on nerve gas attacks in Syria. He pointed out that Litvinenko's symptoms seemed eerily similar to someone undergoing radiotherapy, in which ionising radioactive isotopes are used. The room fell silent as we let this sink in. Had the Russians somehow unleashed radiation inside Litvinenko's body? My mind reeled.

Someone reading the clinical notes pointed out that – six days earlier – Dr Virchis had observed that Litvinenko resembled someone who had undergone chemotherapy. Virchis suggested that the radiology department examine Litvinenko to check for any radioactive sources of poisoning. A day later, they tested his body with a Geiger counter and, on getting no reaction, declared radiation not to be a factor in his condition.

I told the meeting why this could well have been a false result: a Geiger counter cannot detect all forms of radiation. For example, it can't detect alpha rays. Because of their relatively large size – they are helium nuclei – alpha rays travel only a short distance and wouldn't even penetrate a single sheet of paper. They're simply not powerful enough to be registered by a Geiger counter. Yet, if a human ingests alpha rays, they wreak devastation, destroying DNA, ionising the internal organs and shutting them down, leading to certain death.

However, as I explained to the group, the only way to detect alpha ray radiation is through blood and urine. So, we arranged for samples from Litvinenko to be sent immediately to the Atomic Weapons Establishment (AWE) in Aldermaston – the only place in the UK set up to handle such potentially lethal material. The scientists at AWE prioritised the sample, promising results of his blood and urine by Wednesday morning, November 22. But one person couldn't wait that long before spouting off to the media.

The night before the results were due, Professor John Henry told reporters that he stood by his theory that thallium was involved, saying that a radioactive type of thallium could be responsible.

'Radioactive thallium adds a new dimension to this case,' he declared. 'It means that his bone marrow is at very high risk and we have to see how his cells recover.'

Not for the first time, the ego and vanity of an academic floored me. Dr John Henry clearly believed it was more important that he appeared to be correct in his original diagnosis than to admit we were re-evaluating the root cause of his paying client's illness.

By the time we reconvened on Wednesday morning – with an additional guest from the Atomic Weapons Establishment – everyone was desperate to find out, once and for all, what was killing Litvinenko.

The man from AWE declared that Alexander Litvinenko had been poisoned with the radioactive element polonium-210. The unthinkable had become a reality – the Russians had unleashed a deadly radioactive toxin in the heart of the British capital.

Discovered by Marie Curie in 1898, polonium-210 is one of twenty-five radioactive isotopes of polonium, a silver-coloured metal found in uranium ores. A microgram of polonium-210 – about the size of a speck of dust – would be certain to deliver a fatal dose of radiation if swallowed. Once inside the body it spreads quickly, leaving reactive radicals in its path and taking electrons from molecules. Radiation can also damage a victim's DNA, affecting how cells replicate. But more serious poisoning can cause cells to die – a process called apoptosis.

From the moment he took a sip of that tea, there was nothing anyone could do to save Alexander Litvinenko.

The man from AWE went on to explain that polonium-210, a radioactive isotope of polonium that emits alpha radiation, must be ingested or inhaled to cause damage – in other words, you must breathe it in, take it into the mouth or get it in a wound. And because the radiation has a very short range, it harms only nearby tissue. It cannot pass through skin, paper or clothes. If Litvinenko had ingested an alpha-emitting substance, this would explain his symptoms – and the failure to detect radiation from his body. It occurs in very small amounts naturally but is likely to have been man-made through a nuclear reactor not long before Litvinenko's death.

That really hit home. This deadly material had come from a Russian nuclear reactor and they are all state-controlled, which meant only one thing – this had been a state-sponsored hit. But that wasn't what was panicking us most at this point: more pressing was that we now potentially faced outbreaks of deadly alpha radiation all over London.

This lethal toxin had been deployed in a public bar, most likely in a teapot and cup that would've been washed and reused since. God knew how many more people had sat at that corner table. If anyone had touched an object with even secondary polonium-210 contamination and then licked their fingers, they faced a long and painful death. And then there were all the places that Litvinenko and his poisoners had gone afterwards, bringing their deadly polonium-210 traces with them – albeit, in Litvinenko's case, unwittingly.

The task confronting the investigating officers was surely unprecedented in Met Police history. They now had to trace everywhere Lugovoi and Kovtun had been from the moment they flew into the UK until they left, and test everything and everyone they potentially came into contact with for radiation. This meant grounding planes and shutting down hotels and, potentially, Arsenal's Emirates Stadium.

But at least now – three weeks after he'd been poisoned – we were able to tell Litvinenko what he was dying from. Maybe this had been what he'd been clinging on for because, that night, he had a heart attack and had to be induced into a coma, from which he never returned.

Next day, November 23, he died.

His friend Alex Goldfarb read a statement that Litvinenko had pre-prepared, accusing Russian president Vladimir Putin of being directly responsible for his death. The statement ended: 'You may succeed in silencing one man but the howl of protest from around the world will reverberate, Mr Putin, in your ears for the rest of your life.'

Meanwhile, at the Millennium Hotel's Pine Bar, Litvinenko's white ceramic teapot had not been difficult to isolate – it gave off readings of 100,000 becquerels per centimetre squared. The biggest reading came from the spout. Combined with the damage found to the back of Litvinenko's throat and larynx, it was clear that he'd drunk tea laced with polonium-210.

Unsurprisingly, the teapot was put in the dishwasher afterwards and unknowingly reused for subsequent customers – happily with no reports of illness. The table where the three men had sat registered 20,000 becquerels. Half that, ingested, is enough to kill a person.

In the gents' toilets next to the Pine Bar, specialists found 'off-the-scale' contamination in a toilet cubicle. CCTV from the hotel foyer showed both Lugovoi and Kuvton going into those toilets shortly before Litvinenko's arrival, whereas their target didn't go in there at all. Had this been where the assassins had prepared the polonium-210 before spiriting it into the teapot?

Another 'off-the-scale' reading was found in the plughole of the bathroom sink in room 382, Kuvton's hotel room. Remember, he joined the meeting between Litvinenko and Lugovoi in the Pine Bar late. Had he been upstairs dumping what was left of the polonium-210 after they'd tipped some into the teapot?

Scientists found contamination where the suspects had sat on planes and at the Emirates Stadium. Several people – including Marina Litvinenko and staff at the Pine Bar – had been contaminated; thankfully no one suffered any long-lasting effects.

Needless to say, the Forensic Science Service took very little part in detecting and making safe what had become known as the Polonium Trail. But we still had a role in this investigation that would prove highly significant.

After Litvinenko's death, the investigation team approached me wanting to know if the FSS could confirm exactly when polonium-210 had entered his system. By now, Russian authorities were making a show of interviewing Lugovoi and Kovtun. The prime suspects were insisting that it had been Litvinenko who had tried to poison them and his efforts had backfired. As preposterous as this defence seemed, it needed to be knocked down.

We knew that the best way to detect when Litvinenko had ingested polonium-210 was through his hair. Growing at 1.5 centimetres per month, head hair can act almost as a calendar in detecting when the body has ingested alien elements. But Litvinenko had none left by the time he died. We did some digging and discovered that, a few days after Litvinenko had been admitted to Barnet General Hospital on November 3, his hair had started to fall out in clumps. He complained to Marina that he found the sensation of loose hair uncomfortable, so she arranged for a friend and hairdresser to cut what was left and to shave the rest of his head. Someone at Barnet General had the foresight to give Marina a plastic bag in which to store his hair in the event that someone might want to analyse it in the future.

That someone would be Dr Stuart Black at the University of Reading

But Stuart immediately identified a problem. The half-life of plutonium 210 – the term used to describe how long it takes for radioactivity to fall to half its value – is 138 days. As so little had been used to poison Litvinenko, what remained would be virtually non-existent by now. However, he pointed out that every radioactive isotope has a 'daughter' isotope. This 'daughter' is what's left after the polonium has decayed – in this case, lead-206, which is a stable isotope.

When Stuart measured the lead-206 in Litvinenko's hair, it became clear that he had ingested a sudden and lethal dose of polonium-210 on November 1 – the day he'd met Lugovoi and Kovtun at the Millennium Hotel. But he found something else in Litvinenko's hair that didn't fit the narrative and rubbished the Russians' claims that Litvinenko himself had been the poisoner.

His hair revealed that Litvinenko had ingested a much smaller dose of polonium-210 sometime between October 14 and 18 – some two weeks before the fatal dose. Had there been a previous attempt on his life that we didn't know about?

Detectives checked the movements of Litvinenko and his poisoners and discovered that – a fortnight before their fateful meeting at the Millennium Hotel's Pine Bar – the trio had met in London.

On October 16, Litvinenko, Lugovoi and Kovtun had attended the boardroom of a private security firm, Erinys International, with a senior executive called Tim Reilly. The Russians were hoping that Reilly – a specialist in Russian industry – could help them broker a multimillion-pound deal with Gazprom, an energy corporation based in St Petersburg.

At the request of the Russians, Reilly had made tea. Lugovoi and Kovtun kept encouraging him and Litvinenko to drink up. Reilly declined because, as it was a sweltering hot day, he'd already drunk a lot of water from a cooler. Litvinenko also left his untouched.

Reilly told police: 'They kept saying to me, "Well, don't you want tea?" You know, they were joking, saying English people always drink tea.'

When the meeting ended, Litvinenko took his Russian guests, minus Reilly, to his favourite restaurant – Itsu in Piccadilly.

Scientists found high levels of polonium-210 in the Erinys boardroom, particularly where Litvinenko had sat at the table, suggesting that the lethal dose had been somehow secreted into his teacup during the meeting. Reilly was also found to have traces of polonium-210 in his body as well as in his car. Secondary contamination was found at a table in the Itsu restaurant where the trio had sat after the meeting at Erinys.

Reilly revealed that, later on October 16, he fell extremely ill with diarrhoea and 'horrendous, migraine-type symptoms... I felt just dreadful. I've never had an illness like it before and I've never had one since.' Similarly, Litvinenko had thrown up that night. However, neither man knew about the other's 'copycat' symptoms, and both had dismissed their sudden illnesses as some rogue bug. Had they spoken to or even emailed each other, it may well have saved Litvinenko's life: having been spiked once, he surely wouldn't have availed himself of the green tea in the Pine Bar on November 1?

The evidence from Litvinenko's shaved hair confirmed that Lugovoi and Kovtun were the killers. But despite the overwhelming evidence, the Russian authorities refused to extradite either suspect to the UK. The only justice Litvinenko ever got was a public inquiry into his death, which ruled that Vladimir Putin had 'probably approved' his murder.

Credible reports claim that Litvinenko is just one of fourteen suspicious deaths in the UK linked to Putin and Russian agents. Little did I know that I'd end up playing a key role in another.

CHAPTER SIXTEEN

OPERATION DAPHNE
NOVEMBER 10, 2012

It was almost dark as security guard Neil St Clair-Ford drove through St George's Hill, a high-security gated community in Weybridge, Surrey. Spotting something strange on the side of the road, he pulled up to find a middle-aged man in jogging gear lying in a foetal position, pale, cold and displaying 'very faint' signs of life. St Clair-Ford couldn't get a signal on his mobile, so knocked on the front door of a nearby house. Records would later show that the occupant called for an ambulance at 4.45 p.m. St Clair-Ford next rushed to the nearby workplace of a colleague, Liam Walsh, who was ex-Royal Navy and trained in administering CPR. Walsh later told police that, during mouth-to-mouth resuscitation, the prone man had vomited 'greeny-yellow' bile with a strange taste, like 'licking a battery'.

At 4.53 p.m., an ambulance arrived at the scene. Paramedics attempted to resuscitate the man but were unsuccessful. He was pronounced dead at 5.39 p.m.

Police later established that the dead man was one of many

Russian émigrés living in the gated community, which, over the years, has boasted Kate Winslet, Ringo Starr and Elton John as residents. Alexander Perepilichnyy, forty-four, had died 100 metres from the house he shared with his wife and two young children, rented at a staggering £15,000 per month.

Perepilichnyy had been a currency trader in Moscow before moving to the UK in 2009. On his laptop. detectives discovered deals worth up to $500 million. They also traced enquiries to buy a £5 million home on the St George's Hill estate and another in Miami, Florida.

It emerged that the dead man had several life insurance policies adding up to some £8 million. To secure these, he had been rigorously examined and his family confirmed no major health problems, current or past. He'd given up smoking thirteen years earlier, rarely drank alcohol and had recently lost three stone in a health drive.

His wife Tatiana revealed that, on the morning of his death he'd returned from a three-day business trip to Paris feeling a little 'under the weather'. She made him sorrel soup, which clearly did the trick as, a few hours later, he embarked on his late-afternoon run around the gated estate.

However, when detectives looked into his trip to Paris, they found that it had been less business, more pleasure. He'd spent much of the time with his Ukrainian mistress, Elmira Medynska, twenty-eight, whom he had met through a dating website the previous May. She revealed that the night before his death they had gone to an exclusive Japanese restaurant, where he ordered prawns ventura. He sent the meal back, complaining that it 'smelled bad', and ate sushi instead.

Later that night, he threw up three times in their hotel bathroom. She said he emerged 'looking red' but insisting he felt much better. Officers consulted several experts, who said that Perepilichnyy's symptoms were typical of scombroid fish poisoning – caused by bacteria on fish that hasn't been refrigerated properly – from which he would've recovered in a matter of hours.

Police told the media that, as it was an unexplained death, there would automatically be a postmortem. But, as far as they were concerned, a forty-four-year-old man of average build and above-average wealth had simply fallen down and died in the leafy suburb he'd recently begun to call home. All expected the pathologist to open him up and find evidence of a heart attack or something similar.

He didn't.

Dr Norman Ratcliffe found no signs of organ failure or foul play, and couldn't give a cause of death. When this happens – and it's more common than most people think – the coroner must open an inquest. No one could have foreseen that it would take six years of investigations, tests and legal wrangles before this inquest could be heard.

And I got dragged right into the thick of it.

I hadn't even heard about the case when, towards the end of November, I got a call from Nick Craggs, principal SOCO at Sussex Police. The gist of the call was this: another rich Russian had been found dead in mysterious circumstances. Could I organise a case conference along with senior detectives and scientists in order to investigate whether or not the victim had been poisoned? I arranged this conference for the University of Reading, where I was working at the time. The guestlist included Dr Stuart Black and Dr Nick Branch, now also a senior lecturer at the university. Both scientists had been key in the 21/7 failed London bombings and Adam cases respectively. I also suggested they invite Nick Gent from Public Health England – whose call to check Litvinenko for radioactivity ultimately cracked that mystery.

I arranged the meeting for the university's Wager Building, where Dr Stuart Black had his office and which, fittingly, could've been something out of Soviet-era Russia. In a massive, echoey room – in which one entire wall was dominated by a bookcase containing thousands of PhD theses – we sat at a vast old brown table big enough to comfortably accommodate twenty people.

It wasn't long before we found out that police were feeling the pressure. They'd failed to grasp the global importance of Perepilichnyy and his murder until now, several weeks after his death. It turned out that Perepilichnyy was embroiled in all sorts of dodgy dealings in Russia – and had fallen out with some of that country's most powerful figures.

Most of the police's information came from an American called Bill Browder, who insisted that Perepilichnyy had been murdered. So why was an American embroiling himself in the murder of a Russian?

Back in 1996, Browder had recognised golden investment opportunities in Russia. Four years later, his company Hermitage Capital was the best-performing emerging markets fund in the world. Then, around 2005, he fell out with Vladimir Putin and was promptly kicked out of Russia.

According to Browder, some years later he found out that top Russian officials – including judges, senior cops and politicians in cahoots with organised crime – had stolen £150 million of tax paid by Hermitage Capital and siphoned it off to accounts around the world. A Russian lawyer – Sergei Magnitsky – uncovered the scam and was promptly jailed by the authorities. After eleven months in custody, Magnitsky mysteriously died. Perepilichnyy had been involved in the laundering plot but, after fleeing Russia in 2009, decided to switch sides and help Browder expose the scandal.

Two years later – January 2011 – Hermitage Capital filed an application to authorities in Switzerland based on Perepilichnyy's evidence. The Swiss responded by freezing the bank accounts of the Russians allegedly involved in the fraud, now known as the Klyuev gang. But they may not have been the only people who wanted Perepilichnyy dead.

Browder revealed that Perepilichnyy had left Russia owing millions to a firm founded by Dmitry Kovtun, one of the suspects in the Litvinenko killing. According to Browder, Perepilichnyy had recently received several threats to his life – something the dead man's wife Tatiana disputed.

Indeed, Tatiana had insisted from day one that her husband had not been threatened at any point – a stance she maintained throughout the six-year legal wrangles surrounding his death and her rights to his bumper life insurance dividend.

However, Browder claimed that Perepilichnyy's behaviour in Paris had been that of a man fearing for his life. For example, he'd reserved two hotel rooms in different parts of the city for the same nights. According to Browder, Perepilichnyy met a man during the trip who purported to be from the Russian government, but who was in fact an affiliate of a criminal syndicate.

What Browder and several life insurance companies were demanding to know was this: had Perepilichnyy been poisoned? The former hoped this would put pressure on the UK and the US to help him get his money back from the dodgy Russians who'd stolen it; the latter didn't want to fork out £8 million in life insurance.

Now, normally, the police wouldn't be remotely concerned with the dubious fiscal motives of vested interests. But Browder had been resourceful in stirring up a media frenzy about Perepilichnyy's strange death, briefing journalists about the dead man's dark secrets and reminding them of the Russian flair for poisoning.

As Browder put it, the Russian regime 'doesn't like to kill people in easy-to-identify ways', adding: 'Poison is one of their methods because they can do it in a plausibly deniable way.'

Browder's accusations didn't stop there. He suggested that the police failed to thoroughly investigate Perepilichnyy's death in part because they were incompetent and in part because of the enormous influence that wealthy Russians wielded in British business and politics. He told a parliamentary committee that the stolen money Perepilichnyy helped expose had passed through twelve British banks, with many millions of it going towards 'an orgy of spending on luxury goods and services in the UK'.

With such lurid accusations flying about – and their initial inertia in the case exposed – the police felt they had no choice but to officially open a murder investigation. Their first move was to order a second postmortem, eighteen days after Perepilichnyy's death, this time conducted by a Home Office forensic pathologist.

As in the first postmortem, Dr Ashley Fegan-Earl identified no obvious cause of death. He ruled that – providing poisoning could be excluded – Perepilichnyy had died of sudden arrhythmic death syndrome (SADS). This is a quick, unexpected death from cardiac arrest where the cause of the arrest can't be found. SADS is not as uncommon as people may think, claiming between 800 and 1,500 people in the UK each year.

However, Fegan-Earl's report revealed that most of the dead man's stomach contents had been disposed of after the first postmortem. This is not uncommon after hospital postmortems, but still prompted this concluding remark: 'The only proper conclusion that can be posited is that the cause of death is unascertained.'

A few days after the results of this second postmortem, the police wanted to know one thing: how could they prove, once and for all, that Alexander Perepilichnyy hadn't been poisoned?

Having spent years seeking evidence of foul play, it now seemed somewhat surreal being tasked to find the opposite – and to prove a negative.

I told the meeting that the only way to do this was through an exhaustive process of elimination. But there was good news. Due to the unusual circumstances of his death and the fact that there were no signs of foul play or internal injury, we could eliminate the vast majority of poisons right away.

Common sense said that any poison or drug that has to be injected could be ruled out. After all, two postmortems had failed to find signs of violence or a struggle, and would certainly have spotted a needle mark. Similarly, the dead man must have been aware of his vulnerability to poisoning so would not have imbibed anything that smelled, tasted or looked suspicious.

Some poisons require a large dose or repeated doses to be lethal; all of those could be eliminated. Anything with a strong odour or caustic in nature would've been picked up at postmortem, by either damage to the stomach lining or the odour on cutting the victim open. So, we could scratch all those off the list.

Many poisons have a prolonged period between intake and death, but it's only in Agatha Christie books and plays that someone who has been poisoned walks around feeling fine for several hours before suddenly keeling over and dying. In real life, victims suffer first, like Litvinenko. Our man had exhibited no such symptoms, nor were any of the classic side-effects of a poison identified in either postmortem.

Of course, we discussed if he could have been poisoned in Paris. But again, after vomiting in the hotel bathroom, he had seemed fine. By the time he got home, he'd recovered enough to go on a run. Had he been poisoned by one of these slow-burn toxins in Paris, he would've exhibited some symptoms on November 10, both before and after his death.

We could rule out quick-acting poisons, as the victim had been out running for quite some time before he collapsed. I found it hard to believe that a man with enemies like Perepilichnyy would've accepted and ingested anything in the course of his run. Of course, we considered that he may not have had any choice. The Russians are constantly innovating; according to intelligence reports, the FSB have developed cyanide that can be deployed as a mist. Some years earlier, a KGB defector admitted killing a prominent writer by spraying him in a stairwell with a canister hidden in a newspaper. Again though, where were the signs of burning skin around the face? Or the other classic symptoms of cyanide poisoning, convulsions and excessive salivation? A test for cyanide was performed on the postmortem blood sample from Perepilichnyy, with negative results. Besides, would the Russians really have sent someone to break into a gated community and intercept Perepilichnyy's spontaneous jog armed with a canister of some mysterious lethal mist? It was November; a slight breeze and both parties would have wound up quivering, barely conscious on that private road. It just didn't stack up.

As far as I was concerned, no known poison fitted the bill. But I told the meeting that I'd prepare an exhaustive report and subject anything that couldn't be ruled out by common sense to independent scientific testing. Maybe there was some poison or toxin out there that would slot neatly into the narrative of Perepilichnyy's death; if there was, I'd be the first to flag it.

Several months later, Nick Gent, Nick Craggs and I submitted a lengthy and detailed report that analysed every known type of poison and the reasons why they could be discounted, from acids, toxic anions and gases to venoms, warfare agents and ricin. The reasons they were ruled out basically came down to one or more of the following: the symptoms associated with these toxins weren't exhibited by Perepilichnyy, alive or dead; the internal remnants or side-effects of these toxins weren't identified in either of the two postmortems; the sheer impracticality of administering the substance in question, unless by force (remember, the victim's body showed no signs of violent struggle).

Take the classic poison arsenic. If he'd ingested this, there would've been two telltale postmortem signs. One, it would show up in his urine; Perepilichnyy had an arsenic level of approximately fourteen micrograms per litre, which is within the normal range of a fit and healthy person. Second, he would've developed brick-red mucosa, due to severe haemorrhage.

However, to be certain, we did get his blood, urine and stomach contents independently tested for drugs, alcohol or any other possible drug. The only medication found in his system was Viagra.

We also decided to get plant material in his system tested. As we had found out during the Adam investigation, nature can offer up some of the deadliest and most elusive toxins. To test the flora in Perepilichnyy's system, I returned to my tried-and-trusted source of plant-based mischief – Kew Gardens. Little did I know that their resulting report would generate lurid news headlines around the world.

* * *

The problems began in May 2015 – two and a half years after Perepilichnyy's untimely demise – when a misguided journalist got lucky.

The reporter turned up at the Old Bailey for what he thought was the opening of the inquest into the Russian's mysterious death. No one had told him that this was just the pre-inquest review hearing, dealing with logistics like dates and the availability of lawyers and witnesses. The reporter decided to sit in anyway.

At some point in the logistical discussions, a QC called Bob Moxon Browne, representing a life insurance company, said something that made the reporter sit up and start scribbling. According to Moxon Browne, a professor at Kew Gardens had found a chemical in the dead man's stomach associated with a poisonous plant that grows in China, called gelsemium.

'Given that it only grows in China and is a known weapon of assassination by Chinese and Russian contract killers, why was it in his stomach?' asked Moxon Browne.

The police requested that all samples from Perepilichnyy's body be sent to Professor Monique Simmonds at Kew Gardens so that she could conduct more tests. The coroner agreed, delaying the proceedings for another four months.

As soon as the hearing ended, the reporter raced outside to file his story: 'Billionaire Russian Businessman Found Dead Outside Surrey Home Could Have Been Poisoned.'

The opening paragraph read:

A Russian whistleblower who collapsed and died outside his home in Surrey after warning of death threats from the Kremlin had traces of a rare plant poison in his stomach, a pre-inquest hearing has heard.

By that night, reports about the exotic flower that had apparently killed a Russian whistleblower were all over the world's media.

During my days in toxicology, I had come across gelsemium. It comes in three flowering varieties, two of them native to North America and one to China. All three can be deadly. But the most toxic variety, *Gelsemium elegans*, only grows in Asia, where it's known as 'heartbreak grass' because the leaves, if swallowed, cause cardiac arrest.

The first scientific insight into the poison came from none other than Sir Arthur Conan Doyle – who had tested it out on himself! In a paper, published in an 1879 issue of the *British Medical Journal*, the author and physician described self-experimenting with tinctures of gelsemium to test its properties as a poison. He had become curious after using the tincture to treat nerve pain. Noticing that overstepping the advised dose appeared to have no ill effects, he decided to up his intake by a small amount each day.

After taking 9 millilitres, Conan Doyle 'suffered from severe frontal headache, with diarrhoea and general lassitude'. After 12 millilitres – the highest dose he managed – he reported: 'The diarrhoea was so persistent and prostrating, that I must stop at 200 minims [12 ml]. I felt great depression and a severe frontal headache. The pulse was still normal, but weak.'

Initial symptoms from an overdose would typically include dizziness, nausea, blurred vision and convulsions. In larger doses, it causes paralysis of the spinal cord, leading to almost complete loss of muscular power and eventually asphyxia.

But previous cases of poisoning with heartbreak grass had revealed telltale traces of gelsemium alkaloids in the blood and urine of the victim. We found no signs of this in Perepilichnyy. So, what the hell was going on here? Why had it been reported in the pre-trial as if it were fact?

The first tests on plant contents in Perepilichnyy's body had been conducted by the pollen specialist who'd helped me on the Adam case – Dr Nick Branch – along with Professor Monique Simmonds from Kew.

The tests showed that Alexander Perepilichnyy had recently consumed the plant materials sorrel and caraway – both ingredients in the soup he'd eaten after returning home from Paris. Their joint report went on to say that none of the comprehensive collection of 122 plant toxins held at the Royal Botanic Gardens in Kew had been detected in his system.

This is what I reported to the investigation team, closing down yet another avenue of potential poisons. As far as we were concerned, an exotic plant had not killed Alexander Perepilichnyy.

In my opinion, that should have been the end of the plant analysis of his system.

It wasn't.

The barristers at the 2015 pre-inquest review hearing were quoting a subsequent set of findings by Professor Simmonds's that I needed to check out. If this was the case, then where were the traces of gelsemium in Perepilichnyy's urine or blood?

The first thing I did was review Professor Simmonds' work. To identify plant compounds in what was left of the dead man's stomach contents, Professor Simmonds used two techniques. The first: high-pressure liquid chromatography to separate the individual compounds in the stomach contents. The second: mass spectrometry, which reveals the chemical structure, molecular weight and formula of the stomach contents, which we can identify like a fingerprint.

Reporting her findings, Professor Simmonds said: 'In the stomach contents we did detect a signal associated with the mass of a compound in the traces that could be associated with the toxic alkaloids found in gelsemium. Toxic alkaloids from plants belonging to this genus, such as gelsemicine, are known to be fast-acting toxins.'

The reason Professor Simmonds reported the comment above was that a small peak on the chromatogram had the same molecular weight (and molecular formula) as gelsemicine (328 $C_{20}H_{26}N_2O_4$).

As I knew from experience, this didn't necessarily mean that remnants of deadly gelsemicine had been present in Perepilichnyy's gut. Back in the 1970s, I'd spent two years training in mass spectrometry and learned its quirks. As I pointed out to the investigation team, using this system, nitro dimethyl benzene – which is harmful if inhaled, digested or absorbed – has the same molecular weight as paracetamol, which, as we all know, has healing qualities. In short, what Professor Simmonds found in the results certainly did not mean that there were any indications of gelsemium in his stomach.

The researchers at Kew knew this too, and had searched for traces of this toxic plant in the matter recovered from Perepilichnyy's stomach. Their resulting report said they could find no signs of it.

This clarification, however, did not prevent certain barristers – representing those trying to prove that Perepilichnyy had been murdered – claiming in an open court that the dead man had been poisoned. They were no doubt gambling that these claims would garner lurid headlines around the world. After all, a ghostly assassin 'whacking' a Russian whistleblower with some exotic but untraceable Chinese death plant made far better copy than him simply dropping dead. It didn't matter that the scientists had found no trace of gelsemium in the man's stomach contents. Once those headlines were published and broadcast, they couldn't be taken back.

When the inquest finally started in 2018, the John le Carré vibes were fanned further when it was revealed that the home secretary, Sajid Javid, had got involved. Javid invoked a national secrecy law to avoid sharing evidence from two of the UK's spy agencies about Perepilichnyy with the inquest. This left everyone in little doubt that the Russian exile had worked in some capacity for UK intelligence.

As the inquest ground on, I knew that we had to kill off this notion that he'd been poisoned once and for all. The legal team representing the police called another botanist from Kew, Geoff Kite, an expert in the high-pressure liquid chromatography mass spectrometry system used. He confirmed that they had identified an 'unknown compound' in Perepilichnyy's system with the same molecular mass as *Gelsemium elegans*. However, he told the inquest that further examinations had proved 'beyond reasonable doubt' that there was no plant toxin in Perepilichnyy's stomach when he died.

Yes, there was an unknown compound in his gut but, as Kite pointed out, this was not uncommon. In fact, the compound that had caused all this furore had been one of over 300 unidentified compounds found in Mr Perepilichnyy's system.

Still, those parties intent on getting an open verdict from the coroner refused to give up the ghost. Professor Robin Ferner, consultant physician and clinical pharmacologist instructed by Hermitage Capital, gave examples of a myriad of drugs/poisons that he thought could not be excluded.

He quoted paracetamol, antidepressants that – when mixed with certain foods like blue cheese – can be deadly, ecstasy, cancer drugs and fast-acting poisons.

Next, he cited sarin – the compound used to such deadly effect on the Tokyo underground system – VX, which killed Kim Jong-nam at Kuala Lumpur airport, and even warfare agents used in Syria.

I could only assume he hadn't read my report, because I'd dealt with – and dismissed – every single one of these. For a variety of sound scientific reasons, none of them fitted.

Despite this, I still believed that the coroner – Nicholas Hilliard QC – would come back with an open verdict. After all, we couldn't prove that Perepilichnyy had died of natural causes or SADS.

The police knew that an open verdict would lead to a furious backlash against them. Detective Chief Inspector Ian Pollard and his team had taken an absolute kicking during proceedings. Lawyers arguing that Perepilichnyy had been murdered were at pains to emphasise their every failure. And there had been many: the early decision to classify his death as non-suspicious; the fact that police didn't search the area near to where he'd died, take photographs of the scene or harvest local CCTV; their failure to realise in those first weeks that Perepilichnyy had been a whistleblower in a case involving Russia's most powerful figures.

But the single biggest criticism against the police was that a forensic postmortem hadn't been carried out until eighteen days after he died, by which time most of his stomach contents had been destroyed.

No wonder DCI Pollard and his team seemed tense. But they weren't alone.

For me, an open verdict meant we had failed to identify a terrifyingly efficient, mystery poison currently in the hands of Russian assassins. In short, we had failed to do our job.

As we waited for the ruling, a rare moment of levity cheered me. A member of the Sussex Police team told me how, in chambers, one of the barristers hostile to the police had remarked: 'Who is this bloody Ray Fysh anyway?'

Apparently the coroner, Hilliard – whom I had worked with on both of Siôn Jenkins's retrials – turned to the man and said: 'You obviously haven't done much forensic work if you've never heard of Ray Fysh!'

Finally, on December 19, 2018, Hilliard came back with his verdict.

He said it was possible that a 'novel unknown substance' had been used to murder the Russian exile. He made clear, however, that 'if he was killed in this way, it left no trace which could be picked up at postmortem'.

Hilliard added that he could not 'completely eliminate all possibility' that Perepilichnyy had been the victim of foul play. But, he said, 'there is no direct evidence that he was killed or any compelling circumstantial evidence either'.

His final verdict was that Alexander Perepilichnyy had died of natural causes, most likely sudden arrhythmic death syndrome, while out jogging.

It's beyond dispute that Vladimir Putin has personally sanctioned the murder of many people on UK soil. However, unless the Russians have developed the perfect colourless, odourless, tasteless, symptom-free, untraceable and instant poison, Alexander Perepilichnyy wasn't one of them.

CHAPTER SEVENTEEN

OPERATION MINSTEAD
1999 TO 2009

Towards the end of the noughties, a number of high-profile cases came to symbolise the progress we'd made at the Forensic Science Service – at least for me. After I'd spent over a decade as specialist advisor, we were no longer just testing exhibits and samples and sending back the results. We were helping detectives figure out ways to identify and track down culprits. Police forces all over the world now sought out our expertise as we became world leaders in adapting scientific methods from other disciplines to live criminal investigations.

There is one case in particular that really symbolises this evolution, being as it was so long-running that it straddled both eras. It remains the largest and most complex rape investigation in Met Police history, and it lasted seventeen years and cost over £10 million.

But what is perhaps most galling for the police force is not the time it took, or the money it cost, but the fact that if it weren't for a clerical blunder, the case could've been solved fully a decade earlier.

We spent all that time chasing a shadow. However, from a purely forensics perspective, this case forced us to push DNA science into bold new territories that are still being explored today.

I first began working on the periphery of Operation Minstead in 1999. A year earlier, semen found at the scene of a house break-in, burglary, indecent assault and attempted rape of an eighty-one-year-old woman in Warlingham, Surrey, had proved to be a DNA match to the rape of an eighty-four-year-old woman in Shirley near Croydon some six years earlier.

Such violent sexual attacks on two defenceless elderly women were truly disturbing. Both victims had lived alone. The suspect had entered their homes in the early hours by skilfully removing a windowpane or panel. He cut off the electricity, disconnected the landline phone and removed lightbulbs before creeping into the bedrooms of his sleeping victims. Both women awoke to find a powerful torch light shining in their faces and a hand over their mouths. The man, all in black and wearing a balaclava, talked to them gently at first, asking for money, before launching a violent and prolonged sexual attack. In the first break-in, he stole £275 in cash and a Hunter watch. In the second, he ignored cash and jewellery but spent over two hours in the house with the terrified woman. Neither victim could tell us much, just that he appeared to be a light-skinned Black male and spoke with a local accent. All we had were samples of his DNA; his profile wasn't on the national database.

The linked cases threw up a lot of questions. Why would a suspect risk spending hours at a crime scene? And why had there been a gap of six years between the offences?

In 1999, he got busier. Same MO, same victim profiles – all elderly and living alone in the same general area of Croydon, Bromley and Orpington in south London. But this next spree of attacks came with an added chilling twist – he was now sexually assaulting both elderly women and men.

In the space of two summer months, he carried out at least five more attacks, and appeared to be getting cocky. He left a scarf at one home with traces of his saliva. At another, he helped himself to drinks. Then he brought beer to the house of another victim, leaving a part-empty can behind. However, when he flashed his penis at one elderly woman, she quickly put a dent in his burgeoning confidence.

'What would your mother say if she could see you now?' she scolded.

Detectives were convinced that, by challenging the suspect, this plucky pensioner had saved herself from sexual assault. However, the very next night, he broke into another property and launched a vicious rape on an eighty-eight-year-old woman. The victim suffered a perforated bowel as a result of the attack, almost dying during six hours of surgery and living out the rest of her life in agony.

Back at the lab, in these initial stages of the investigation and my early days as SA, we performed our role of corroborating evidence with distinction. For example, after a rape in Addiscombe, near Croydon, we managed to obtain a DNA profile from semen in a bowl of water that was used by the offender to wash the victim's nightdress.

Our toolmark experts set to work on his entry points into these properties. They found that, when microscopically compared, the toolmarks on the window beading at six properties directly corresponded. If police apprehended the suspect and he still had this tool in his possession, it would indisputably prove him to be the burglar. But that was just the thing: we were relying on the police to catch him first. Only then would our forensic work pay off. I wanted us to be doing more. But I'd have to bide my time.

As it stood, detectives had little to go on except the suspect's DNA. Victim descriptions had been vague – he was a Black male, possibly light-skinned, maybe of mixed race, aged thirty to forty, softly spoken and athletically built. A size-ten Nike shoe impression had been found at one scene. The rest was all circumstantial. He seemed to have knowledge of old people living alone. The paltry sums he stole suggested that he didn't rely on the spoils of these burglaries, so he must have had some sort of a job. Another striking observation by his victims was how skilled he'd been in handling them, raising them by the elbows and supporting the smalls of their backs and even, in one case, expertly removing a woman's false teeth. Did he work in a care home or at a local hospital? Was he a carer? Unless his DNA profile suddenly appeared on the national database for another offence, the police were at a loss as to where to start.

The feeling of helplessness in this case was especially acute for me. My elderly parents lived in his target area of south-east London and, like so many of their trusting generation, rarely locked the doors. When visiting, I'd walk down the side of the house, through the ground-floor basement and up to the first floor, to find Mum in the kitchen without a single locked door having blocked my path.

'You've done it again, haven't you, Mum?' I'd protest. 'You've got to lock the doors and windows.'

I'd told her all the gory details about the man the media had by now dubbed 'Night Stalker' and she'd been truly horrified. I even heard her say to friends: 'Isn't it terrible what's happening to those old people?'

Yet, when I'd hound her about security, she'd just shake her head and say, 'Oh that's not going to happen to us, Ray.'

Just to be sure it didn't, I rang and called around a lot more often than usual.

For some reason, after the vicious rape of the eighty-eight-year-old in August 1999 the offender stopped again, this time for over two years.

When, in 2002, the attacks resumed, Detective Superintendent Simon Morgan had been put in charge of solving the case. His deputy was Will O'Reilly, whom I'd been working closely with on the ongoing Adam investigation. By now, almost three years since I last worked on Operation Minstead, I'd gained a fresh perspective on my role as specialist advisor. Having helped drive the forensic efforts in the Sarah Payne and Adam cases, I felt like I'd 'seen the light' in terms of how I could help senior cops struggling with tricky, long-running cases. So, I contacted Detective Superintendent Morgan and asked for a meeting, bolstered by the knowledge that Will O'Reilly would vouch for me.

Simon met me at the incident room in Lewisham. I was struck immediately by his youthful, college-boy looks, which seemed so at odds with his permanently worried expression. I'd learned to read senior cops quickly and could tell that Simon was a hardened, old-school detective. He was perfectly polite and pleasant, but I sensed a lack of trust and faith in what I was telling him about the Adam case and how we could apply the same strategies to Operation Minstead.

Perhaps some of my initial ideas about using forensics to lead the charge seemed a bit pie in the sky for a detective dealing with the day-to-day practicalities of finding a rapist. Back then, many senior cops had the mindset that a scientist's place is in the lab. They just couldn't see what a boffin might bring to the day-to-day rough-and-tumble of an incident room when they already had so many hard-bitten detectives vying for their time. I got it: what I was offering was new and, to someone like Simon, untested.

So, as I sat at his desk in his office next to the starkly lit incident room, I made things clear from the outset; he was the boss and I'd be in his hands. I'd make suggestions but it was completely up to him whether or not to act upon them. I wouldn't be remotely offended if he didn't. And then I delivered the promise that always swung even the most hard-bitten coppers – I'd make sure that all his exhibits and samples got fast-tracked through the FSS lab.

Simon leaned back in his chair, all the while surveying me: 'OK then, Ray. Let's give it a few weeks, see how we get on.'

And so, I had to prove my worth and win the trust of yet another senior cop – all part of the service! To be fair to Simon, he let me in on all the ongoing conversations about leads and seemed genuinely open to ideas, so long as they were good ones.

In terms of identifying who this suspect was, detectives were already doing all the standard investigative stuff – checking out sex offenders not on the National DNA Database and anyone arrested for burglary, trespass or voyeurism. An intelligence-led screen was also in place. However, the target population's distrust of the police was making this a slow process.

A major source of debate continued to be the long gaps between his offences, from 1992 to 1998 and 1999 to 2002. Where had he been? He may have been in prison between 1992 and 1998; after all, as we had found out during the hunt for the M25 Rapist, it wasn't until 1999 that people being released from prison were automatically sampled and put on the National DNA Database. However, this also meant that he couldn't have been in prison between 1999 and 2002, or he would be on the database. Maybe he'd moved abroad? So we cross-referenced his DNA with every international database we could find. We also considered things like the armed services and mental health institutions, but to no avail. We were struggling to get a break; we needed to try to build a picture of this man through any means possible.

Unable to pin down the man himself, we turned our attention once again to the crime scenes in the hope that they might yield some vital clue to help identify the perpetrator. What became clear was that the suspect preferred detached or semi-detached houses or bungalows on quiet suburban streets with side access to the rear garden. Presumably he would hide in the garden behind a bush or a law wall, watching his target through the window until lights out. But how did the suspect have such an intricate knowledge of south London suburbia? And how had he known that all these vulnerable, elderly people lived alone?

Police included these factors in an exhaustive list of suspect characterisations. The man we sought was a gerontophile – someone with a sexual attraction towards the elderly. The fact he knew where these victims lived meant he was likely to be a home-calling professional of some sort – a delivery driver, taxi driver, salesman, odd-job man – but who also had regular interaction with the elderly. So, a doctor, paramedic, nurse or a care home worker were added to the list. When it came to intelligence-led DNA screening of potential suspects, men with jobs like these would be bumped up the order.

We were also acting on titbits picked up by the victims during their ordeals. At one scene, the suspect let slip that his mother had died in 2000, so police were combing through the death records of women in south London whose ages matched this scenario. In a couple of offences, he'd mentioned that he needed money to 'get back to Brighton', so we were making detailed enquiries on the south coast. Another victim said that the suspect had worn motorcycle gloves. Traffic cameras were pored over and every male holder of a motorcycle licence in south London and Brighton – there were more than 15,000 of them – scrutinised. During another offence, he was picking cash out of a bowl when the female victim said, 'Please don't take that, that is the church's money.' Amazingly, he put it back. Was the suspect a member of a church or a religious group, perhaps lapsed in his faith? Had going door to door on behalf of a religious organisation given him the perfect cover to check out elderly people living alone? Yet another lead to pursue...

No detail was too small or insignificant.

Victims described the suspect as having a 'sweet' smell. Had this been the result of a particular type of hair product, or maybe cannabis? Some diabetics don't have enough insulin to utilise glucose in their systems, resulting in sweet-smelling breath.

Away from the incident room, behavioural psychologists were looking into the bizarre mindset of a man whose relationship to his victims seemed to be almost schizophrenic. He could commit acts of unspeakable violence against his victims, but then appeared to crave relationships with them, displaying flashes of apparent tenderness and a conscience. He sexually assaulted these old people, then spent up to four hours in their company before thanking them and kissing them goodbye. He could overpower his victims with ease, yet fled whenever one of them stood up to him. He stole from their homes, but mostly small amounts of cash and objects of little value like ornaments – trophies, in other words. He occasionally took a victim's pulse – in the manner of a man used to doing so – and had twice said: 'I'm really sorry, I won't do this again.'

But he did, and several times, carrying on undeterred throughout 2002 and 2003. In the more violent cases, he left his DNA at the scene. And through our tool and fibre experts and his unique MO, we were now linking him to dozens more break-ins and sexual assaults. The police held workshops for elderly people in each of the hot spots, offering advice to people living alone about how to be safer. Heartbreakingly, many who attended admitted sleeping during the day so that they could stay awake all night on high alert.

After what was now over ten years of this man being on the loose, Met Police bosses were growing embarrassed by our continued failure to apprehend this suspect. The pervading attitude seemed to be: 'You've got all these officers and resources, and you can't even catch a burglar!' Because to the outside world that, in essence, was all this guy seemed – a burglar who, when the opportunity presented itself, lived out his twisted sexual fantasies.

In truth, we were drowning in suspects. The more leads we pursued, the more names got added to the list. When the crime team finally pulled together their list of 'persons of interest', it numbered more than 21,500 men. And with every call from the public, that list got longer.

Sometime around the end of 2002, Simon had called me with a short but very big question: how can we whittle down the number of suspects? By now, I'd really grown to like and respect Simon. Despite always looking worried, he sucked up the pressure from above admirably so that his team could remain focused and confident.

Simon and I agreed to continue screening mixed-race men aged between twenty-five and forty in south London. Meanwhile, around this time – 2002 to 2003 – we were having some success in the Adam case, tracing the boy's ancestry to a relatively small tranche of the African continent. Could we do the same with this suspect? Of course, in Adam's case, we had the torso of a child, which gave us bones to work with. In this case, all we had was a DNA profile. So, the next question was, how far can we push the information held in this suspect's DNA profile?

I returned to my old friend, the geneticist Andy Urquhart.

Since before the Adam case in 2001, Andy had been researching whether DNA could reveal key details about a suspect: for example, the colour of their skin. Using DNA profiles of known ethnic groups that he'd obtained from all over the world, Andy was busy building a database that was resulting in some compelling statistical data. For example, he found some number sequences in Night Stalker's DNA profile that were a thousand times more likely to come from an RC3 or Afro-Caribbean than an RC4, which is Asian, and 2,000 times more likely to be RC3 than RC1 or Caucasian.

Of course, this still didn't tell us anything very specific about his ancestry, but the result at least confirmed what all those elderly victims had told us – that our suspect was Black.

In our quest to push this further, we came across a hi-tech research company based in Sarasota, Florida, claiming to be 'the world's first recreational genomics testing service'. For a fee of around £300, DNAPrint Genomics Inc. offered a map to a client's ancestral origins and racial make-up, with results delivered on CD. 'Uncover Your Personal Anthropology!' urged the company's promotional material. Encouragingly, among their clientele were a number of US law enforcement agencies.

Simon Morgan flew to Florida to see this outfit for himself. He discovered that the scientists there tested for 177 DNA markers – compared to the 10 we used for our DNA database. These markers – single nucleotide polymorphisms, frequently called SNPs – had been selected out of the many millions that make up human DNA as they show the most ancestral variance. According to Simon, the company had some impressive blind tests to back up their claims. That was enough for us: we sent them a sample and willed them to find something, anything, that would help us progress.

Several weeks later, the US researchers reported identifying three separate strands of DNA in the rapist's sample. The mingling of these strands was 82 per cent sub-Saharan African, 12 per cent Native American and 6 per cent European, with no trace of an Asian component. According to DNAPrint Genomics, this combination of bloodlines pointed strongly towards the rapist's origins being the Caribbean. As a result of colonisation by Europeans and the import of slaves from Africa, that particular genetic mingling occurs only in this region.

This detailed analysis proved crucial to our next steps. We took the results to the genetic epidemiologist considered the world's finest – Professor Paul McKeigue at University College Dublin. He supported the findings and added some valuable elimination tips: this suspect couldn't be from a solely African ancestry, and we could exclude anyone with a European parent or grandparent. This was a massive breakthrough. We could now eliminate all Black males of African origin in London and focus purely on Black men from the Caribbean who didn't have European parents or grandparents. At a stroke, this slashed our 'persons of interest' list by almost 5,000 and this meant we could conduct a much more focused DNA screen on suspects in the south London area.

However, as this was the first time that such a test had been used in the UK, we thought it only wise to test its validity. In spring 2004, we came up with the idea to conduct voluntary tests on over fifty staff at Scotland Yard known to have Caribbean heritage. The benefits were obvious: the sample would be unusually reliable because serving Met Police staff would have no reason to lie about where they came from. And we could do it quickly. The so-called Night Stalker usually got busy in the summer months and we wanted to try to catch him before his next spree.

Then, a problem. A newspaper reported that, after receiving representations from the Metropolitan Black Police Association (MPBA), Scotland Yard's top brass scrapped the idea. However, after initial misgivings about the highly sensitive nature of racial profiling, the MPBA relented.

The staff samples were sent to DNAPrint Genomics for profiling and the results forwarded blind to Professor McKeigue for his interpretation. McKeigue's set of results matched the perceived ancestry of the volunteers extremely closely, proving that their system worked.

Intriguingly, Professor McKeigue told us that if we could obtain DNA samples from a few hundred people of Caribbean extraction, we may be able to statistically narrow down Night Stalker's ancestry to a specific island. Of course, this research is never going to convict anybody, but it seemed like vital new learning and an area with mind-blowing potential.

Meanwhile, our more focused DNA screen continued. That spring of 2004, a letter from the Minstead team had been hand-delivered to hundreds of Black Caribbean men in the south London area who fell into the profile of the suspect. The letter explained that the police intended to take samples from some 1,000 people 'who fit the suspect's description' for comparison with the offender's sample. Emphasising that this was intended to eliminate the innocent, the letter assured recipients that their legal rights would be carefully safeguarded: if a voluntary sample proved to be negative, it would be destroyed.

Following the refusal of 125 of these men to take part in the proposed mass screening programme, another letter from the Minstead team urged recipients to 'consider that the suspect is likely to refuse a voluntary sample'. It ended with what some interpreted as a veiled threat, informing those who hadn't complied that police would be 'reviewing the circumstances surrounding your refusal'.

The *Voice* newspaper, which serves Britain's Black community, reported the experiences of a thirty-nine-year-old electrician, Andy Holder, who accused the police of 'bully-boy' tactics when he objected to providing a sample. Under the headline 'Do Not Agree', the *Voice* quoted Holder saying he was threatened with a court order. The issue was then raised by Lynne Featherstone, a Lib Dem member of the Greater London Council. When it emerged that five of the men who'd refused to provide a sample had been arrested, civil rights group Liberty took up the cause.

In autumn 2004, Night Stalker struck again. We found more fibres from his clothes at the scene and, dumped in a nearby hedge, a pair of gloves bearing his DNA as well as that of an unidentified woman. After launching more attacks in the spring of 2005, he went under the radar again.

2006 – 14 YEARS AFTER NIGHT STALKER'S FIRST ATTACK

By 2006, Night Stalker had attacked ninety-eight victims that we were aware of, raping at least four of them and indecently assaulting a number of others. The youngest victim had been sixty-eight, the oldest ninety-three. Although the majority were women, he had attacked ten men, sexually assaulting at least one of them. As we were beginning to find out, many of the victims felt too embarrassed to tell the police if they'd been raped or sexually assaulted. In some cases, we only found out after they had died: they had confided in a friend or relative and sworn them to secrecy.

Simon Morgan made a point of personally meeting all the victims and, later, attended many of their funerals. He seemed particularly haunted by the words of one lady before her death: 'The one thing I need to know before I go is who it was and why he did it to me.'

But by this time – 2006 – the investigation had stalled. Police had eliminated 10,000 of the 21,500 'persons of interest'. The police were still flagging up offenders and calling me at all hours seeking a quick-turnaround DNA check. None was a match. An appearance by Simon on *Crimewatch* – his third during Operation Minstead – generated 150 calls but no fresh leads of note. We were stuck.

This suspect had been terrorising south London unchecked for fourteen years. With our knowledge of past long-running investigations, Simon and I suspected that – when we did finally identify this offender – we'd find that we made a mistake somewhere along the line. That we'd missed something. And with the investigation having taken so long, there would almost certainly be an inquiry into our performances. So, I kept checking and re-checking all of our work. I spent weeks and possibly months going back over all of our tests and results, over and over. Where a DNA sample was just a few numbers out, we put it through the system again in case the numbers had been mistranscribed.

I badgered my contacts in academia for ideas about what else we could do with the suspect's DNA, especially now we had such a comprehensive profile from the US genetics company. Could we use this data to detect congenital health conditions or mental disorders? Could we generate a composite image of the suspect through the facial traits revealed by his DNA? I was fifteen years too soon: scientists in the Netherlands are currently looking into constructing e-fit images purely from DNA data.

So, with that route blocked, I went old-school and looked into more traditional forensic opportunities. I discovered that, up until 2002, a lot of the victims' bedding and other exhibits had not been examined. The primary goal until that point had been to get a DNA profile of the suspect. We went back through all of it searching for anything we might be able to work with – a hair, fibres, marks – but drew another blank.

By now, 2006, he'd 'vanished' again for the best part of a year and counting. We began to wonder if – in between his prolific crime sprees in London – he moved back to the Caribbean. The decision was made for a team of us to make a brief visit to Trinidad and Barbados. First, we could make appeals for information through the media; second, we could liaise with local police. Perhaps they had similar offences on their records, or an offender with a similar description and MO.

Simon Morgan and some senior detectives went out first, arriving in Trinidad on the Wednesday night. Kate Campbell from the Yard's press office and I travelled Thursday and, on account of delays, didn't reach the hotel until 5 a.m. Friday. After two hours' sleep, we met the others for a breakfast briefing before undertaking an intense day of media interviews. That evening, we had a couple of beers at the hotel bar while cringingly watching ourselves on the TV news. The others went out for a meal but I headed straight upstairs for room service and bed. And that was about all of the island I saw.

That Sunday, a British newspaper ran photos of some of Simon's team relaxing by the pool in swimming trunks, and Simon and I having a beer at the bar, under the headline 'The Frying Squad'. The subheading read: 'Soaking up the sun in Trinidad… how Scotland Yard's finest are hunting for the Night Stalker.' The piece implied that we were enjoying a glorified holiday at taxpayers' expense. Of course, it was nonsense. Sure, we had a few beers when we weren't on duty, but we'd all worked hard on that trip, generating lots of publicity and connections to local police. I felt especially indignant on Simon's behalf. He'd dedicated years of his career to this case, giving it his all in the face of some real stick from bosses, colleagues, the media and the public. He carried the whole thing on his shoulders, somehow managing to keep up morale among his flagging officers. No one could've done more or worked harder, yet here he was being subjected to what I considered to be public ridicule.

As 2006 drew to a close, it seemed that Night Stalker hadn't struck for the entire calendar year. How we all hoped that, for reasons we might never know, his reign of terror had ended for good.

2009 – 17 YEARS AFTER NIGHT STALKER'S FIRST ATTACK

By 2009, Night Stalker was back with a vengeance, terrorising the elderly of south London. I still got regular calls from members of Simon's team saying: 'We've got him this time, Ray, we're certain. Can you turn around a quick DNA profile?'

I lost count of the number of times I had to call them back with bad news.

Crucially, though, the suspect had become greedy. He'd been taking the bank cards of victims and demanding their pin numbers. In August 2009, a CCTV camera caught the suspect using the cash card of an eighty-eight-year-old Polish man he'd burgled in Thornton Heath. Months later, he appeared at the same ATM, fresh from another burglary. As he'd been masked both times, the footage appeared to be evidentially useless. However, when reviewing the later CCTV, one eagle-eyed officer spotted the reflection of a bus in a shop window. The bus was tracked down and found to be fitted with cameras. Police trawled through the CCTV footage the bus had recorded. In it, a dark Vauxhall Zafira was spotted near to that cash machine at the time the offender had used the cards. They were getting closer…

On Sunday evening, November 15, 2009, a Zafira was spotted parked in the Shirley suburb of Croydon – the very place where Night Stalker had begun his campaign of terror seventeen years earlier. Except this time, more than seventy undercover officers were staking out several streets following a recent burglary. An organised stop of the vehicle was ordered and the driver arrested.

It was just after 1 a.m. when I got the call at home from DS Adam Spier.

'Ray? We've got him, we've definitely got him.'

'Yeah. Yeah' – I yawned – 'of course you have.'

'No, it's definitely him,' insisted the voice on the other end.

He told me briefly about the arrest and it did sound promising. So, I gave the lab a call. We had 24-hour DNA profiling available. I asked them to do it quicker if at all possible. We've never turned a test around faster. At about 7.30 a.m., as I sat at the kitchen table drinking tea, the result came through.

I called Simon right away.

'Simon, this time you really have got him,' I said.

I don't think I've ever enjoyed imparting a piece of good news more. Simon remained silent. God knew what was going through his mind, but I could imagine those many long years of anxiety just tumbling away.

Delroy Grant, fifty-two, was arrested wearing two pairs of jeans, three T-shirts and a long sock for a belt; he was clearly planning to shed the top layer as soon as he'd committed whatever horrors he had planned that night.

Officers searched his car and found Night Stalker's kit: a grey balaclava, latex gloves, a bolt cutter, pliers and black woolly hat. In the boot, a hammer, pincers, a towel, a blue jumper and a crowbar with his DNA and which perfectly matched the marks left at a recent burglary scene.

While his fingerprints were being taken, Grant said to a detective: 'I don't know why you're bothering, I always wear gloves.' Now, if that's not a 'hands-up' – gloved or otherwise – I don't know what is. Incredibly, while giving a DNA swab to another detective, he tried to pin the blame for the rapes on his estranged son, pointing out that their profiles would be similar.

Despite this, his arrest shocked relatives and friends. They considered him a loving family man, pointing out how he'd selflessly given up work as a cab driver to care full time for his wife, a multiple sclerosis sufferer.

Other personal details proved an uncanny match to our original list of suspect characteristics: not only was he a carer and a taxi driver, he'd also once been an active Jehovah's Witness. We got it right genetically too: Grant was originally from Kingston, Jamaica.

At his trial, Grant claimed he'd been 'fitted up' by his embittered ex-wife, who had kept samples of his bodily fluids, semen and saliva, and paid burglars to plant it at Night Stalker crime scenes. Bearing in mind that she and Delroy had split in 1980, this meant his 'ex' had discovered DNA profiling before Professor Alec Jeffreys!

As laughably improbable as these lines of defence might seem, they were enough to sway two members of the jury. Delroy Grant was found guilty only after Judge Peter Rook QC agreed to accept a majority verdict of 10–2. Convicted of three rapes, one attempted rape and seven indecent assaults, Grant was sentenced to four life terms and a minimum of twenty-seven years.

After the trial, we found out why Delroy Grant had proven so elusive to Operation Minstead since 1999. That year, a member of the public had reported a car near the scene of a burglary in Bromley, Kent, which turned out to be registered in his name. However, due to a clerical error, the DNA sample of another Delroy Grant who lived in Hackney, east London, was mistaken for that of Delroy Grant from Brockley Mews and he was eliminated from enquiries. This blunder left Grant free to continue his sick campaign against solitary elderly people for another ten years. We never stood a chance of identifying 'Night Stalker' Delroy Grant because he'd been mistakenly eliminated from the inquiry just as we were starting to work on it. Buried among 40,000 other suspects, he didn't come to the notice of the enquiry team again until he was caught.

CHAPTER EIGHTEEN

OPERATION HOLBROOK – OCTOBER 2008

They say necessity is the mother of invention. Our desperate need to make something happen in really challenging investigations like Minstead, Adam, the 2005 terror attacks on London and the poisoning of Litvinenko saw us pushing ourselves and forensic science to the limits.

The most gratifying legacy of all this was that, by the late 2000s, we could use this learning and knowledge to solve three unrelated high-profile murders of young people that would never have been cracked otherwise.

In October 2008, children playing in woodland just outside Hastings, East Sussex, stumbled upon what appeared to be a human skull with its lower jaw missing. They told their parents who, in turn, alerted the police. SOCOs carried out a detailed search of the area, finding about 90 per cent of the victim's skeleton, including the fibula, pelvic bone and left femur.

Nick Craggs, the principal SOCO at Sussex Police, called to tell me about the body. I was pleased to learn he had drafted in our old friend Lucy Sibun, the forensic archaeologist who eight years earlier had performed such a vital role in preserving the shallow grave of Sarah Payne.

Lucy deduced that no attempt had been made to bury the body, which had been lying out in the open for several months and had got scattered by animals. No clothing or personal possessions were found in the fingertip search.

Meanwhile, the forensic pathologist found a metal plate in the victim's left femur that showed it had suffered a severe break in recent years. The removal and examination of the plate revealed a unique serial number and, in hospital records, the identity of its recipient. Victoria Couchman, nineteen, had three years earlier broken her leg in a road traffic accident that claimed the life of her seventeen-year-old brother Dean.

A mother of one, Victoria had lived with her dad, Tony Couchman, forty-seven, less than a mile from where her skeletal remains were found. For some reason, she hadn't been reported missing.

In attempting to establish cause of death, forensic pathologist Dr Kenneth Shorrock found no evidence of a fractured skull or broken ribs. Neither did he find bones damaged as they would be in the course of a stabbing.

In his postmortem report, he said: 'Victoria was a young woman and a common way to kill young women is to strangle them. In my view strangulation is a distinct possibility.'

Neighbours described Victoria as a devoted mum who used to spend hours playing with her toddler. However, they also reported a darker side to her domestic life. People who knew the Couchman family described how Tony often blamed Victoria for the crash that killed her elder brother Dean, even though she had been merely a passenger in the car.

A neighbour last saw Victoria outside her dad's home 'sometime in May 2008', when she had complained that he was 'too controlling'. Another neighbour visited the house later and had asked after Victoria.

'She's gone out,' Tony had brusquely declared.

Neither neighbour had seen her since. All activity on Victoria's mobile phone had ended on May 16, 2008. Her final texts confirmed that she had been with her dad at this time.

Detectives turned their attention to Tony Couchman, who had eleven previous convictions ranging from theft to firearms offences. When asked why he hadn't reported his daughter missing, Tony said he feared social services would take away Victoria's child – his grandchild. He claimed that Victoria had vanished on previous occasions and was on 'a final warning' from social services – something they denied.

Investigations revealed that, twelve days after Victoria had vanished, Tony had sold his car. He also claimed to have lost the mobile phone that he was using at the time of Victoria's disappearance. Detectives seemed convinced that both items had contained vital clues to Victoria's fate, which was why he'd disposed of them. Five days after Victoria's body had been found, officers arrested and charged her dad on suspicion of murder.

But they now had a problem.

In February 2009 – four months after the discovery of Victoria's skeletal remains – I found myself on the road to Brighton for a meeting with the officer in charge, Detective Chief Inspector Adam Hibbert, and Nick Craggs, principal SOCO at Sussex Police. I enjoyed working with Adam, a dedicated and smart detective with a wicked sense of humour.

Upon my arrival, he barked: 'Have you had a drink, Ray?'

'No, I haven't,' I said defensively, wondering why he'd thought I was tipsy.

'Someone get Ray a drink!' he called out to the office at large, obviously meaning a tea or coffee.

As soon as we sat, Adam bowled a question I wasn't expecting.

'How accurate can we be at determining Victoria's time of death?'

Of course, we've all seen those TV dramas where the inappropriately jolly pathologist confidently declares – normally while peeling off a pair of latex gloves – that the suspect died between six forty-five and eight the previous evening.

It really isn't like that…

The truth is, pathologists hate being asked for a time of death as they know how utterly impossible it is to say, given traditional methods of analysis. One of these 'methods' involves taking the rectal temperature of the dead person, subtracting it from their live temperature of 98.6 degrees Fahrenheit, then dividing the difference by two. This system isn't as random as it sounds: it follows an official 'standard cooling curve' formula that a dead body will lose 1.5 degrees Fahrenheit per hour. But it does fail to account for so many potential contributing factors: was the body inside or outside, wet or dry? What was the air and ground temperature? The body weight and clothing?

There are other methods – like testing *rigor mortis* – but this too can be affected by so many *in situ* variables.

Of course, neither of these methods could be applied to Victoria's skeletal remains.

'Why do you need to establish Victoria's time of death?' I asked.

'As you know, Ray, the last time Victoria's mobile phone had been used was on May 16, 2008,' Adam explained. 'However, we've now been alerted to evidence that Victoria may have still been alive three months later, in August 2008.'

'What sort of evidence?'

'That August, she apparently posted several messages on her Bebo social media account. Her mother, Fiona Masters – who's separated from her dad – also says she got some texts from Victoria that same month, saying that she'd left Hastings and set up home with her new boyfriend in another part of England. There are also some friends of Victoria's claiming they saw her around Hastings town centre in the August of 2008. Of course, this exonerates Tony – who, by the way, we think is behind both the Bebo entries and the texts. But we can't prove it.'

'But proving that Victoria had died the previous May would sort all this out?'

'Exactly, Ray. But is it possible?'

I knew that Dr Stuart Black at the University of Reading had carried out research with forensic pathologist Dr Ben Swift into the decay of radioactive isotopes to determine the postmortem interval, or time of death. So, I decided to give him a call.

'In terms of working out Victoria's time of death,' Stuart told me, 'the isotopes that could help us are the radioactive isotopes lead-210 and polonium-210, both of which we ingest daily through our normal diet.'

This took me aback. My only experience of the radioactive element polonium-210 was that it had killed Alexander Litvinenko.

'Believe it or not, Ray,' said Stuart, 'there are minute traces of polonium-210 in our bones. It reaches a steady low state from the time we are about twenty weeks old and doesn't change until you die.'

He told me that the lead-210 isotope, on the other hand, has a very different life cycle inside our bodies.

'We take lead-210 into our bodies every day,' he said. 'In fact, the amount of lead-210 we consume in the UK through food and air pollution is monitored by the Food Standards Agency, which publishes its findings each year.

'The level of lead-210 in our bones rises gradually from the time we're born until we reach about forty, when it levels out, and this is reflected in lead isotopes in our bones. At the time of death of a normal adult, the lead-210 level is far greater than the polonium-210 level.'

All this seemed easy enough to grasp. What I was struggling to figure out was how these two things were connected and what they might reveal about Victoria's time of death.

Stuart spelled it out: 'After you die, your lead-210 level declines because you are no longer taking in food and air and through normal radioactive decay. Lead-210 has a half-life of 22.3 years. Here's the thing though, Ray: polonium-210, which has a half-life of 138 days, is the daughter isotope of lead-210, so the concentration of polonium-210 increases as lead-210 decays postmortem.'

I knew the rest from my toxicology days and couldn't stop myself jumping in:

'And these changes are steady and consistent after death because the radioactive half-lives of these isotopes are not affected by environmental changes like temperature. So, by measuring the ratio of polonium-210 to lead-210 in a dead body...'

We said the next bit in unison: 'We can calculate how long the person has been dead.'

Everything Stuart needed to make this happen I had sent over to the University of Reading. In July 2009, we analysed Victoria's bones, got a ratio of polonium-210 to lead-210 and did the maths. Calculated from the day of analysis – July 3, 2009 – the results indicated a postmortem interval of 415 days, plus or minus 11 days for margin of error.

It had been 413 days since Victoria Couchman was last seen alive on May 16, 2008. Our tests proved overwhelmingly that she had died in May 2008 and could not have posted those messages or been seen in Hastings three months later. Once again, reaching out to academia and isotope research had helped crack a case. Remember, stable isotopes had helped us isolate the region in West

Africa where Adam had come from. Now radioactive isotopes had assisted us in calculating a time of death.

Tony Couchman was charged with murder and perverting the course of justice. Tragically, in January 2010 – two days before he was due to stand trial – he slashed his wrists while in custody at Lewes prison and died. We'll never know if our isotopic evidence would've convicted him.

But similar analysis would get justice for another grieving family.

OPERATION TABLOW – MAY 2010

On the evening of May 3, 2010, twenty-one-year-old Nathan Allen was hanging out with friends on Desmond Street in New Cross, south London when three men on bicycles rode into their estate. One of the men indicated he had a gun, sending Nathan and his gang scattering in different directions. The gang chased Nathan, cornering him in Ludwick Mews and opening fire.

Enid Scott, seventy-two, had been watching TV in her ground-floor flat when she heard a pounding on her back door and pleas for help. She felt too scared to answer, so called the police. Nathan managed to dial 999 too, gasping: 'Been shot – in my lung – I can't breathe. Quick – on Ludwick Mews – I'm in a back garden. Ludwick Mews, New Cross.'

They would prove to be his final words.

He was pronounced dead in Enid's back garden at about 9 p.m. Four bullets were recovered from the scene: one from Nathan's chest, two from his clothing and a fourth from the headrest of a Vauxhall Astra parked nearby. All were .22 bullets.

As is standard in gang shootings, there were no witnesses and no weapons recovered. However, police picked up intelligence that the shooting had been the result of an incident earlier that evening when a motorcycle had driven 'too close' to a local woman and her three-year-old daughter. The aggrieved woman had called local hardman Curtis Quashie and asked 'for something to be done'. He and two members of the Anti-Shower Gang went in search of the man they believed had ridden the offending motorcycle, Nathan Allen of the rival Shower Gang.

After Nathan's death, police searched the home of Quashie, twenty-two, and found three unused .22-calibre bullets in his kitchen. With no other evidence, police asked me if these three bullets could be connected to the four recovered from the murder scene. It felt like a long shot: the three recovered from the house and the four fired at the scene were all illegal and, as such, had probably come from a variety of sources. These bullets could've come from anywhere around the world before winding up in New Cross.

Franco Tomei, a very experienced firearms expert at the lab, tried to compare the bullets found at Quashie's home with those at the murder scene, but found the spent bullets too impact-damaged and deformed. Franco was, however, able to help with the first stage of my forensic plan – by getting hold of .22 bullets for me to analyse, 192 of them no less!

Again relying on isotopic analysis, I discovered that bullets manufactured in different parts of the world had their own distinct lead ratio or signature. In short, the isotopic ratio of lead in any bullet will reveal if it was made in the USA, Asia, Europe or the UK.

Lead-isotope-ratio analysis first revealed that the bullet recovered from Nathan's chest in the postmortem had an identical isotopic lead ratio to the one that ended up lodged in the Vauxhall's headrest. This held no evidential value – after all, both bullets had been fired from the same gun at the murder scene – but it did offer welcome 'proof of concept'.

We then received better news. The lead isotopic ratio of a bullet recovered from the waistband of Nathan's grey hoodie proved identical to one of the bullets recovered from Quashie's kitchen. This was a promising start but, to convince a jury, we needed a stronger connection. We decided to push the science further.

Our next step was to chemically compare the reference bullets provided by Franco to those found at the scene of Nathan's shooting and in Quashie's kitchen. This involved Dr Stuart Black and a postgrad student spending months carefully drilling out each bullet, extracting the contents and finding ways to test their elemental composition – with a total of thirty-six elements quantified.

The work proved painstaking but the results spectacular: the bullets from Quashie's kitchen were found to be chemically identical to the bullets fired at the scene. None of the other reference bullets analysed from our sample of 192 came close to being a match in both lead isotope ratio and elemental composition.

The prosecution already had strong circumstantial evidence against Quashie and two associates. Mobile phone records revealed the three suspects calling each other before the murder. CCTV showed the trio on their way to the scene. A witness in a nearby shop belatedly came forward to report seeing the suspects moments before the shooting, one of them with a gun tucked into his tracksuit bottoms.

Now, forensically, we could show that the bullets found in Quashie's kitchen were identical in chemical make-up and lead isotopic ratio to those fired at the scene of Nathan's death.

It proved enough to convince the jury. The trio were found guilty of murder; Quashie was sentenced to twenty-four years, his cohorts to seventeen each. But this wasn't the most tragic case in which we applied techniques developed at the Forensic Science Service during my time as specialist advisor. There can be only one candidate for that…

OPERATION PASTEL – SEPTEMBER 2011

Early in 2013, I was contacted by an officer from South Yorkshire Police struggling to find an independent forensic lab willing or able to help.

'How did you hear about me?' I asked.

'Word of mouth,' he said, 'what I'm told is that you take on the cases no one else wants.'

I invited him to brief me about his 'problem'. By the time he'd finished, I would've done the work for nothing. Because what happened to four-year-old Hamzah Khan is simply unthinkable in twenty-first-century England.

The discovery of the crime came down to the diligence of a young police community support officer, Jodie Dunsmore. She'd returned to the house of single mum Amanda Hutton, forty-three, and her eight children in the Heaton area of Bradford on several occasions in response to complaints by neighbours of antisocial behaviour. On each occasion, she'd failed to get in. However, on September 21, 2011, Jodie was in no mood to be thwarted again.

At first, she'd noticed dead flies on the windowsills. When repeated raps on the front door generated no response, she got down and prised open the letter box – only to be knocked back by a rancid smell. The officer now made one thing abundantly clear to the occupants inside – if someone didn't open this door, she was going to kick it in.

Finally, the door groaned open. Amanda Hutton stood there with flies buzzing about her matted hair, seemingly oblivious to the eye-watering stench emanating from behind her.

Jodie's suspicions were instantly heightened by the ominous smell and soon called for backup. She wanted this house searched and some sort of order restored.

As police officers waded through piles of rubbish, food waste and faeces downstairs, their colleague acting sergeant Richard Dove took himself into Amanda's relatively uncluttered upstairs bedroom. From the top of a travel cot, he began removing piled-up objects like bedding, shoes and clothing. And that's when he made the horror discovery. His right hand shook wildly as he tried to comprehend the sight before him – the mummified body of a small child clutching a teddy bear.

The child's bones poked out from beneath the skin, and the duvet was coated in maggots, pupae cases and insects. There were flea eggs on the child's hands and head.

Later, as Amanda was being driven to the police station, a police officer said to her: 'You know what's been found, don't you Amanda?' to which she replied: 'He died two years ago on December 15.'

Later, Amanda Hutton told police that the boy was her youngest son, Hamzah Khan, born in 2005. She fled his dad after several incidents of domestic abuse, which police had attended, taking her eight kids with her. On December 14, 2009, Hamzah – then aged four – had become unwell. Next morning, she was at a pharmacist getting medicine for the sick child when she received a panicked phone call from an older child telling her to come home at once.

The officer who'd come to see me about this case went on: 'She explained that when she returned, Hamzah was near to death. She sought to revive him but to no effect.

'She described placing Hamzah into his cot, making plain that she had treated his body with dignity. But instead of dialling 999 or a doctor, she ordered in a pizza. And she went on claiming child benefit for the boy right up until the time we found him, almost two years later.'

Amanda told officers that it was only since Hamzah's death that she'd resorted to drinking heavily, often consuming a bottle of vodka a day. However, as the officer from South Yorkshire put it: 'The fact they found Hamzah, a four-year-old boy, in a Babygro designed for an infant aged six to nine months suggests she'd been drinking heavily for a lot longer than that.'

South Yorkshire Police charged Amanda Hutton with manslaughter, claiming that, as a result of her neglect, Hamzah had been allowed to starve to death. At the time he was found, the boy weighed just four pounds five ounces.

As the officer put it: 'Amanda Hutton failed to provide her child with the nourishment that he needed to survive, so she killed him.'

However, despite obvious signs of neglect and starvation, police and prosecutors faced a problem. Subsequent analysis of Hamzah's bones had shown the presence of osteoporosis – the skeletal disorder where bones become brittle and bend and break easily. Amanda Hutton was claiming that, from the age of eighteen months, Hamzah had developed 'thin, bandy legs' – a classic early symptom of osteoporosis. Her defence were planning to argue that Hamzah's malnutrition could have arisen through 'some naturally occurring condition' like osteoporosis, and not through the neglect of his mother.

The detective wanted to know if I could prove that Hamzah Khan had died from malnourishment.

I knew from my ally in academia, Dr Stuart Black, that the study of carbon and nitrogen isotopes in bones, teeth and hair was used in archaeology to determine the diets of ancient peoples. Once again, this is because 'we are what we eat' – these isotopic values reveal how much fish, meat, dairy and crops a person has consumed, and when and from where they came. Each food type leaves its own unique signature in isotopes – and Stuart was able to direct me to academic charts revealing what these signatures were.

However, as far as any of us knew, this specific knowledge had never before been applied to a criminal forensic investigation.

During her trial at Bradford Crown Court in October 2013, Amanda Hutton admitted that Hamzah had been underweight but insisted she was not overly concerned. Two of her older children, including Qaiser, now twenty-two, had also gone through stages of being poor eaters and skinny when they were little but had since 'filled out'. Strenuously denying that Hamzah had starved to death, Amanda insisted that she overcame the problem of him being 'a fussy eater' by feeding him calorific nourishment drinks rather than solid food, right up until the time of his death.

It was now up to me to show otherwise.

Using the carbon and nitrogen isotopic signatures in Hamzah's hair and bones, I'd constructed a graph showing his animal protein intake during the last years of his life. The results showed, in particular, a low nitrogen isotope value in his bone (around 6.4 per cent), indicating a low intake of animal protein that reduced to nothing during his final weeks. It was clear that the poor boy had simply starved to death.

The jury convicted Amanda Hutton of manslaughter by gross neglect and she was sentenced to fifteen years.

* * *

In the cases of Hamzah Khan, Nathan Allen and Victoria Couchman, all other investigatory avenues had been exhausted when forensic scientists took the lead. Using techniques pioneered by the Forensic Science Service and the academics at the University of Reading over the previous fifteen years, forensic scientists did what everyone else had failed to do – prove the cases against the suspects. That is the legacy of the FSS appointing specialist advisors in 1996 to help drive forensic science forward.

Yet neither the Nathan Allen nor Hamzah Khan cases had been taken on by the FSS. Indeed, the agency that nurtured and supported so much groundbreaking research, development and expertise would never benefit from the legacies of its visionary approach to forensics.

That's because, early in 2011, the government announced that it was closing us down.

The news caused an outcry. The police weren't happy. A cross-party House of Commons Science and Technology Committee report warned that 'proper consideration' had not been given to the impact of this decision on the criminal justice system. The report also accused ministers of not looking for any viable alternatives to shuttering the FSS. Could it have been run more efficiently, for example?

Let me give you the answer to that question. When I joined the Met Lab in 1971, the deputy director Dr Bobby Jones still did casework in his expert field of arson. By 2011, as specialist advisor for major crime, I was the highest rank at the FSS that dealt with casework. Above me were eight grades who were purely managerial. I received six police commendations during my time spent as a specialist advisor, but not once did any of the senior managers meet me and congratulate me.

Of course it could've been run better.

But that's not what the government wanted. The FSS was 'losing' £2 million a month. As far as the politicians were concerned, it didn't matter that it had become the envy of the world, or that it provided a vital non-profit service to what many consider a basic human right – a rigorously fair judicial system. But it is said that politicians know the cost of everything and the value of nothing. None of this was worth £2 million a month to our politicians. By closing it down and letting private companies charge police for forensics services, the government was saving money.

Who cared about the inevitable consequences further down the line?

What private company, for example, would've taken on cases

like Hamzah Khan or Nathan Allen? There isn't a business plan or model in the world that would allow for such niche and painstaking scientific work. If companies can't afford to take such cases on, then justice suffers, victims suffer and dangerous criminals walk free.

And so it came to pass.

In May 2019, a report published by the House of Lords Science and Technology Committee warned that the forensic science services in England and Wales were 'inadequate'.

The report warned of declining standards, which could lead to crimes going unsolved and an erosion of public trust in the criminal justice system. It also revealed that, as a result of police forces outsourcing work to unregulated providers to save money, three of the largest and most reputable labs were on the brink of financial collapse. The committee attributed the decline in forensic science standards to two things: one, an absence of high-level leadership, a lack of funding and an insufficient level of research and development; two, the abolition of the Forensic Science Service in 2012. The FSS was then providing 60 per cent of forensic services to police forces in England and Wales.

Everyone who understood the justice system – police officers, lawyers, judges – had predicted this back in 2011. Undeterred, the government set the closure date for March 31, 2012.

I didn't even last that long.

The FSS stopped taking new cases in October 2011. As this had been my bread and butter for the previous fifteen years, I suddenly found myself with nothing to do. Sneaking out early minus a fanfare truly appealed to me so, forty years after I first joined the Met Lab, I offered to walk. They couldn't get shot of me or my salary fast enough.

I made it clear that I didn't want any presentations, speeches, not so much as a supermarket sponge cake sliced in my honour. That would prove to be my final order as specialist advisor.

On my last day, I shared a tearful cuddle with Bridget March, the heroine of 7/7, and quiet handshakes with my closest colleagues. Clearing my desk, I came across a file from Operation Greenfinch – the so-called 'Bedsit Murders' of Wendy Knell and Caroline Pierce in Tunbridge Wells in 1987 – and felt a pang of regret that I'd never found their killer.

I then bailed early just in case, and drove home in stunned silence.

Yes, I was bitter.

I felt bitter about all the sacrifices Jackie and I had made for this organisation: all those missed holidays, spoiled special occasions and lost weekends. All those disruptive phone calls in the middle of the night and late drives home.

I felt bitter on behalf of all those great scientists in the FSS and in academia who had given so much to us out of their sheer love for science and their unshakeable belief in the importance of what the FSS stood for and did.

I felt bitter about all the efforts we'd made and lengths we'd gone to to make the Forensic Science Service the best in the world. What would happen to all this learning and groundbreaking science now?

I organised a farewell 'do' at the Pineapple pub in Lambeth, inviting all the scientists whom I respected, retired and working, police and SOCOs from the Met, Sussex and Kent, as well as a few other special guests.

On the day, for old times' sake, I took the train into Charing Cross station – the same journey I'd made when I first started working at the Met Lab in the summer of 1971. Back then, I couldn't afford a tube or bus so used to walk to Holborn. That evening, I decided to do the same, heading up the Strand, then taking a left. In the early 1970s, Covent Garden was a proper fruit and veg market awash with vans, porters, trolleys and stalls. Amid the hum of brisk, spit-and-a-handshake trade, I remembered the sounds and smells of the market mixing with characteristic scent of pubs, open early for the all-night workers and last night's 'never-say-die' party animals. These days, it's become such a soulless altar to global brands that I had to remind myself where I was.

As I approached Holborn, I realised that this had been where I got my first taste of proper Italian coffee and cask ale. Now, of course, those family-owned cafes and old-school local pubs are long gone, replaced by chains.

How sterile, corporate and homogenous it all now seemed. How unrecognisable from the neighbourhoods I'd fallen in love with forty years earlier. I hailed a taxi and got the hell out of there, making my way to the Pineapple.

It was a good old London boozer and – despite having had pangs of dread – I thoroughly enjoyed the night. I felt grateful for the chance to properly say thanks and goodbye to many colleagues, scientists, police officers and SOCOs I held dear, and to reassure friends that my departure wouldn't change anything.

Highlights included a gift from my FSS colleagues of an enlarged, framed photo of me aged eighteen. Then, something I didn't see coming. The counter-terrorism police presented me with a framed crest of their unit – the famous bell, book and candle – which now accompanies my other career honours on the wall of my garden shed.

Jackie joined me on this special occasion. We left the Pineapple just before the last bell, in time to catch one more quiet drink in a pub around the corner.

'You deserve all this and more,' she said, 'you gave your life to that job.'

'Yeah, well, this was the job of my life, Jackie. I wouldn't have traded it for anything.'

EPILOGUE

A question I'm often asked since I left the Forensic Science Service is: 'What's the one that got away?'

Most expect me to say Adam. But I feel like we identified some of the key players in that crime, and they were punished – albeit for people-trafficking. Others are surprised to learn it's not Billie-Jo Jenkins.

Both of those cases frustrated and disappointed me. But the case that preyed upon my mind as I walked out of the FSS one last time in October 2011 was the so-called 'Bedsit Murders' of Wendy Knell and Caroline Pierce almost a quarter of a century earlier. Little did I know that the forensic work we had done on this case would finally catch up with their killer...

After my days in the FSS, I became a lecturer in forensic science at Canterbury Christ Church University, as well as running a crime scene analysis course at the University of Reading. This gave me a chance to dust down my old personal files on Adam, Sarah Payne and the M25 Rapist and teach a new generation how forensics had cracked those cases.

How I hoped that one day I could lecture them on Operation

Greenfinch – the official name of the investigation into the 'Bedsit Murders'. But it would have to be solved first.

* * *

Back in 1987, both young women had complained about a 'peeping Tom' prowler. Wendy, twenty-five, was raped and battered to death in her bedsit – the pathologist couldn't say in what order. Caroline, twenty, vanished one night from outside her flat less than a mile from Wendy's. Three weeks later, her body was found in a waterlogged dyke some forty miles away. She was wearing just a pair of tights.

One of the few things we could deduce with any certainty was that whoever killed Wendy and Caroline had been stalking them, so we thought he must've been a local. If so, even if he'd since moved to the other end of the country, there was a chance he'd still have relatives in the area. In 2001, we worked with Kent Police on an intelligence-led screen, but got no matches.

Returning to the case in 2003, we extracted a DNA profile from semen on a towel that lay under Wendy's head. This provided a partial match to the DNA profile of the offender. We re-examined the tights worn by Caroline Pierce but, after three weeks lying in a flooded ditch on Romney Marsh, they didn't yield any DNA.

In 2004 and 2007, we conducted familial searches on the National DNA Database but failed to identify any relations of the offender. As 2007 marked the twentieth anniversary of the murders, *Crimewatch* broadcast a segment about the case, but calls from the public proved futile.

In 2010, we took yet another stab at finding a familial match in the National DNA Database. One of the frustrating things about this process is that, as soon as you've performed the search it's out of date, because more DNA profiles will have been added. It was another bust. On leaving the FSS, I took comfort in the fact that Kent Police would keep reviewing the case. I just hoped that they'd identify the offender before Wendy's elderly parents, Bill and Pamela, passed away.

* * *

In 2012, I returned to the role of reporting officer for a private forensics company. However, for me, no job could match the buzz of specialist advisor and I soon moved on. I started working at the University of Reading where, along with my old sparring partner Dr Stuart Black, I carried out forensic examinations in the cases of Alexander Perepilichnyy, Nathan Allen and Hamzah Khan.

I felt saddened by the death of Bill Knell in 2017 and the fact that, on the thirtieth anniversary of the murders, we'd failed to fulfil his dying wish. His wife Pamela had said at the time: 'It was so hard for him, for both of us. I told him at the hospice because he kept hanging on, "Why don't you let go and go and find Wendy?" And then he died around midnight. He is up there with Wendy and all his brothers and sisters.'

I still had contacts at Kent Police, who assured me that the case had not been forgotten. In fact, it was about to get a new lease of life.

Although I'd retired from police investigations, my previous work on this case ensured that – when Detective Superintendent Ivan Beasley revisited it in 2019 – I was kept abreast of developments. Using a new technique called sperm elution, a private company was finally able to extract a DNA sample from the tights worn by Caroline Pierce. It proved a strong partial match to the DNA profile found at Wendy Knell's bedsit, connecting the cases scientifically for the first time.

Meantime, the DNA profile from Wendy's duvet cover was upgraded to a DNA17 profile, which decodes sixteen areas of DNA (32 alleles), making it much more informative. Back in 2005, we had also obtained a Y-chromosome DNA profile from the semen sample. Using these references, Detective Superintendent Beasley conducted another familial search through the National DNA Database.

Once again, they used parameters like age and geography to whittle down a list of thousands to ninety individuals. Officers travelled all over England, as well as to Northern Ireland and Scotland, tracing these people and taking samples.

On November 16, 2020, Kent's senior crime scene investigator Emma Jennings got a call confirming a very close match to the DNA17 and Y-chromosome profiles. In fact, the match proved so close that it might be what you'd expect from a close male relative of the suspect.

Incredibly, his DNA had been entered onto the system in 2011 – the year after we conducted our most recent familial search of the DNA database.

We had missed him by a matter of months.

It turned out that the man had given the sample after a minor offence. He had two brothers. Records show that one of them – David Fuller – had convictions for burglary in the 1970s. Police also found that, at the time of the murders, David Fuller had lived just over the border from Kent and was working in Tunbridge Wells. In the early hours of December 3, 2021, officers turned up at Fuller's three-bedroom family semi in Heathfield, East Sussex.

'Oh, blimey,' declared the sixty-seven-year-old dad of two on answering the door.

Police arrested Fuller and took a swab for DNA analysis. Now, thirty-three years on, we could do nothing but wait for the result and hope that we had finally unmasked the killer of Wendy and Caroline.

David Fuller's DNA profile turned out to be an exact match to that found on Wendy Knell's duvet and Caroline Pierce's tights.

We had him!

But what he been up to since 1987? Common sense says a man as sick as this doesn't suddenly stop carrying out depraved acts. Officers searching the home he shared with his family were about to find out.

An upstairs box room acted as his home office. It was monitored by a CCTV system and had access to the loft via a hatch. It very quickly became clear that Fuller was a hoarder. More than 3,500 exhibits were seized from the office and loft, including computers going back to the late 1970s, mobile phones as old as twenty years, handwritten diaries, 34,000 photo prints, negatives, slides and camera rolls and 3,500 digital storage devices.

A dedicated team of 100 officers and staff was created to investigate, and spent five months sifting through the material.

Inside an office wardrobe, police found a handmade box screwed to the back. They opened it to find four more hard drives. When officers viewed these drives, Fuller's deviant secret life was finally laid bare.

Fuller had filmed himself sexually abusing dead women and girls. By the time detectives had worked through all the footage, they had found evidence of him violating 102 deceased victims aged between nine and 100. He stored records of his serial sex offending on computer folders with titles including 'Necro Lord', 'Register', 'Deadly', 'Deadliest' and 'Best Yet'.

The folders contained names, numbers and dates, as well as images of a mortuary logbook used to create his own record of those whom he'd defiled. He also kept a detailed diary of his sex assaults, penned in his own handwriting. Fuller was found to have researched many of his victims after the attacks via Facebook.

The footage and images of abuse dated back to 2008 but detectives believe this merely signifies when Fuller had switched to digital devices. He had worked at two hospitals as an electrician since 1989, which gave him an access-all-areas swipe card that included the mortuaries. Colleagues revealed that he'd favoured the late shift, which would've left him free and unsupervised to carry out his twisted acts.

Detectives were able to identify eighty-two of the dead victims. It left police in no doubt that, as they'd feared at the time, Fuller had performed necrophiliac acts on his murder victims, Wendy Knell and Caroline Pierce.

Fuller was charged with both murders. Despite the strength of the DNA evidence, he denied everything. According to Fuller, he didn't know the murder victims, Tunbridge Wells or Romney Marsh. But his hoarding and meticulous record-keeping soon gave him away. Documents and diary entries from his home revealed that his previous addresses included Guildford Road – he had once lived just two doors from where Wendy Knell had been murdered. They even found photograph sleeves from SupaSnaps – the shop Wendy managed in Tunbridge Wells.

Now that they had Fuller in custody, detectives were able to revisit evidence from the Wendy Knell crime scene and use it in a new way. Because of his convictions for burglary in the 1970s, David Fuller's fingerprints had been on file. However, the partial fingerprint found on the Millets carrier bag at Wendy's bedsit had been too poor in quality to run through the system. But with Fuller in custody, fingerprint specialists could now physically compare his print to the one found on the bag – and confirm it was his. Furthermore, detectives found an old photo of Fuller from the 1980s in which he wore a pair of Clarks shoes, the sole of which matched the bloodied footwear mark on Wendy's blouse.

Even the manner of the burglaries for which he'd been convicted in the 1970s connected him to Wendy's murder. A so-called 'creeper burglar', Fuller had climbed through the windows of his victims – which is he how he'd accessed Wendy Knell's bedsit.

There was more. On the night of Wendy's murder, two

motorists reported a blue hatchback car being driven erratically close to the scene at about 1.10 a.m. Records showed that, at the time of the murders, Fuller had owned a blue Fiat Uno.

Fuller's lifetime of keepsakes also connected him to the murder of Caroline Pierce. He'd once lived at an address just round the corner from Caroline's flat and had dined at the restaurant she managed. Detectives discovered he had connections to the Romney Marsh area, where Caroline's body had been dumped. Both sets of his grandparents and other close relatives had lived there. Fuller regularly visited the area to indulge his dual passions of birdwatching and bike-riding. Indeed, the cycle club he belonged to had a route through Romney Marsh that went right past the site where Caroline Pierce's body had been found.

When Fuller's trial started at Maidstone Crown Court on November 1, 2021, I followed it closely through the media. Fuller was admitting responsibility for killing Wendy and Caroline but denying the murder charges on the grounds of diminished responsibility.

Three days later, he changed his plea to guilty. He also admitted a further 51 offences related to sexually abusing at least 102 victims in the mortuaries of Kent and Sussex and Tunbridge Wells hospitals over more than a decade.

On the thirty-fourth anniversary of the discovery of Caroline Pierce's body, Fuller was sentenced to two whole life orders for the murders and handed concurrent sentences totalling twelve years for the sexual abuse of the deceased women.

He joins Levi Bellfield – killer of Milly Dowler, Marsha McDonnell and Amélie Delagrange – as the only criminal in UK legal history to be serving two whole life orders.

Pamela Knell, Wendy's elderly mother, somehow found the strength to attend the trial proceedings. I can only hope that she derived some sense of closure and comfort from Fuller's conviction.

Once again, how privileged I felt to have played a minor role in catching a killer.

ACKNOWLEDGEMENTS

Kind words such as 'thank you' can be short, easy to say and sometimes devoid of any real meaning, but in my case I really want to express my sincere gratitude to the people below.

My first thank you goes to my late mother and father, for the love, care and support given to me during my education – I know the sacrifices made by both.

To the producer/writer Emma Shaw, thank you for planting the idea in my head of writing a book about my career as a forensic scientist. In turn, this led to my introduction to James 'Jim' Nally – the writer of this book (also a producer and writer). Jim is just the most wonderful wordsmith. How he transforms my ramblings during many meetings into readable logical text is real magic. We also managed a few laughs along the way and I now consider him a firm friend.

For turning this idea into reality, I'd like to thank Ellie Carr and all at Bonnier Books. Thank you for believing in this project.

In a forensic context I have been lucky to work with several scientists from the Metropolitan Police Forensic Science Laboratory, Forensic Science Service and academics within universities. All of their knowledge, skill and experience was immense, there are too many to name, but you know who you are and I thank you all for sharing your extensive expertise with me. Also, I would like to say a very special thank you to all the scientists who worked long hours and with such dedication on both the 7/7 and the 21/7 London Transport bombings. Bridget March and her team showed the world how the laboratory could work 24 hours a day, producing results which led them to be an integral part of the investigations.

From the world of academia, I would like to especially thank Dr Stuart Black who really was introduced to the role of the expert witness when he took on the work in the 21/7 London Transport bombings.

I also had the pleasure of working with a number of Senior Investigating Officers (SIO's), the detectives working as part of these investigation teams and the tremendously skilled Scenes of Crimes Officers. During these normally high-profile investigations, I spent some considerable time with these investigators – thank you all for allowing me into your world and showing trust in me in order to the share details of the investigations with me, some of which were highly confidential. I have named some of you in this book, but there are so many so if I have missed you out, please forgive me.

I hope in some small way I have helped in solving these complex investigations. It is I think worthy of note that through this work I can say that I have become close personal friends with some of the police staff, occasionally sharing the odd beer together. And in that smaller group, I'd like to namecheck Andy Baker, Will O'Reilly, Nick Chalmers and Simon Morgan.

Last, but certainly not least, I am thankful beyond words for the love and support I received from Jackie, my wife. I was lucky to have met Jackie when she was somewhat reluctantly transferred to the laboratory from the Metropolitan Police Civil Staff. She has totally supported me in my work, even when I missed her birthday celebrations. Thank you.